Bible and Ethics in the
Christian Life

A New Conversation

Bible and Ethics in the Christian Life

A New Conversation

BRUCE C. BIRCH,
JACQUELINE E. LAPSLEY,
CYNTHIA MOE-LOBEDA, AND
LARRY L. RASMUSSEN

FORTRESS PRESS
MINNEAPOLIS

BIBLE AND ETHICS IN THE CHRISTIAN LIFE
A New Conversation

Cover image: Thinkstock / Abstract grunge of cityscape by Grandfailure
Cover design: Lauren Williamson

Print ISBN: 978-0-8006-9761-7
eBook ISBN: 978-1-4514-3854-3

The paper used in this publication meets the minimum requirements of American National Standard for Information Sciences — Permanence of Paper for Printed Library Materials, ANSI Z329.48-1984.

Manufactured in the U.S.A.

Contents

Part III. The Bible, Ethics, and the Moral Life

Figures

Preface

This volume has a history. In the early 1970s, Bruce Birch and Larry Rasmussen decided to teach a seminary class together on the Bible and ethics at Wesley Theological Seminary. Initially, they were convinced that the processes used by Christians to discern the meaning and significance of the Bible for their lives and the processes Christians used for moral discernment and decision-making had many similarities and often overlapped or exercised mutual influence in the Christian life.

They also agreed, as a personal discipline related to the course, that they would try to write something for publication out of their work together. They imagined something like a journal article. However, in the actual preparation of the class, and somewhat to their surprise, they could find very few published resources to use for course reading or to place on the bibliography of the syllabus. Although ethicists used biblical materials and Bible scholars sometimes drew implications from their exegesis for contemporary moral issues, only a handful of scholars had systematically looked at the methodological issues of relationship between Scripture and ethics, either historically or in the contemporary life of the church.

Instead of a journal article, they ended up writing a book entitled *Bible and Ethics in the Christian Life* (Augsburg, 1976). In that volume, they profiled in a single chapter the only six scholars who had published works systematically exploring the methodological issues of relationship between the Bible and Christian ethics. They ended up emphasizing the importance of the Bible for ethics both in character formation (being, identity) and in decision-making/action (doing, conduct). This means that the Bible is significant not just as a source of explicit moral admonitions but as an inheritance of diverse and complex traditions that shape us as people and communities in worship, study, and discipleship.

In 1989, Birch and Rasmussen published a revised edition of their book, and they found some significant changes in the conversation about the Bible and ethics. So many new works had been published in a remarkable decade of interest in Scripture and ethics that they could no longer summarize this in a single chapter. Instead, they engaged these new works, as reflected in footnotes, in updating their own perspectives on the issues in relating Bible and ethics. Perhaps most visibly, they added an entire chapter on community as the necessary context within which Scripture originated and within which Scripture must be appropriated for the moral life. This seemed like a clear omission from the first volume.

The expansion of interest and publication around the relationship between the Bible and ethics has continued. There is now rich and more nuanced literature exploring this relationship. Oxford University Press recently published, as part of their Online Bibliographies project, a large annotated bibliography on "Biblical Ethics" that contains over 200 items.[1]

More recently, Birch and Rasmussen were asked if they would consider a third edition of their volume. Almost forty years, a biblical generation, had passed since initial publication, and the world had changed dramatically. So, they offered an alternative: a new book. That alternative is the volume the reader now holds in hand. Birch and Rasmussen are joined by two new partners, both of whom have been a part of this expanding and ongoing conversation around the relationship between the Bible and ethics: Jacqueline Lapsley of Princeton Theological Seminary and Cynthia Moe-Lobeda of Pacific Lutheran Theological Seminary. Joining Birch of Wesley Theological Seminary, and Rasmussen, emeritus at Union Theological Seminary, they bring the voices of a new generation of scholars into the conversation.

This is not, however, a revision of the earlier volumes in this lineage. It cannot be. As will be made clear in the introduction, we are faced with a dramatically altered context for our reflections on Bible and ethics. The reality of the Earth itself has changed, affecting the well-being of human and nonhuman parts of God's creation. The

1. Bruce C. Birch, "Biblical Studies: Ethics," *Oxford Online Bibliographies*, March 10, 2015, http://tinyurl.com/y9jzvyzf.

reality of the church has changed, facing us with new complexities and configurations in the body of Christ for our time.

Our authorial team tried to revisit the entire question of how we are to understand the relationship of Scripture to ethics for Christians in a new day. We are in conversation with the previous work represented by half of our team, but we consider new voices and new questions, as represented by two new conversation partners. Our intention has been to open ourselves to new realities and new possibilities in the conversation. We have sought to listen to voices sometimes pressed to the margins of the conversation. We have sought to reflect the diversity of God's world in a way that transcends traditional patterns of thinking about Scripture and ethics. Yet, we understand that much of what we write cannot do justice to the richness of the present conversation that is unfolding in the global context of altered Earth and church. We hope our work can be seen as representative of an even wider conversation into which our volume invites its readers.

We want to express special thanks to Jessica Rigel for editorial work on the entire manuscript. We also express special thanks to James Klotz, and to Odja Barros for sharing her biblical study experience with Flor de Manacá, which is the basis of an important section in chapter 8.

The subtitle for this volume is "A New Conversation." As coauthors, we have enjoyed and been illumined by this new conversation among ourselves, but we intend the title to be much more than that. We would hope the title can be heard as an invitation to join with us in "a new conversation." The conversations of the past, stretching from biblical times to the present, can undergird us, but the conversation about how we engage our foundational traditions in the Bible as resources for our contemporary moral life, in character and conduct, must go on anew for every generation. Some of us joined this conversation a generation ago; some of us joined it more recently. We invite our readers to continue it into the next generation.

Bruce C. Birch
Jacqueline E. Lapsley
Cynthia Moe-Lobeda
Larry L. Rasmussen

Introduction: A New Conversation

Reading Scripture for the Christian moral life takes place across dramatically changing landscapes, creating a new conversation for the Bible and ethics. One altered landscape is the planet and its human world. The other is Christianity and the church.

OF BIBLICAL PROPORTIONS

The planetary changes are epochal and probably deeper and more extended in space and time than we yet realize.

How epochal? "Doomsday predictions can no longer be met with irony or disdain," writes Pope Francis.[1] Events are happening that feel like a hike through Revelation.

Ask the scientists. One of them is Craig Childs, explorer, naturalist, and author. In the frontispiece of his book *Apocalyptic Planet: Field Guide to the Future of the Earth*, he defines "apocalypse":

> The word "apocalypse," from the Greek *apokalypsis*, originally referred to the lifting of a veil or a revelation. The common definition as a destructive worldwide event is more recent. In this book, it is both.[2]

Childs put on his boots, packed his maps and journals, and explored how Earth is tending in view of changes already in motion. The nine locations he chose "unveiled" (*apokalypsis*) where nature is headed if

---

1. Francis, *On Care for Our Common Home: Laudato Si'*, ed. Sean McDonagh (Maryknoll, NY: Orbis, 2016), para. 161.

2. Craig Childs, *Apocalyptic Planet: Field Guide to the Future of the Earth* (New York: Vintage Books, 2012), frontispiece.

current trends continue or some wild card events—mass extinctions, super volcanoes, or dramatic sea-level rise—take the community of life by surprise, as they have in ages past, whether humans were present or not. (Most often they were not.) The table of contents mirrors Childs's findings and reads like extremes of, well, biblical proportions:

1. Deserts Consume

2. Ice Collapses

3. Seas Rise

4. Civilizations Fall

5. Cold Returns

6. Species Vanish

7. Mountains Move

8. Cataclysm Strikes

9. Seas Boil[3]

Childs's account, however valid, is only one. Other scientists—geologists, biologists, climatologists, and oceanographers—have theirs. Varied as they are, they converge at a single point: our cumulative human presence is now sufficiently powerful to alter our centuries-long relationship to the rest of planetary creation and our social world.

For the first time, humanity is now the single most decisive force of planetary nature itself. We are altering the carbon content and dynamic in the atmosphere and the oceans, effecting acidification of the oceans, and resetting the planet's thermostat. We are sending species to eternal death at a quickening pace. We have reengineered more rocks, soil, and landscapes in the last century than have volcanoes, earthquakes, and glaciers. We have modified the flows of most rivers and changed the water catchment areas of the world. We may, in fact, be initiating a new geological epoch, already christened "the Anthropocene" by some (because of the dominance of human activity).[4] Its tattoo appears to be climate volatility, social uncertainty, and

---

3. Ibid., TOC.

4. There is a rapidly growing selection of literature on "the Anthropocene" and on "geo-engineering," all of it based in the prominence and dominance of human activity in shaping planetary processes and systems. *The Economist* made it their feature story in the May 26, 2011,

a grave threat to life. This contrasts with the late Holocene, whose mark has been climate stability sufficient to allow, even promote, the flourishing of life. Not least, the late Holocene has hosted all human civilizations to date, from 11,000 BCE to the present, as well as the birth of world religions and writing of all the world's scriptures.

In short, the human imprint is everywhere. All the systems of the natural world are either currently embedded as part of human systems or profoundly affected by those systems. This includes places humans do not live—the high atmosphere, the ocean depths, the high polar regions.

How far-reaching is this imprint? Elizabeth Kolbert concludes that we are now a co-evolutionary force. "We are deciding, without quite meaning to, which evolutionary pathways will remain open and which will forever be closed. No other creature has ever managed this, and it will, unfortunately, be our most enduring legacy."[5]

If this is so, we have entered upon a new era of human responsibility. Never have our choices, actions, and way of life had the height, depth, and power they do now.

For Bible and ethics, the questions would seem to be these: What dialogue shapes the contours of moral imagination and human responsibility when no terrain goes untouched by both human goodness and human molestation? What dialogue facilitates human character and conduct when, as never before, our collective reach is "exercised cumulatively across generational time, aggregately through ecological systems, and nonintentionally over evolutionary futures?"[6] What biblical and present understandings of ourselves help generate a capacity to take a stand not only for present and future generations of humankind but for the community of life as a whole? Do not the parental elements of life itself—earth, air, fire, and water—make moral claims upon us for their health and well-being,

---

issue on "The Anthropocene: A Man-Made World." A widely read op-ed piece in the *New York Times* led its author, Roy Scranton, to expand it as a short book, *Learning to Die in the Anthropocene: Reflections on the End of a Civilization* (San Francisco: City Light Books, 2015). Elizabeth Kolbert's work, *The Sixth Extinction: An Unnatural History* (New York: Henry Holt, 2014), incudes "Welcome to the Anthropocene," 92–110. Of special import for philosophy and theology is Clive Hamilton, *Defiant Earth: The Fate of Humans in the Anthropocene* (Cambridge, UK: Polity, 2017). In Christian ethics, one of the earliest and most thorough works is Willis Jenkins, *The Future of Ethics: Sustainability, Social Justice, and Religious Creativity* (Washington, DC: Georgetown University Press, 2013); see Jenkins's introduction, "Ethics in the Anthropocene," 1–15, as the lead-in to subsequent chapters.

5. Kolbert, *Sixth Extinction*, 268–69.

6. Jenkins, *Future of Ethics*, 1.

rather than only we upon them, for ours? What kind of Bible and ethics exchange retrieves, renews, even creates Christian practices for living the faith amidst these anthropocene powers? What manner of living chooses "life and blessing" over "death and curses" so that our "descendants may live" (Deut 30:19–20), and live well, in a world we will not see but whose contours we profoundly shape?

Nor are climate change, limited water resources, monster storms and wildfires, the loss of biodiversity, and other changes to the planet the only challenges we face. Because ours is not only a planet but a "world," these interact with other stark realities "of biblical proportions": a world population of 9 billion human beings by 2050; terrorism and the militarization of societies (including police forces); extreme inequality and poverty; global health issues; heightened "us versus them" conflict along racial, ethnic, class, gender, and religious lines; more refugees, asylum seekers, and displaced persons than at any time since World War II; and the incapacity of governments to address these as they interact and impact one another. Most fundamentally, the global human economy is at war with the economy of which it is part and upon which it is wholly dependent—namely, nature's. The world that has been built up over five hundred years of conquest, colonization, industrialization, urbanization, and commerce is found to be unsustainable, inequitable, and increasingly self-destructive. Not without reason, then, "apocalypse" appears in secular discourse and common conversation, even among scientists. It is no longer the domain of religious texts and arcane scriptures alone.

RELOCATED CHURCH, CHANGING CHRISTIANITIES

The second transformed landscape is Christianity and the church.

Here is a glimpse via Wesley Granberg-Michaelson, in *From Times Square to Timbuktu: The Post-Christian West Meets the Non-Western Church* and his essay "Navigating the Changing Landscape of World Christianity."[7]

> For one thousand years Christianity's center of gravity—meaning the point at which an equal number of Christians around the globe were found to the north south, east, and west—remained in Europe. Then,

7. While in the following excerpt "Global North" and "Global South" have largely geographic connotations, we recognize that the terms increasingly are used to indicate not geographic locations but social location. In this volume, we use these terms in the latter sense.

from 1910 to 2010, it moved from Spain to a point near Timbuktu, Africa. This is the most rapid geographical shift in all of Christian history. And for the first time in 1000 years, more Christians were living in the Global South than the Global North.

In 1910, 2% of Africa's population was Christian. Today, one out of four Christians in the world is an African while in Asia Christianity is growing at twice the rate of population growth. Asia's present 350 million Christians are projected to grow to 460 million by 2025. Already in China alone it is estimated that, on any given Sunday, more people attend worship than in the United States. Add to this that Latin America, together with Africa, holds 1 billion of the world's Christian community, with trends that continue to grow. At the same time the percentage of the world's Christians found in Europe and North America fell from 80% in 1910 to 40% a century later. Among evangelicals the shift is even more dramatic: 90% were found in the U.S. and Europe a century ago; today 75% of evangelicals are in the Global South.[8]

This is Christianity breaking away from its millennium-long geographical and cultural center in the Euro-West. Even the Roman Catholic Church, while headquartered in Rome, finds two-thirds of its 1.2 billion members (16 percent of the world's population and half the world's Christians) in Asia, Africa, and Latin America. And those 1.2 billion are led, for the first time in 1,200 years, by a pope from the Global South, Francis. Nor should we fail to note that another large communion of 260 million, the Orthodox churches, have never regarded themselves as "Western."

But the most bracing demographic change is the astonishing rise of Pentecostal and Charismatic churches,[9] together with growing evangelicalism and newly established independent churches. To cite only the first mentioned: while in 1970, "about 5% of Christians identified themselves as Pentecostal," as of 2015, one out of every four Christians in the world is Pentecostal and/or Charismatic. "80% of Christian conversions in Asia are to Pentecostal forms of Christianity," with "about 25% of all Pentecostals" now in Asia. Africa is home to almost one-third of the world's Pentecostals while

---

8. Wesley Granberg-Michaelson, "Navigating the Changing Landscape of World Christianity" in *A Ministry of Reconciliation: Essays in Honor of Gregg Mast*, ed. Allen Janssen (Grand Rapids: Eerdmans, 2017), 122–23. See also Wesley Granberg-Michaelson, *From Times Square to Timbuktu: The Post-Christian West Meets the Non-Western Church* (Grand Rapids: Eerdmans, 2013), 7–12; and Todd M. Johnson and Kenneth R. Ross, eds., *Atlas of Global Christianity: 1910–2010* (Edinburgh: Edinburgh University Press, 2009), 50–53.

9. Granberg-Michaelson, "Navigating the Changing Landscape," 124.

Latin America finds Pentecostalism "growing at 3 times the rate" of its long-established Catholicism.[10] Christianity itself is on the increase globally. It grew 2.4 percent from 2000 to 2010. But its Pentecostal/Charismatic stream is growing at four times Christianity's overall rate of increase.[11] (The Pew Forum on Religion and Public Life in 2011 gave 504,040,000 as the number of Pentecostal and Charismatic Christians, 26.8 percent of the world Christian population.[12])

The Atlas of Global Christianity concludes that "Pentecostalism . . . became the main contributor to the reshaping of Christianity from a predominantly Western to a predominantly non-Western phenomenon in the twentieth century."[13]

Yet, "Western," "Euro-Western," and "non-Western" are deceptive designations if their meaning is solely geographical. Rather, there is a global intermingling of diverse Christian peoples and their Christianities. In the world's large cities, for example, congregations that were once geographically east, west, north, or south may all be neighbors, mirroring the movement of peoples and their cultures or subcultures around the world. Timbuktu has arrived in Times Square, to recall Granberg-Michaelson's title. Pick your city and experience diverse cultures, subcultures, and spiritualities residing cheek-by-jowl as neighboring Christianities. Nor are they alone. They belong to an interfaith mix of multiple streams of Judaism, Islam, Hinduism, Buddhism, and others.

A salient point is that these Christianities are notably "non-Western" as cultures. They are not Euro-American or "mainline." For most of them, the community holds primacy over the Euro-West's primacy of the individual. Bodily and mythic experience is as valid a path to truth as rational, factual, scientific inquiry. Material and spiritual worlds interpenetrate one another with ease, in contrast to a common Western separation of spirit and matter, or natural and supernatural. While in Europe and North America, or at least in the parts of them that are shaped by dominant culture, a strong secular temper reigns—a "post-Christian" world—and formerly mainline

10. Ibid., 124–25.

11. Ibid., 124.

12. "Christian Movements and Denominations," Pew Research Center, December 19, 2011, http://tinyurl.com/h3ek9pb. See also "The Global Religious Landscape," Pew Research Center, December 18, 2012, http://tinyurl.com/qg97qjy.

13. Johnson and Ross, *Atlas of Global Christianity*, 100.

religious communities are numerically in decline, globally the world is more religious, not less.

This can be said differently. What is happening is the indigenization of Christian faith in other than Euro-Western cultures. Even the Pentecostalism brought by missionaries of Pentecostal denominations in the West is not the Pentecostalism of newly independent churches in Africa, India, and China. The latter have incorporated their own cultural values and artistic expression together with their own emotional and spiritual worlds. Their faith travels with them when they move or are moved around the globe.[14]

In short, the movement of Christian peoples and their cultures has brought non-Western churches into the West in a way that does not readily assimilate into what has been the dominant Euro-Western Christian temperament or mindset. They may, however, assimilate with minority temperaments in the West. The historically black and Hispanic churches of evangelical and Pentecostal persuasion are examples.

With this array of changing and diverse Christianities now more mobile than ever, and with non-Western churches taking up residence in the post-Christian West, is there anything they share? Is there any common "treasure in an earthen vessel" they all look to for wisdom and guidance? Is there any authority they all turn to and claim? There is. But it's not the same music or liturgy. Nor is it the same traditions, food, leadership, or polity. It's the Bible. The Good Book is their one common source and guide in matters of faith and life.

Yet, is it the same Bible, read in the same way? On the face of it, the answer is "no." And if that is so, if the reading of Scripture reflects the diversity of the Christian communities themselves, there is all the more reason for "a new conversation" (this book's subtitle), a conversation especially attentive to *method*: method in biblical interpretation, method in ethics, and method in relating Bible to ethics.

With the decentering of Christianities from the Euro-Western world comes invaluable knowledge and insight into the Bible and ethics. God reveals Godself to the world in new ways through the worldviews, epistemologies, and life experiences of different peoples in highly varied social locations. The Bible opens up in different

14. Sandra S. K. Lee, "Christianity by Major Tradition, 1910–2010," in Johnson and Ross, *Atlas of Global Christianity*, 76.

ways, and new insights emerge about its relationship to the moral life when it is read with lenses other than Euro-Western and when different forms of knowing interact in probing the Bible and its relationship to the moral life.

Two profoundly important challenges have emerged in the last three decades as Euro-Western Christians have listened to theological voices from Africa, Asia, Latin America, and nonwhite North America. One challenge is a deepening awareness of the terrible role that Christianity in general and the Bible in particular have played in the colonization of Africa, the Americas, and parts of Asia. South African theologian Allan Boesak says it with piercing honesty:

> The nations of the rich North had as their goal the theft of land and people, oppression, slavery and genocide, all with the express intent of exploitation, deprivation and enrichment. Invasion and colonization went hand in hand with domination and subjugation, and the Christianization of the people was unthinkable without the demonization of their culture and beliefs, that wide open door to the eradication of their history and their physical annihilation. . . . Central to it all was the Bible, the source of an all-encompassing justification of acts unspeakable in their cruelty, and the sanctifier of bigotry, hatred and greed so deep it could only exist and endure through the most obstinate *denial*.[15]

This challenge does not delegitimize the Bible as central to the moral life of Christians. It does, however, demand that Euro-Western Christians refuse this ongoing "denial," and it demands that all Christians interrogate, with faithful diligence and courage, *how* we read the Bible and its implications for how we are to live in this world. That is, our method of reading the Bible and of relating it to the moral life matters; method may be—in fact—a matter of life and death.

The Bible itself may be the doorway into that faithful honesty. For "the *logos*, the living Christ, is the truth (John 14:6)"[16]—and the truth will set us free. As Lutheran Brazilian theologian Vítor Westhelle points out, in New Testament Greek, the word for truth is *alētheia*. "The prefix *a*- denotes a negation of *lēthē*, that means, of oblivion

---

15. Allan Boesak, "Babblers to the Rabble, Prophets to the Powerful: Mission in the Context of Empire" (keynote address, consultation sponsored by the Council for World Mission, Bangkok, May 29–June 2, 2017); italics ours.

16. Vítor Westhelle, "Freeing the Captives: Speaking the Truth" (paper delivered at Multicultural Theologians Seminar, Mystic Lake, MN, July 29–August 1, 2008).

or concealment. The word *alētheia*, therefore, means the denial of oblivion."[17] The word of God—the living Christ—undoes denial and concealment of uncomfortable realities; it reveals or tells the truth. A primary role of the church—as the body of Christ—is viewing history truthfully so that we may live in the present and future more faithfully.

A second challenge pertains to the indigenization of Christian faith in cultures around the globe. Just as the spread of Christianity in the colonial era went hand-in-hand with the imperial projects of Europe and, later, the United States, the rapid relocation of Christianities to the non-Western world in the last five decades also is accompanied by market interests and influence. The wave of fundamentalist Christianity around the globe rides a current of commercial interests and often serves those interests. The Bible itself is commercialized to serve the global market. Brazilian theologian Nancy Cardoso points out that "the bigger Bible publishers are owned by big conglomerates of non-Christian media. . . . Zondervan, with a catalogue of more than 500 different Bibles and with the control of 35% of the [Bible] market, was bought in 1998 by HarperCollins, which is part of News Corporation, Rupert Murdoch's media empire."[18] That media conglomerate also owns Fox News.

Our point here is that celebrating and honoring the movement of Christianities around the globe and the growth of indigenous Christianities means also questioning how that movement and the understandings of the Bible it promotes are influenced by interests that perpetuate the values of Western capitalism and culture. Again, we are not calling the Bible itself into question. Rather, we mean to call to the fore the crucial role of intentionality and self-awareness in reading and interpreting the Bible and its implications for how we are to live.

A NEW CONVERSATION

What shall we say in conclusion?

First, right under our feet and over our heads, something of enormous consequence is happening. The planet is being changed in

17. Westhelle, "Freeing the Captives".

18. Nancy Cardoso, "The Bible: Globalized Commodity in the New Strategies of Neocolonialism" (paper presented at consultation sponsored by the Council for World Mission, Bangkok, May 29–June 2, 2017).

ways it has not for hundreds of thousands of years, and humans are the causal force. The human world that has brought on this change is caught up in it and adds its own tumult, violence, and confusion. While Earth is one, from both a scientific and biblical view, the world most definitely is not. Moreover, Christianity is in the midst of its own profound transformations. All these deeply altered landscapes tally as a civilizational and moral-spiritual challenge of epic proportions: how do we move from unsustainable industrial civilization to a civilization that allows the survival, indeed flourishing, of human and other-than-human life together, a civilization that is marked by social equity in its many forms?

Second, there is an emerging consensus. Suffice it to cite Roy Scranton:

> In order for us to adapt to this strange new world, we're going to need more than scientific reports and military policy. We're going to need new ideas. We're going to need new myths and new stories, a new conceptual understanding of reality, and a new relationship to the deep polyglot traditions of human culture that carbon-based capitalism has vitiated through commodification and assimilation. . . . [W]e will need a new way of thinking our collective existence. We need a new vision of who "we" are.[19]

This book is a modest part of that immodest rethinking of our collective existence and identity. It ventures a new, or renewed, conversation for Bible and ethics, a conversation among those for whom both Bible and ethics do matter, or might matter, in a world deemed sacred.

19. Scranton, *Learning to Die*, 19.

PART I

The Bible as Moral Witness

1.

A Two-Part Consensus

This new conversation must begin with an initial treatment of the Bible as a moral document or, more accurately, a collection of moral witnesses. Yet, even this new conversation is based on "an important two-part consensus, held by biblical scholars and ethicists alike."[1] This consensus consists of two claims. First is the claim that *Christian ethics is not synonymous with biblical ethics.* The second is that *the Bible is somehow formative and normative for Christian ethics.*

This two-part consensus is an important starting point. From it has sprung in the last two to three decades a rich literature of voices reflecting on the distinction between Christian ethics and biblical ethics, and on the fuller understanding of the complex and sometimes divergent ways in which the Bible exercises its formative and normative role in Christian moral life. In many ways, this entire volume is intended as a contribution to that ongoing conversation, growing

---

1. Bruce C. Birch and Larry L. Rasmussen, *Bible and Ethics in the Christian Life*, rev. and expanded ed. (Minneapolis: Augsburg Fortress, 1989), 11, 14. Hereafter cited as Birch and Rasmussen, *BECL*, rev. As the preface to this volume makes clear, this new conversation revisits a topic taken up by Birch and Rasmussen's earlier work. However, we intend the discussion of this volume to be in no way dependent on familiarity with that earlier work. It is useful for readers to know that this discussion stands at a point following over thirty years of new literature on the relationship between Scripture and ethics. Yet, we believe the two-part consensus described here and in that volume is still basic to all of that literature as a starting point.

This chapter builds upon and further develops work previously published in Bruce C. Birch, "Ethics in the OT," in vol. 2 of *The New Interpreter's Dictionary of the Bible*, ed. Katharine Doob Sakenfeld (Nashville: Abingdon, 2007), 338–48.

from that consensus and our assessment of where that conversation has come and might profitably continue.[2]

BIBLICAL ETHICS AND CHRISTIAN ETHICS

There are a variety of reasons why biblical ethics and Christian ethics cannot be equated. The first is that the term "biblical ethics" itself has suffered from a variety of meanings and usages, and this has resulted in some confusion in the literature. "Biblical ethics" can be used to refer to different arenas within which the Bible's relationship to ethics might be explored. Each of these arenas provides a different angle of vision on that relationship and faces different questions and problems.

The Bible for all Christians includes the Old Testament (Hebrew Bible) and the New Testament (the Greek canonical writings of early Christianity),[3] collections of writings drawn from a span of as much as fourteen hundred years, collected and handed on through generations. Thus, in dealing with the Bible we are always dealing with a text. That text varies somewhat in differing manuscript traditions and is read by most church members in various translations from the original Hebrew, Aramaic, and Greek. Nevertheless, even in an age of technological media, the Bible remains a text to be read, interpreted, and appropriated.

One of the arenas where interest in the Bible and ethics has focused is on the world behind the text. The focus of studies in this area is on discovering, describing, and assessing the morality of the social contexts and communities out of which the biblical texts were produced. In the mid-twentieth century, there were some who thought they could describe either a unified or developing system of Israelite morality in the Old Testament (OT).[4] Such efforts are now largely

2. Allen Verhey has offered a thoughtful reflection on this two-part consensus and the fuller discussion of its implications and elucidation in "Scripture and Ethics: Canon and Community," *Union Seminary Quarterly Review* 58, no. 1–2 (2004): 13–32.

3. For Roman Catholics and most of Eastern Orthodoxy, the books of the Apocrypha would also be considered Scripture and part of the Bible. Although this volume writes from a Protestant perspective, the methodological issues of relating the Bible to Christian ethics remain largely the same. Only the field of texts used in the life of the church would be expanded in other traditions. Since this volume is not aimed at interfaith readership, we have kept the usage of the terms Old and New Testament as they still appear in most Christian Bibles.

4. Johannes Hempel was a very influential proponent for finding a historically developing system of morality in Israel related to various social strata in Israel's life (peasants, pastoralists, urban dwellers, royal noble classes). See Johannes Hempel, *Das Ethos des Alten Testament* (Berlin: Töpelmann, 1938), and Johannes Hempel, "Ethics in the Old Testament," in vol. 2 of

abandoned because of new appreciation for the complex diversity of the OT. Individual texts are moral witnesses out of a variety of social contexts but may be reflective of a common majority opinion (the Decalogue) or be a minority voice declaring the popular morality bankrupt or ignored (Jeremiah).

> The Old Testament is evidence for, not coterminous with, the life and thought of ancient Israel; Old Testament writers may at times state or imply positions that were the common currency of ancient Israelites, but they may also propound novel, or controversial, or minority positions. . . . The mistake is . . . to assume that *extant* evidence is also *typical* or *complete* evidence.[5]

In New Testament (NT) studies, some have sought to find the outlines of a Jesus-movement morality that predates the NT literature and the concerns of the early church. But the only NT literature we have is from the diverse communities of the early church, and we have no direct access to Jesus that does not reflect the concerns of these early Christian communities to shape their moral life in response to Jesus.[6]

More recent interest in biblical ethics as recovery of the morality of communities in biblical times has focused on the use of social scientific methods, which have been helpfully applied to deepen our understanding of the morality reflected in certain sets of texts, or particular voices of moral witness, without trying to synthesize these understandings into some larger unified or developmental understanding of the morality of the OT or NT. Such studies deepen our

---

The Interpreter's Dictionary of the Bible, ed. George Arthur Buttrick (Nashville, Abingdon, 1962), 153–61.

5. John Barton, "Understanding Old Testament Ethics," *Journal for the Study of the Old Testament* 3, no. 9 (October 1978): 46, 49.

6. We want to acknowledge the wide breadth of early church communities and their perspectives on Jesus. Our NT is the final result of a long process of identifying the writings that would be accepted by the wider church as scriptural canon. Many gospels and other early Christian writings that were not included in the canon survive even today. These are important witnesses to the breadth of theological perspective in the early centuries of the Christian era. Some of these reflect early communities and viewpoints that continued, in some cases, for centuries. Study of these writings enriches our understanding of the dynamics out of which the canonical collections emerged and the present-day branches of the Christian faith formed. None of these other ancient writings, however, are formally recognized by any contemporary church community as part of its scripture or as authoritative for theological beliefs or faith practices. See Hal Taussig, *A New New Testament: A Bible for the Twenty-First Century Combining Tradition and Newly Discovered Texts* (Boston: Houghton Mifflin Harcourt, 2013), for a full discussion of this extracanonical literature and an argument for its importance.

understanding of the world that produced our biblical texts, but these are only glimpses of the multifaceted moral world of ancient Israel and the early church. There is no biblical ethics that can be discovered behind the text and simply adopted as Christian ethics.

The term "biblical ethics" might also refer to the world of the text created by the formation of the canon. Both Old and New Testaments have gone through a process whereby witnesses to the community's experience of God have taken a variety of written forms, which have then been selected for preservation and inclusion in larger collections of texts until the result is an authoritative canon given scriptural status through ongoing generations. The study of biblical ethics in a canonical context goes beyond an inquiry into the origins of biblical texts. Moral dialogues are created within the canon. The ethical witness of biblical texts takes multiple forms when placed within the canon: agreements, tensions, continuities, contradictions. In the context of the canon, biblical ethics creates a new moral world that transcends the moral world behind individual texts.

For example, the moral concern to feed the hungry will draw perspectives across the canon from texts as diverse as manna in the wilderness, laws from rural/tribal Israel, prophetic mandates for Israel returned from exile, Jesus's teaching on the priority of the poor, and Paul's collection for the church in Jerusalem. The goal is not to replicate any of those contexts in our own response to the hungry but to allow these witnesses to all inform the moral context, choices, and actions of those who read these testimonies as Scripture.

Thus, the community that claims the canons of the OT and NT as Scripture enters a new conversation on biblical ethics that engages the moral world of the canon in all its complexity, in dialogue with the faith community's own complex and highly diverse world through generations. In this way, biblical ethics as canonical moral witness becomes central to Christian ethics but is not synonymous with Christian ethics. We will have more to say later about the function of the canon.[7]

A further obvious reason why biblical ethics cannot be synonymous with Christian ethics is that biblical communities did not confront some of the moral issues and social forces that shape our lives today. The Bible does not begin to imagine some of the moral issues that are part of modern life in the twenty-first century.

---

7. We will expand on the nature and importance of the canon in chapter 2.

In 1973, Stanley Cohen and Herbert Boyer first spliced genetic material from one microbe into another to create a bit of life that never existed before. James Watson and Francis Crick had, in 1953, determined the chemical arrangement of DNA (deoxyribonucleic acid), a double helix strand that carries the hereditary blueprint of all living things. In 1987, the United States Patent and Trademark Office decided that patents for new life forms can be extended from microbes to higher life forms, including (new) mammals.[8] In 1988, the Office determined that companies holding patents on new animal forms can require farmers to pay royalties on the animals and their offspring through the seventeen-year life of each patent.[9]

The ancient peoples of the biblical communities did not possess the knowledge and power to manipulate the very building blocks of life itself. It is we who have "cracked" the genetic code and positioned ourselves to create new life forms. "Cellular engineering," "gene-splicing," "genetic counseling," "biotechnology," and "bioethics," relatively new terms in the dictionary thirty years ago, are now commonplace and have spawned major industries. These human initiatives have resulted in increased human power unforeseen by the biblical communities, but like all increases in human power, they carry corollary moral responsibility.

Nor did those ancient biblical communities know the terms "climate change," "global warming," "acid rain," or "species extinction," all realities that drastically affect the moral landscape and the discussion of ethical response. In spite of some climate change deniers, scientific evidence is clear that human beings have proven capable of damaging their planetary environment in ways threatening to the continued well-being of life on Earth. These results of the exploitation of creation stand alongside the capacity of humans to cataclysmically destroy life on this Earth through weapons of mass destruction and nuclear, chemical, and biological weapons. Such moral realities were not on the horizon of biblical communities. Nor could they have foreseen the reality of nearly 8 billion people pushing the very carrying capacity of the planet, to say nothing of the pressures, economic and political, this volume of population places on the quality of life worldwide and the suffering that results.[10]

8. "New Life: The Promise and Risk of Genetic Engineering," *New York Times*, June 8, 1987.

9. Keith Schneider, "Farmers to Face Patent Fees to Use Gene-Altered Animals," *New York Times*, February 6, 1988, http://tinyurl.com/ycy44nob.

10. Larry L. Rasmussen has argued that such realities demand a new perspective for Christian

While there is much in human nature that binds us all together across vast stretches of time and culture, and much moral wisdom and folly that makes its way from age to age, it is yet undeniable that Christian ethics today must find its way amidst moral questions that never appeared on the horizon of biblical ethics. Christian ethics cannot be a synonym of biblical ethics when ethics includes unprecedented moral issues.

Even when a moral issue stays much the same in its basic outline, the context is so altered that the biblical response no longer applies directly. Hunger and starvation are gruesome realities, and people starved in the ancient world in the same way biologically that people do now. Cells died in an excruciating process of physiological deterioration, then as now. But addressing the *causes* of hunger and working to alleviate it are very different in our time. Although political realities could affect the availability of food, the biblical world still suffered from drought and crop failure that often left populations without food available from any source. The Joseph story in Genesis is remarkable for its unusual description of planning and making food available across national borders, not the norm of the era. Today, most hungry people are hungry because they are poor and do not have access to food, not because food is unavailable. Pursuing poverty's causes in the modern world leads into a set of local, regional, and international arrangements of trade, finance, and economic and political realities more complex and far-reaching than people of the biblical world could have imagined. The basic moral issue of responding to the needs of the hungry remains, but the context and response will be considerably altered compared to those of biblical times.[11]

A final reason biblical ethics cannot be considered synonymous with Christian ethics lies in Christian affirmations about the character and activity of God and the nature of our faith in response to God. Both Judaism and Christianity insist that they are *historical* religions. The God they worship is a God who has made the divine self present

ethics: *Earth Community, Earth Ethics* (Maryknoll, NY: Orbis, 1998), and *Earth-Honoring Faith: Religious Ethics in a New Key* (Oxford: Oxford University Press, 2013).

11. Cynthia Moe-Lobeda, although dealing with a much broader range of moral issues than hunger alone, has written about the radically changed moral reality of our world while maintaining a solid biblical grounding. What makes this possible is one of the central questions of this volume. See Cynthia Moe-Lobeda, *Healing a Broken World: Globalization and God* (Minneapolis: Fortress Press, 2002), and *Resisting Structural Evil: Love as Ecological-Economic Vocation* (Minneapolis: Fortress Press, 2013).

in particular times and places in an ongoing way. This is the force of ancient Israel's claim that God had "come down to deliver" from bondage in Egypt (Exod 3:7) and is not only a God of Israel's memory but is a God who is constantly "about to do a new thing" (Isa 43:19). This God of ongoing historical relationship for Christians becomes known in the incarnation ("The Word became flesh and dwelt among us," John 1:14). Jesus is seen as the embodiment of the claim of Isaiah that God in Christ is Immanuel ("God with us," Isa 7:14; Matt 1:23). The Scriptures are the testimonies of varied communities in ancient Israel and the early church seeking to discern "a word from the Lord" for their own times and circumstances. The Scriptures are not repositories of timeless truths simply to be applied in the generations after the biblical period, thus relieving future generations from the effort to discern God's "new thing" in their own times and places. Scripture as the record of these testimonies to the character and action of God plays a role in future moral life for the community of faith, as we seek to explore in this volume, but such ancient moral testimony cannot be torn from its moorings and simply applied to modern moral challenges as if God had ceased to act and reveal the divine self with the end of the biblical period. Scripture cannot be transported as changeless content across centuries and applied in an unqualified way to different circumstances and different modes of life and thought in the generations stretching from biblical times to our own era. God is incarnate, as "God with us," in our present world as well as the biblical world. God as spirit, ongoing in our midst, enables "new things" and not simply replication of the old.

One of the most dramatic examples of such historically ongoing revelation of God's character and will can be seen in the multiple instances where we find ourselves in a completely different place in moral judgments on particular issues from those made or accepted by biblical communities. Christian ethics today does not find sound justification for accepted biblical codes on slavery, the treatment of women as personal property, capital punishment for a greatly broadened range of offenses, or the limited catalog of proper gender roles or sexual relationships. Time and much serious, painful moral struggle has rendered some "ancient good uncouth."[12]

In a word, the ethics of biblical communities are not and cannot be

---

12. This phrase was penned by James R. Lowell in a poem protesting American involvement in the Mexican War in 1845: "time makes ancient good uncouth." The poem was set to music by Thomas Williams and became the widely sung hymn "Once to Every Man and Nation."

the same as Christian ethics for us. It is precisely *because* they are not the same that the issues arise that are addressed by this book.

THE BIBLE AS FORMATIVE AND NORMATIVE

This brings us to the second part of the double consensus mentioned at the start of this chapter, which is this: the Bible is somehow formative and normative for Christian ethics. But in what ways formative and normative?

To foreshadow a fuller discussion to come, let us simply note here two inescapable realities. Even though Christian ethics cannot be synonymous with biblical ethics, ethics cannot be Christian without reference to and foundation in the biblical witness.

On the one hand, the Bible is our only source for the foundational story of God in Jesus Christ and in the Spirit. That Gospel story (in four testimonies) is self-consciously rooted in the God of Israel and the sweep of a story with God at the center that stretches from creation to deliverance to covenant community to kings and prophets to exile and restoration. It extends beyond the story of Jesus to the formation of the church, in the power of God's Spirit, and the early witness, from Paul to John of Patmos, out of that early church. Outside the OT, NT, and a few noncanonical early Christian writings, there are only traces of the story that gives Christian faith and the church their identity.

On the other hand, if the Bible is the foundational story for Christian identity, it is also the source of tensions, with prevailing cultural realities throughout the generations. The community that looks to the Bible as the source of identity-forming story often finds itself an alternative to the communities of prevailing cultural contexts.[13] Thus, the Bible has carried the power to *create* moral problems that may not be problems for those who are not influenced or shaped by Scripture. Almost from the beginning of the church, tensions emerged between loyalties to God and to earthly principalities and powers. Could Christians acknowledge Caesar when "Jesus is our king" (Acts 17:7)? Could Christians take up arms for the state or make offerings to Caesar? Is there not a stark choice between two masters, God and mammon (Matt 6:24; Luke 16:13)? The fundamental loyalty of Jews

---

13. See this point made forcefully in Walter Brueggemann, *The Prophetic Imagination*, 2nd ed. (Minneapolis: Fortress Press, 2001).

and Christians to a *faith* community rather than to a *civic* community raised innumerable problems and tensions that have carried forward from biblical times to our own, with traditions making different moral choices in these matters, but all in dialogue with biblical identity.

AGENDA

If biblical scholars and Christian ethicists are generally agreed on these two matters—Christian ethics is not a synonym for biblical ethics, yet the Bible is a shaping force for the Christian moral life—then the issue becomes this: What is the relationship of Scripture and ethics in contemporary communities of faith, in theory and in practice? What is the range of options available in response to this question and how may those options be assessed? These questions, and a host of secondary ones, coalesce into an agenda for this book.

In the next three chapters, we begin with a discussion of the Bible itself as a moral witness: its foundations in community, the nature of its authority for the moral life, and the interpretation of its texts for the sake of the moral witness and ecclesial practice of the church.[14]

1. What is the effect of understanding the witnesses of the biblical text not as isolated, individual voices but as community testimonies that, even if originating in particular persons and events, are claimed by the community for preservation and passed on to future generations? What results when these testimonies are coalesced into a canon that creates new conversations on the nature of God, community, and witness so that future generations automatically have a common base for identity and reflection on what it means to be the people of God and, for the purposes of this volume, a moral community?

2. What is the authority of Scripture for formation of moral character and the shaping of moral conduct? How authoritative are nonbiblical sources of insight? Is the authority of Scripture somehow different from the authority of other sources? What is the relationship of these various sources? What controls might constrain people from simply choosing among biblical and nonbiblical sources in accord with convictions already held?

14. In this new conversation, we have made a conscious decision to begin with clarification of the nature of the Bible as a moral witness and then proceed to understandings of Christian moral life and the nature of Christian ethics and its concerns. This is a reversal of order from the previous editions of Birch and Rasmussen, *BECL*.

3. Beyond discussing the nature of the biblical witness and the understandings of biblical authority, how does the Christian community actually use Scripture as a resource for the moral life? What kind of exegesis is appropriate to this task? How important are the original form, context, and meaning of biblical texts? Are all materials equally important or appropriate? How do we choose among the bewildering diversity of viewpoints and types of literature in the Bible? What is the relationship of one biblical reference to the whole of Scripture? Does the existence of an official "canon" of Scripture make a difference for how we use Scripture in moral matters? Does the nature of different biblical resources and divergent witness to particular issues suggest different ways in which they might be linked to the moral life? What are those ways and how do individuals and communities make use of them?

We take up these complex questions in the chapters that follow.

2.

Foundations of the Biblical Text in Community Witness

Community is a key category for understanding the relationship between Scripture and ethics as developed in this volume. Community, at its simplest, is a synonym for social relatedness, but we are a part of many different communities: families, cultures, nations, neighborhoods, cities. However, we are not only participants in various communities, we are, in them all, moral agents. By this we mean that human beings are creatures of morality by nature. Both in character and in conduct, we reflect the moral influences and communities that have shaped our being and our doing, for better or for worse.

[The Bible] assumes that all persons are moral agents. Who we are and how we act is considered to be a matter of moral accountability. The collection of witnesses that form the canon . . . presumes to affect moral agency. The . . . canon is not just the fortunately preserved literature of interesting ancient communities. It seeks to form communities of moral agency within which individuals [in community] are brought into relationship with the character, activity, and will of God as witnessed by these collected testimonies from ancient Israel [and the early church]. . . . The formation, preservation and transmission of this literature as canon imply that its intention is to form communities of moral agency in relationship to God through succeeding generations.[1]

1. Birch, "Ethics in the OT," 340.

We will further argue that the human communities responsible for the present canonical witness of Scripture understood themselves not only as social communities but as in community with all of creation. To covenant with God the creator is to also be related in commitment to wholeness (*shalom*) with the land, the nonhuman inhabitants of the Earth, and the elements of the cosmos itself (Genesis 1-2; Psalms 8, 104). A more nuanced discussion of community and moral agency in Christian ethics remains for a future chapter.[2] This chapter and the two following seek to show the centrality of community and moral agency to the foundational biblical texts of the OT and the NT, and to the experience of God to which they witness. These gave birth first to the faith of Israel and then to the early church.

THE FORMATION OF THE TEXT IN COMMUNITY

One of the helpful developments in recent biblical studies has been the full recognition that every text originates in a social context. Moral insights are not simply the product of inspired individuals isolated from social communities. Whatever the role of individual authors or witnesses, their testimony had to resonate with some wider social community or these texts would not have been handed on to succeeding generations. Nor can moral insight be abstracted from the text as nuggets of moral truth or timeless moral principles, separated from the communities that affirmed and passed on these texts. In both the OT and the NT, there is no private or individual moral testimony that is not related to the moral commitments of wider communities that valued and passed on these texts. "There is no private morality which is not also in its varying commitments, a public morality. The [Bible] knows nothing of the notion that morality could be a purely private and individual affair."[3]

One of the fortunate developments in recent biblical scholarship has been the increased use of social scientific methodologies to add precision and definition to our understanding of the particular social

2. It should be noted that this chapter draws on material from ch. 2 of Birch and Rasmussen, *BECL*, rev., 17–34. However, as the chapter title implies, the focus there was on Christian ethics as community ethics. While still highlighting the importance of community as a category for our "new conversation," we now choose to begin with the community dimensions of the Bible itself as a moral witness. Chapter 9 will address the importance of community in Christian ethics.

3. Ronald E. Clements, *Loving One's Neighbor: Old Testament Ethics in Context* (London: University of London Press, 1992), 13.

contexts out of which individual biblical texts arose. Sociology, cultural anthropology, socioeconomics, social history, and social archaeology have all added nuance and depth to our understanding of individual voices witnessing through the preserved texts of the OT and NT. This has been extremely valuable in understanding the social circumstances that occasioned the witness of many texts. But accompanying this development has also been a recognition that broad, synthetic, or developmental patterns in describing the ethics of particular biblical times or places are virtually impossible. What may have been a minority and persecuted voice in its own time (e.g., Jeremiah) ends up in the same canon as Proverbs, which probably originated in the teaching of the privileged. The letters of Paul ultimately overwhelm any witness out of the earliest Jerusalem church community. What all of these texts in the diverse collections of both Testaments have in common is that a wider community found these testimonies to experience with God worthy of preservation beyond the time of their originating social context. The community claimed these testimonies as valued beyond their own immediate time and place.

CONGREGATION, NARRATIVE, AND MORAL FORMATION

The preservation of texts beyond their originating social context witnesses to the intended formation of an ongoing community in relation to the experience of God witnessed in those texts and assumed to be continuously at work in the experience of subsequent generations. "The contribution of the Bible to ethics is at the level of community-formation, not primarily at that of rules or principles."[4] There is a dynamic interrelationship between the experience of a God who has chosen to relate to human history and the formation of a story that shapes a people and its way of life in relation to that God. It is the Bible as Scripture that grounds and connects God, community, and an ongoing way of moral life.

Several helpful observations can be made about aspects of this relationship of God, community, and ethics. These are overlapping rather than discreet points in that dynamic relationship.

4. Lisa Sowle Cahill, "The New Testament and Ethics: Communities of Social Change," *Interpretation* 44, no. 4 (1990): 395.

The biblical communities of faith were initially congregations when they were called into being in both the OT and the NT. Both at Mount Sinai in the Exodus accounts and in Moses's recollection of that time in the speeches of Deuteronomy, Israel is referred to as an "assembly" or a "congregation" (e.g., Deut 5:22). Moses could address the entire assembled people. Likewise, the earliest church consisted of a congregation in Jerusalem that formed from those apostles, followers, and new converts who heard Peter's Pentecost sermon and were empowered by the Spirit (Acts 2).

Soon, both Israel and the early church expanded much beyond those who could be gathered in a single congregational assembly. Yet, many understandings of what it meant to be God's people or the body of Christ continued to have congregational assumptions. In large part, both Israel and the early church went from originating congregation to multiple congregations, but not as self-sufficient entities. Congregations—local bodies of the faithful—were related to a common God and, therefore, to one another. Paul, who wrote powerfully about belonging to one body, does so addressing the congregations in Rome, Corinth, Galatia, Ephesus, Philippi, Colossae, and Thessalonica (some dispute Ephesians and Colossians as genuinely Pauline, but the letters present themselves as such). John's Revelation on Patmos is a letter to seven congregations in western Asia Minor—in Ephesus, Smyrna, Pergamum, Thyatira, Sardis, Philadelphia, and Laodicea. The assembly was both local and ecumenical.

In the OT, the earliest periods were characterized by priests and worship in many locales. When worship became more centralized in the temple, its life was often dominated by kings and the powerful. The temple was ultimately destroyed as a part of the Babylonian exile, seen by the prophets as God's judgment on covenant disobedience. During the exile, the institution of the synagogue returned Israel's faith to the local congregations, and although the temple was rebuilt only to be destroyed again in 70 CE, it is the synagogue that has endured as the primary community of faith for Judaism from the Second Temple period to the present. In the NT, in spite of some tension between Paul and his gentile mission with Peter and the church in Jerusalem, the Christian faith spread throughout the world as new congregations were established and nurtured by apostolic witnesses.

Because of these beginnings as congregation, our biblical faith is strongly insistent on a faith that has meaning in the life of local communities seeking to live in relationship to God. Attempts to focus faith on the larger trans-congregational institutions of religious life have always met with a challenge from prophets or apostles who called for expressions of faith that included and addressed the needs of local communities of faith (e.g., Hosea's concern for the people of the land while kings and priests focus on the [concerns] of palace and Temple, or Paul's letters to struggling young [gentile] churches in spite of conflicts with authorities in Jerusalem).[5]

Whether we look at the formation of a people of God in the exodus/ Sinai covenant tradition, or at the cross/resurrection/Pentecost account of the birth of the church, the experience is the experience of divine power as a power for "peoplehood." The beginning experiences for both Jewish and Christian ethics are the experience of God as the One who generates community and the One who is experienced in community, as its deepest source and meaning.

Moreover, community was the commanding moral matrix for both Israel and the early church. When faith community members asked questions about character and conduct, they did not ask the imperious question later philosophers would sometimes pose: "What is the universal good, and what action on my part would be in accord with it?"[6] Instead they asked: "What character and conduct is in keeping with who we are *as a people of God*?" Identification with the faith community was central to the moral life; the community itself was the matrix.

The moral life is not even its own subject in Israelite and Christian

5. Bruce C. Birch, "Memory in Congregational Life," in *Congregations: Their Power to Form and Transform*, ed. C. Ellis Nelson (Atlanta: John Knox, 1988), 21.

6. The broad stream of moral philosophy that has flowed from the Enlightenment has, in the United States especially, carried individualism and universalism as its core notions. What can be known for sure (epistemology) and what can be done about it (ethics) are to be discovered by autonomous and rational individuals shorn of their attachments to traditions and other parochial influences, including religious ones. All that truly counts in the quest for morality is what individuals have in common as rational beings in quest of the good and their duty to it. By way of contrast, the nature of Christian ethics grounded in Scripture is intrinsically a community ethic of a particular people of God embedded in a particular history. This is at odds with the Enlightenment-based tradition of moral philosophy, in spite of its richness and our indebtedness to it for such treasures as the Universal Declaration of Human Rights. An important analysis of two contrasting and sometimes conflicting moral languages in American culture—individualistic and communitarian, or individualistic and "biblical and republican"—is found in Robert N. Bellah, Richard Madsen, William M. Sullivan, Ann Swidler, and Steven M. Tipton, *Habits of the Heart: Individualism and Commitment in American Life* (Berkeley: University of California Press, 1985). For a discussion of the fate of community and morality in the United States, see Larry L. Rasmussen, *Moral Fragments and Moral Community: A Proposal for Church in Society* (Minneapolis: Fortress Press, 1993), esp. ch. 3, "Hard Journey, Uncertain Outcome," 34–60.

origins. There is very little interest in either the OT or NT in "moral- ity," per se, as a separate topic or in some abstraction called "the moral life." Rather, morality and ethics were dimensions of community life in which the concern was how a people of God were to live with one another and with those outside the community of faith. The broader interest was faithfulness toward God as the way of life of a people. The "moral life" existed for the sake of, and as part of, community faithfulness.

The OT has often been caricatured by Christians as "law," usually implying that its stress is on personal obedience to the will of God, especially as expressed in commandments and rules. But even com- mandments and rules are in the service of a larger concept of commu- nity, formed by God's initiative and bound to God in covenant. The Hebrew word for law, *torah*, has a larger meaning than that of rules or commands. Indeed, the word *torah*, with the formation of a scriptural canon, is applied to the whole of the Pentateuch, the first five books of the OT from Genesis to Deuteronomy. This encompasses far more than law code and commandment. It includes Israel's testimony to its formative experience with God from creation to promised land and the process within that story of becoming a covenant community of the people of God.

> The best way to approach the Old Testament ethical system as "Torah" is to remember that the purpose of the Old Testament is not primarily to give information about morality . . . but to provide materials which, when pondered and absorbed into the mind will suggest the pattern or shape of a way of life lived in the presence of God. . . . *"Torah" is a system by which to live the whole of life in the presence of God, rather than a set of detailed regulations to cover every individual situation in which a moral ruling might be called for.*[7]

Exodus 19:3–6 is a key passage for understanding Israel as a covenant community. Such a community is only possible as a response to what God's grace has already done in deliverance out of bondage in Egypt (v. 4). Obedience to God's voice and keeping of covenant with God (v. 5) will be a part of the covenant life, but the goal is not individ- ual, righteous moral agents. The goal is, as a part of God's care for the whole of the Earth ("the whole earth is mine," v. 5b), to become

---

7. John Barton, "Approaches to Ethics in the Old Testament," in *Beginning Old Testament Study*, ed. John Rogerson (London: SPCK, 1983), 128; italics in original.

a "kingdom of priests" and a "holy nation" (v. 6). The goal has to do with the vocation of a community that reflects relationship with God, a God who delivers slaves. Much could be said about these phrases to define community—at the least that the role of a priest is to stand between God and the people, mediating both ways. A priest carries the people's concerns to God and mediates God's care to the people. Imagine the vocation of an entire kingdom committed to stand between God and the world. What a moral vocation! Covenant community is a matter not of privilege but of participating in God's promise to Abraham to "be a blessing to all the families of the earth" (Gen 12:3).

To be "holy" is not limited to cultic matters but, at minimum, is to be set apart.[8] The opposite of "holy" is not "profane," it is "ordinary." This people will not be like other peoples (see discussion below about the community of God's people as alternative community). Its vocation will be to reflect the reality of its God. "For I am the Lord who brought you up from the land of Egypt, to be your God; you shall be holy, for I am holy" (Lev 11:45). These same concepts of community vocation in relation to God are picked up by the NT in 1 Peter 2:9 as ways of thinking about the community of the church. The Gospel of Matthew, well known as the most Jewish Gospel, contains the Sermon on the Mount (Matthew 5–8), a lengthy presentation of Jesus's teachings as Torah instruction, and a teaching for becoming people of the Way.

Paul's comments to the Thessalonica community illustrate well the NT appropriation of the moral life as a part of community faithfulness in relation to God. This first letter of Paul is the earliest example of Christian writing that we possess. It is an epistle of moral exhortation grounded in a call to community vocation.[9] Paul opens with thanks for their life together lived in the power of God as "work of faith, labor of love, and steadfastness of hope" (1 Thess 1:3). He notes that they observed the life he and his companions lived among them and become "imitators of us and of the Lord" (1 Thess 1:5–6). The letter is filled with praise for the life they are living and admonitions to show this spirit not only to one another but to those outside the

---

8. For a fuller discussion of the holiness of God as a defining reality for Israel's moral vocation, see Bruce C. Birch, *Let Justice Roll Down: The Old Testament, Ethics, and Christian Life* (Louisville: Westminster John Knox, 1991), 148–51.

9. Wayne A. Meeks, *The Moral World of the First Christians* (Philadelphia: Westminster, 1986), 125.

community and in solidarity with Christian communities elsewhere. The moral life is not for the sake of individual moral achievement but, in a key phrase, "a life worthy of God who calls you" (1 Thess 2:12), a life pleasing to God (1 Thess 4:1).

Morality here, in this earliest Christian letter, as in all Scripture, exists as part of and for the sake of the community's vocation as a community of faith in God. Morality's purpose is to aid and abet living "a life worthy of the God who calls you." God, community, and person are the inseparable living elements of the moral life. The interest is less in discreet moral acts than in a way of life that results in a community reflective of the life of God.

Community faithfulness to God and others is frequently portrayed in the simple terms of a "way of life." The followers of Jesus were called "people of the Way" even before they were called "Christians" (Acts 9:2) just as Jesus himself was presented as "the Way" (John 14:6). The roots are deeply Jewish, since in Judaism much of the community's task was instruction in the Way, using the written and oral Torah (cf. Ps 1:6). What Meeks says of apostolic and other early Christian writings pertained already to Hebrew Scripture: "[They] had as their primary aim the shaping of the life of [the faith] communities."[10] "The Way" denoted a particular pattern of living, the instruction and training required for this (called "discipleship" or a following in the Way), and the continuous remembering and retelling of the formative stories, the Jesus story itself above all (cf. Acts 18:24–26).

In sum, both Judaism and Christianity conceived of the moral life as the practical outcome of the community's faith, as shown in the sorts of lives members of the community, and the community as a whole, lived. To be a Jew was to learn the story of Israel and the rabbinic traditions well enough to experience the world from within those stories and to act in accord with that experience as a member of an ongoing faith community. Similarly, to be a Christian was to learn the story of Israel and of Jesus and the ongoing church traditions well enough to experience the world from within those stories, and to act in keeping with that experience, as a member of that community.

In discussing the intersection of God/community/way-of-life, we have focused on the latter two of this trio. We will turn attention now to the reality of God as both the initiator and the continuing

10. Ibid., 12.

partner with the faith community in its moral life. We will then consider the nature of biblical story as the context within which this trio come together and continue to influence succeeding generations.

There is no unified system of theology or ethics to be discovered in the Bible. Its voice, literatures, and perspectives are simply too diverse.[11] However, what is common to all of Scripture is that it has all been preserved as testimony to the experience of God in the lives of persons and communities. The texts of the OT and the NT, as we have argued, are the witness out of community preserved for future generations, but not as testimony to the history and social reality of ancient communities as such. The Bible is composed of texts that *witness to the character and conduct of God in the experience of Israel and the early church*. It is the moral life of God, God's being and doing, that gives rise to the covenant community of Israel and, in the persons of Jesus Christ and the Holy Spirit, gives birth to the church. And these communities, in turn, give us witness in the diverse voices and texts of the OT and NT so that the reality of a life lived fully in the presence of God can be made possible for subsequent generations down to our own.

In the OT, the Exodus experience of God's deliverance out of bondage is the birth story of the people Israel. It is the prelude of God's initiative that makes covenant community possible. In the Exodus passage we discussed above, 19:3–6, God's message to the people through Moses begins, "You have seen what I did to the Egyptians, how I bore you on eagle's wings and brought you to myself." In the OT canon as it is now arranged, we learn that God's work in deliverance and covenant making has been preceded by the divine work of creation and promise (Genesis). In the OT understanding, the covenant community of Israel is not a human achievement or the historically observed product of social forces. Covenant community is a divinely offered relationship that invites a way of life lived in communion with God. The community's moral character and conduct is a response to God's initiative of grace. The key is always knowledge of God and Israel's faithful response. To break covenant is not simply the sum total of unfaithful acts; it is to lose touch with the knowledge of God and the divine reality that called the community into being. "There is no faithfulness or loyalty, and

11. How to use the Bible as a resource for the Christian moral life, in spite of this diversity, or even with such diversity as an asset, will be the subject of chapter 4.

no knowledge of God in the land . . . my people are destroyed for lack of knowledge" (Hos 4:1b, 6a).

> Neither the text itself nor the community that produced the text nor the story of Israel told in the text would provide a sufficient basis for Old Testament ethics as a shaping influence beyond its originating context. God is the reality behind all bases of ethics in the Hebrew Bible. All moral responses are understood as responses to the reality of experience in relation to the character and activity of God. It is the ability of story, community, and text to point to God and give testimony to the reality of God at work in the world that is decisive.[12]

Thus, the knowledge of God in the OT is prior to and encompasses the knowledge of God's will. God had already been known in creation, giving promise, deliverance out of bondage, guidance, and protection through the wilderness before giving any commandment or law. Through most of the twentieth century, treatments of ethics in the OT focused on the revealing of the divine will as the basis for ethics, both in the OT texts and in their use for contemporary ethics. Moral norms were sought and located in the Decalogue, the law codes, and in explicit moral admonitions such as the prophets. This tended to reinforce the caricature of the OT as relatively rigid law over against NT Gospel, as if the OT was not rich in testimony to God's freely given grace.[13]

Even a widely admired work by Eckart Otto,[14] with a title suggesting a magisterial treatment of theological ethics in the OT, limits its focus only to legal and wisdom texts. He argues that these are the only texts dealing with explicit moral norms in ancient Israel and that to go beyond such texts is to confuse ethics in the OT with the history of Israelite religion or OT theology. This, of course, leads him to argue against any sort of "application" of insights, from ethics in the OT to contemporary ethical concerns. As a result, his work, although extremely valuable for understanding legal and wisdom texts in their originating contexts, lies outside the concerns of this volume, for there is no room for reflecting upon the wider dialogue of these texts

12. Bruce C. Birch, "Old Testament Ethics," in *The Blackwell Companion to the Hebrew Bible*, ed. Leo G. Perdue (Oxford: Blackwell, 2001), 301–2.

13. Even some more recent and relatively sophisticated treatments of the Bible and ethics characterize the OT as centered in commandment and therefore primarily deontological in character, e.g., Thomas W. Ogletree, *The Use of the Bible in Christian Ethics* (Philadelphia: Fortress Press, 1983).

14. Eckart Otto, *Theologische Ethik des Alten Testaments* (Stuttgart: Kohlhammer, 1994).

within the whole of the Hebrew canon or the use of these texts as a part of Scripture for subsequent generations.

Obedience to God's will and the role of commandment do play an important role in the OT, but only in relationship to a God who is more than the maker of ethical rules. We cannot separate moral demand from relationship to the person of God. We have already referred to Barton's notion of ethics in the OT as a way of life lived in the presence of God (see n. 7). Brevard Childs argues that ethics in the OT is characterized less by obligation than by communion with God. Commandments rest on prior relationship to God.[15]

In the OT, the knowledge of who God is and what God has done is the precondition to OT ethics. Further, the character and conduct of God are interrelated and equally important. It is widely recognized that the deliverance from bondage in Egypt (Exodus 14–15) is a decisive act of salvation by Israel's God. In a widely used phrase, it is one of God's "mighty acts." But this saving conduct is preceded by important moments of self-revelation in the Exodus story. In Exodus 3–4, God reveals to Moses a divine reality that sees affliction, hears cries, and knows suffering. Exodus 6, with its constant recurring phrase, "I am Yahweh," connects the very identity and character of God with Israelite suffering (and also exilic suffering since this chapter probably received its final shaping during the Babylonian exile). When deliverance comes, it is understood as consistent with who God is at the very divine core of God's being. Brueggemann writes of Exodus 6, "As much as any text in the Exodus tradition, this one invites reflection upon the character of the God of Israel. . . . God's very character is to make relationships, bring emancipation, and establish covenants. . . . Israel is not always Yahweh-connected, but . . . Yahweh is always Israel-connected, and will not again be peopleless. . . . The God of Israel is defined by that relatedness."[16]

Throughout the OT canon, examples can be multiplied of this interrelatedness of divine character and conduct expressed in relationship with Israel as God's covenant partner. This is the precondition to moral reflection on ethics in the OT, either as a witness

15. Brevard S. Childs, *Biblical Theology of the Old and New Testaments: Theological Reflection on the Christian Bible* (Minneapolis: Fortress Press, 1993), 684.

16. Walter Brueggemann, "The Book of Exodus: Introduction, Commentary, and Reflection," in vol. 1 of *The New Interpreter's Bible*, ed. Leander Keck (Nashville: Abingdon, 1994), 736–37.

throughout the diversity of the canon in rich dialogic ways or as a part of the way in which Scripture serves as a moral resource for subsequent generations.

The NT is consistent with what we have been pointing to as the underlying reality of God, in character and conduct, in the OT. But the decisive new shape of that divine reality is in the incarnation of "God with us/Immanuel" in Jesus Christ (Isa 7:14; Matt 1:22–23). "In the beginning was the Word, and the Word was with God, and the Word was God. . . . And the Word became flesh and lived among us" (John 1:1, 14, cf. also John 14:8-14). "In Christ, God was reconciling the world to himself" (2 Cor 5:19).

Jesus Christ, in the power of the Spirit, becomes the focus of experience with the reality of God in both character and conduct. In the earliest NT witness, in the letters of Paul, the focus of the experience of God in Christ was on cross and resurrection and on the continuing power of God through the Spirit. With the addition of Gospels to the shaping of a NT canon, Jesus's life and ministry gave new dimension to the life of God in Jesus Christ, living and ministering among human realities. Jesus blessed the poor, healed the sick, accepted the outcast. He modeled the love of God and neighbor in his very being and demonstrated the conduct that grows out of one who lives fully open to the presence of God.

A large portion of the Bible is taken up with narrative texts that tell the story of Israel's experience with God; the Gospels' story of the birth, ministry, death, and resurrection of Jesus Christ; and the account in Acts of the formation and life of the early church. But even those materials in the OT and NT that are not narrative texts presuppose a story of Israel formed as God's people (even wisdom literature uses the name of Israel's God and knows of that God, Yahweh, as Creator) or the church as arising because of the story of Jesus eventually given textual form in the Gospels. Although the Bible contains a wide variety of materials, those materials are framed by a story that begins with creation, encompasses the story of Israel as God's people, finds the fullness of God's reality in our midst in Jesus Christ, narrates the formation of the church in the power of God's Spirit, and anticipates the eventual consummation of God's purposes in the final end of history and coming of God's reign. It is this framing of the entire canon of Scripture in a story of God's reality in human experience that is most formative of the community of faith and its moral life through ongoing generations. This makes the narrative texts of the Bible foundational for the shaping of moral community.[17]

It has now been a generation since Stephen Crites's famous essay, arguing convincingly that human experience is itself inherently narrative in form,[18] and Hans Frei calling attention to the "eclipse of biblical narrative" in eighteenth- and nineteenth-century hermeneutics.[19] In Christian ethics, the work of Stanley Hauerwas represented a new generation arguing that, especially in the arena of the moral life, story is the most appropriate form for the community to remember and reinterpret its past, particularly its foundational biblical past. In so doing, he argues, communities of faith are shaped as communities of character.[20]

In the OT, there are, of course, many genres of material other than narrative texts, but we would argue that these are preserved and made available to subsequent generations in the community of faith precisely by their incorporation into Israel's narrative story. Law codes, collections of wise sayings, apocalyptic visions, liturgical collections, and prophetic utterances are all made available to later generations because they are seen as originating in, or related to, the stories of Israel. These stories detail how Israel came to be the recipient of God's grace in transforming ways that led to life lived as God's people sharing in God's mission in the world. Those narrative texts include the stories of the Pentateuch, the historical books, some stories of prophets like Isaiah and Jeremiah, and the stories of Daniel, Jonah, Ruth, and Esther. But these stories are not preserved for entertainment or informational background. They are stories that have shaped Israel's understanding of its own identity and origin in the experience of a God that has chosen to partner with them in covenant and incorporate them into a divine mission that began with creation and continues until the final end of the age (Daniel). These stories shape

---

17. See a more detailed argument along these lines in Bruce C. Birch, "Old Testament Narrative and Moral Address," in *Canon, Theology and Old Testament Interpretation: Essays in Honor of Brevard S. Childs*, ed. Gene M. Tucker, David L. Petersen, and Robert R. Wilson (Philadelphia: Fortress Press, 1988), 75–92.

18. Stephen Crites, "The Narrative Quality of Experience," *Journal of the American Academy of Religion* 39, no. 3 (1971): 291–311.

19. Hans W. Frei, *The Eclipse of Biblical Narrative: A Study in Eighteenth and Nineteenth Century Hermeneutics* (New Haven: Yale University Press, 1974).

20. Stanley Hauerwas, *The Peaceable Kingdom: A Primer in Christian Ethics* (Notre Dame: University of Notre Dame Press, 1983), 39.

the community of Israel and individuals within that community as moral agents whose character and conduct are consciously affected by incorporation into the story. Their narrative accounts of their life as part of this story include successes and failures in the effort to live faithfully in the presence of God.

In the OT, such narratives function as shapers of moral identity in several ways.

First, the stories approximate the moral complexities of human life. We do not exercise our role as moral agents in the neat frameworks of separate laws or aphorisms but in overlapping and often conflicting claims and values in social contexts. Narratives approximate this messiness of human life yet show models of central characters making their way, not without mistakes and repercussions, but nevertheless living out a [life in relation to God] that has dignity and integrity. Second, this complexity of ethics in the midst of life is not lived alone but in relationship to a God who is engaged in the processes of historical experience with us. The portraits of this engagement vary from period to period of Israel's storytelling life, but the overall picture is of a God that values human beings [as well as all creation] and has made a special covenant partnership with Israel for wider purposes than mere gratification or self serving purposes. From creation to promise, to deliverance, to covenant, to settlement, to kingship, to judgment, to exile, to restoration—the sum of Israelite narrative traditions is a story that communicates God's valuing of life in general and Israel as divine partner in particular. How that relationship is lived and understood varies greatly in the telling but reflects the complexity that rings true for human experience in general. Third, the narratives have a power to transform and call persons and communities beyond the minimum ethical standards that might be defined by law codes or wise teachings. Qualities of love, justice, righteousness and compassion surprise us in the actions of God and the characters of the story and inspire readers of these stories through the generations to a similar pondering of the ways in which their own lives might reach beyond the ethical minimum. We might forgive as did Joseph. We might be willing to sacrifice all as was Abraham. We might aspire to be persons after God's own heart as was David, and be willing to repent when confronted by our own violence and its effect on our families and others—as was David. The characters of the narratives are both more and less than commandment demanded, and God in these stories is both agent of accountability and unrestrained lover and renewer of relationship. Each of the great themes of these narratives is deserving of full treatment as ethically significant, and (we cannot here) do them justice. We can only point to the growing recognition of the power of narrative to shape community moral identity as it yet does today through the canon handed on to the generations.[21]

Story as conveyed by narrative text is equally important in the NT but has a more central focus and functions in a slightly different way. The focus, of course, is on the story of Jesus as presented in the Gospel narratives, and then upon the apostles as, in the power of the Spirit, they establish the early church to witness to their own transformation by encounter with Jesus. The focus is less on narratives that reflect the diversity of human experience in relation to the presence and activity of God than on God in Jesus demonstrating the full potential of a human life lived in complete accord with the presence of God. That life has the power to transform other human lives, and, beyond the main focus on Jesus, we do hear stories of lives transformed as well as lives that fall short of what they are called by God in Jesus to be (e.g., Judas, the denial of Peter). The narratives of Acts are themselves witness to the power of the Jesus story to transform lives even after the living Jesus has left them.

In spite of their importance, there are far fewer narratives in the NT—basically four Gospels and Acts. But these texts reflect less than a hundred years of experience, from the beginning of Jesus's ministry to the end of Paul's story in Rome. The NT largely closed because there ceased to be eyewitnesses on which narratives could be based, and these all focused on one central life and its impact—the life of Jesus. As an aside, this may be why the stories of saints and martyrs in the early church were so important in the postcanonical centuries.

A good portion of the NT consists of the letters of Paul to early gentile churches and the letters of other early apostles and Christian leaders, rather than narrative texts. The NT ends with the apocalyptic visions of Revelation. But even this literature presupposes a story. Richard Hays, after a descriptive survey of NT texts from the perspective of ethics, turns to the "synthetic" task and argues, "the unity that we discover in the New Testament is not the unity of a dogmatic system. Rather, the unity that we find is the looser unity of a collection of documents that, in various ways, retell and comment upon a single fundamental story."[22] He goes on to define the shape of this

21. This section is quoted from a discussion of ethics in narrative, contained in Birch, "Ethics in the OT," 346; slight changes indicated in brackets.

22. Richard B. Hays, *The Moral Vision of the New Testament: Community, Cross, New Creation; A Contemporary Introduction to New Testament Ethics* (San Francisco: HarperSanFrancisco, 1996), 193.

story by the themes of community, cross, and new creation.[23] Hays's discussion of these themes is enormously helpful but largely dependent on texts from the Pauline letters. Even in his descriptive survey, he begins with Paul as the earliest Christian texts and frequently refers back to Paul even in his treatment of the Gospels.[24]

There is surely a reason that the eventual shapers of the NT canon wished us to read the Gospels and Acts before coming to the letters of the early church. Even the Gospels set the story of Jesus within a larger story that begins with creation in Genesis, and the genealogy of Jesus is intended to suggest that Jesus is not the beginning of a new story but the culmination of a larger story of God's work to redeem a broken world. We cannot leap to cross and resurrection as the main locus of moral significance for the Jesus story. Jesus's life and ministry are morally significant, and his announcement of an "upside-down kingdom,"[25] demonstrated in care for the poor, healing of the sick, acceptance of outcasts, liberty for the captives, and justice for the oppressed (cf. Luke 4:18–19), gives cross and resurrection climactic moral significance.

Our contention is that the entire canon, especially in its narrative texts, is a God-centered story that shaped the moral identity of both the covenant community of Israel and the early church, transformed by Jesus and empowered by the Spirit. That narrative story includes what God has done through Israel, continues as God incarnate in Jesus Christ, and then focuses on God's people in the ongoing church. Generations down to the present have been given moral identity by encounter with God through this story and have lived transformed lives because of that encounter. "The perennial Christian strategy, someone has said, is to gather the folks, break the bread, and tell the stories."[26]

It should be apparent from the discussion above that the Bible as a moral resource functions as more than a repository for explicit rules and commands to be applied to our ethical behavior, although many still attempt to use the Bible in this way. Moral norms in the Bible arise from imitation of God's character and conduct, as seen in God's

---

23. Ibid., 196–98.

24. See the critique of Hays on this point by Verhey, "Scripture and Ethics," 23–25.

25. This phrase was popularized by Donald B. Kraybill, *The Upside-Down Kingdom* (Scottdale, PA: Herald, 1978).

26. On this and other matters of community formation and leadership, see Larry L. Rasmussen, "Shaping Communities," in *Practicing Our Faith*, ed. Dorothy C. Bass, 2nd ed. (San Francisco: Jossey-Bass, 2010), 117–30, the quotation is from p. 119.

covenant relationship with Israel and in God's incarnate life, death, and resurrection in Jesus Christ. Moral norms do also arise from obedience to God's revealed will for covenant community, not as commitment to eternal rules but as making concrete in moral conduct what it means to be God's people or followers of Jesus.[27]

The imitation of God (*imitatio Dei*), as a basis for understanding the Bible's function as a resource for the moral life, has long been recognized and claimed in relation to the NT as the imitation of Christ (*imitatio Christi*). Popular forms of this may be related to rule-based ethics (e.g., What Would Jesus Do? bracelets). But from the earlier devotional classic by Thomas à Kempis, *Imitation of Christ*, to sophisticated contemporary treatments of Jesus as moral model, such as John Howard Yoder, *The Politics of Jesus*, there has been wide recognition that in Jesus Christ, God has modeled what human life can be in its full created potential. The moral significance of Jesus is not in abstracting rules from his teachings but in "putting on Christ," to use the Pauline phrase. Philippians 2:5–7 captures it well, "Let the same mind be in you that was in Christ Jesus, who, though he was in the form of God, did not regard equality with God as something to be exploited, but emptied himself, taking the form of a slave, being born in human likeness. And being found in human form he humbled himself and became obedient to the point of death—even death on a cross." Even in Jesus's teachings, he often taught in ways that invited his followers into a way of life rather than laying down simple rules for living. To love the neighbor may be a commandment, but deciding who the neighbor is and how to love him or her is not just to obey an explicit rule. So Jesus told a parable that invites further reflection on a neighbor-oriented life rather than a rule to check off (Luke 10:25–37). And Jesus surrounded his teaching by his own life, constantly attentive to the needs of neighbors and subversive of dominating powers. Imitation of Christ has a long and rich tradition in Christian moral reflection.[28]

For the OT, however, it has been much more common in Christian theology and ethics to limit consideration of ethical resources to

27. There is, perhaps, in the scriptural texts on creation and wisdom, a notion of moral life as fitting to the natural patterns of order in a world God created as good even though it has become broken. Some have seen here an analogy to natural law. We will not discuss this option more fully here, but see especially Barton, "Approaches to Ethics," 113–30.

28. A good example of this in recent Christian ethics is Allen Verhey, *Remembering Jesus: Christian Community, Scripture and the Moral Life* (Grand Rapid: Eerdmans, 2002).

explicit moral commands and instructions. It has been traditional in discussions of ethics in the OT to focus on obedience to the revealed divine will as the primary basis for ethics in ancient Israel and among those who turn to the witness of ancient Israel for moral resources in subsequent generations.[29] The result has been attention to the Decalogue, law codes, prophetic moral admonition, and wisdom teachings. Much of this limited treatment of the OT as an ethical resource is related to the caricature of the OT as rigid "law" while it is the NT that emphasizes God's grace in "gospel." Needless to say, none of the shaping influence of Israel's story, just discussed above, receives attention.

Our contention is that even important texts of explicit moral command, such as the Decalogue, would have no meaning apart from Israel's prior experience of God's character and conduct as reflected in Israel's story of encounter and relationship with God. The Decalogue is introduced with a reference to God's previous deliverance of Israel: "I am the Lord, your God, who brought you out of the land of Egypt, out of the house of slavery" (Exod 20:2). Scholars have increasingly recognized the importance of the imitation of God's character and conduct (*imitatio Dei*) as an important basis for the moral address of the OT.[30] In the stories of the OT, God is constantly revealing new facets of the divine character and acting in ways that demonstrate the concrete moral reality of divine character. "For I am the Lord who brought you up from the land of Egypt, to be your God; you shall be holy, for I am holy" (Lev 11:45). In Micah 6:1–8, the prophet voices God's testimony in a court drama with Israel and recites examples of God's gracious actions toward Israel (vv. 3–5) and dramatically concludes the court scene with a verdict, "He has shown you, O mortal,

---

29. See, e.g., Ogletree, *Use of the Bible*, 47–48: "The moral life of the ancient Israelites . . . is bound up with a sense of their concrete history. Within this basic frame of reference, deontological motifs are dominant. What we principally find are specifications of those duties and obligations which are requisite to the ongoing life of the people."

30. It was Martin Buber (*Kampf um Israel* [Berlin: Schocken, 1933], 73) who called early attention to the "imitation of God" as central to the character of Judaism. But it has only been in recent years that scholars interested in ethics in the OT have begun to give serious attention to *imitatio Dei* as a major source of moral norms both with the OT and as it is used as moral resource by the contemporary church. These include Birch, *Let Justice Roll Down*, 125–26; John Barton, *Ethics and the Old Testament* (Harrisburg, PA: Trinity Press International, 1998), as well as several earlier publications by Barton; Paul D. Hanson, *The People Called: The Growth of Community in the Bible* (San Francisco: Harper & Row, 1986), 30, 44; Harry P. Nasuti, "Identity, Identification, and Imitation: The Narrative Hermeneutics of Biblical Law," *Journal of Law and Religion* 4, no. 1 (1986): 9–23.

what is good; and what does the Lord require of you but to do justice, and to love kindness, and to walk humbly with your God" (v. 8). God's people are to model their life after what they have experienced as the life of God who chose relationship to Israel. Even the legal codes appeal at times to this imitation of God as model for Israel's character and conduct: "[God] executes justice for the orphan and the widow and . . . loves the strangers, providing them with food and clothing. You shall also love the stranger, for you were strangers in the land of Egypt" (Deut 10:18–19). The implication is that God has committed the divine presence in human history to patterns of moral character and conduct that serve to model the moral life of the community of Israel who enters covenant partnership with God.[31]

In both the OT and NT, *imitatio Dei/Christi* does not imply that we simply try to do what God or Jesus have done. Indeed, some of the divine and christological actions are impossible for us. We cannot part the seas, bring manna in the wilderness, or walk on windblown waters. But through the testimony of Israel and the early church in the witness of biblical texts, we can enter into the reality of God and Christ in ways that shape and form our character as moral agents and communities. We enter into the life of God in ways that transform our own lives as moral agents and communities, and that transform the broader social structures of which we are a part. In seeing the life of biblically shaped Christians, the world should see God and the fullness of God in Jesus. Perhaps such seeing of God is what being created in the "image of God" in Genesis 1:26 was all about in the beginning of the biblical story.

Obedience to the revealed divine will does also play an important role as a source of moral norms in the OT and NT. A large part of the OT reflects an understanding of covenant relationship established between God and Israel. This relationship is characterized by important moral norms that are to govern both God and Israel's relationship to one another and the wider world. These include justice, righteousness, steadfast love, compassion, and faithfulness, all contributing to the establishment of shalom.[32] But these are not allowed to remain

---

31. For some examples see Bruce C. Birch, "Moral Agency, Community, and the Character of God in the Hebrew Bible," *Semeia* 66 (1994): 23–41; and Bruce C. Birch, "Divine Character and the Formation of Moral Community in the Book of Exodus," in *The Bible in Ethics: The Second Sheffield Colloquium*, ed. John W. Rogerson, Margaret Davies, and M. Daniel Carroll R. (Sheffield: Sheffield Academic Press, 1995), 119–35.

32. See Birch, *Let Justice Roll Down*, 145–97, for a detailed discussion of the covenant relationship, including discussions of these covenant categories.

abstract ideals. The practice of these moral qualities of life are spelled out concretely for Israel in commandment and law code, and shaped by the guidance and admonition of priest and prophet who boldly spoke to interpret God's will. These expressions of divine will are not rigid and eternal truths. The law codes change and develop. The leaders speak God's will for given times and contexts.

> Obedience to God's revealed will is not blind obedience, but is rooted in trust that God is faithful to the divine commitments to steadfast love, justice, righteousness and compassion. . . . God's people can be (both held accountable) and renewed as moral agents in obedience to covenant, and in some sense the OT suggests a continual process of commitment, accountability, and renewal of covenant partnership. . . . Obedience is not to an arbitrary power but grows out of enduring relationship in a life lived by the community in the presence and purpose of God. Thus, even obedience to divine will in the OT has both deontological (duty oriented) and teleological (purpose oriented) elements, and both are encompassed in a theology of shared relationship and moral agency.[33]

The NT also knows something of revealed divine will, especially in the teaching ministry of Jesus. The Sermon on the Mount (Matthew 5–8) and the Sermon on the Plain (Luke 6:20–49), as well as the lengthy teaching passages in the Gospel of John, contain some fairly directive advice on the ethics of the kingdom and the moral path of those who choose to follow Jesus. But just as often, Jesus taught in parables or in rabbinic discourses that challenged listeners to draw their own moral conclusions or to ponder moral patterns of behavior they may have thought were settled in a rigid way by Jewish law. Paul and other Christian writers in the NT often gave very specific moral advice to the specific churches they wrote to. But their intention was seldom to lay out eternal truths or rigid rules for moral behavior. In fact, Paul often showed a considerable flexibility in taking context into account, such as his famous advice in 1 Corinthians 8:9 on eating meat offered to idols: "Take care that this liberty of yours does not become a stumbling block to the weak." The ethical course of action may depend on its effect on others rather than its adherence to some divine absolute. Such explicit moral teaching is not so much an example of revealed divine will as the reflection by Paul and other NT writers on what a life would look like when lived

---

33. Birch, "Ethics in the OT," 343.

in relationship to the revealed divine presence in Jesus Christ, and especially in light of cross and resurrection.[34]

In various ways, we have been exploring in this section the interrelationship of God, community, and way of life reflected in the biblical tradition. We began with community/congregation/peoplehood as the necessary context both in the origins and reading of Scripture as a moral resource. Now we must return to this category of community in light of our discussion of the reality of God's character and conduct reflected in the biblical story.

We are clear that the community of Israel was formed under the conviction that it should reflect the character and conduct of the righteous, just, and compassionate God who knew their sufferings (Exod 3:7) and brought them up from the land of Egypt in its own moral character and conduct. Israel understood that if mighty Yahweh identified with the powerless and dispossessed, so, too, should we as the community of Yahweh. Radical love and caring justice are not optional acts of voluntary piety; they are at the heart of what it means for us to be a people of this God.[35]

The people of God are called to become a community that is radically alternative to the other communities they have known because theirs is a radically alternative God. The key to this pattern of community morality is the experienced character of God, who is here a God of the oppressed. The outcome of the process is a community that consciously tries to become an alternative to the community of oppressive power that it had known in Egypt. Covenant community with the compassionate and righteous God was defined in contrast to the imperial community of the Pharaoh, and other great cultures of the ancient Near East, where the power of the nation paralleled the power of its gods. When Egypt was weak, its gods were weak, and when Egypt was strong, its gods were strong. The power of the gods was measured by the strength of the nation's military might, economic strength, and cultural achievement, and access to the gods was mediated by an elaborate priesthood that was in partnership with a royal power who considered himself to be a god.

In such a world, it was unimaginable that a god should hear the groans of the dispossessed and freely enter a covenant relationship with slaves, who had no standing or power. There was a revolution

---

34. See the detailed discussion of this throughout the writings of Paul in Hays, *Moral Vision*.

35. See the discussion in Bruce C. Birch and Larry L. Rasmussen, *The Predicament of the Prosperous* (Philadelphia: Westminster, 1978), esp. ch. 4, "Deliverance," 80–98.

in gods, followed by a revolution in social arrangements, when these slaves fashioned a community to reflect the character of their God. That was an alternative to the practice of the nations of the period.[36] The texts of the narrative traditions that follow reflect a strong sense of peoplehood focused in relationship to God as "a kingdom of priests" and "a holy nation" (Exod 19:6), albeit precisely as a community that was not meant to be "like the other nations" (the desire of the elders in 1 Samuel 8). As in every community, the texts also reflect unmistakable evidence of human frailty and error, and narrow, unjust, and corrupting perspectives and practices. With kingship, the hated ways of the Pharaoh would, in fact, find their own counterpart later in Israel itself. It was at least as difficult to get "Egypt" out of "Israel" as "Israel" out of "Egypt." This ironic reality nonetheless does not alter the deep insistence upon finding a way to give social form to the experience of God. Such a community-creating and community-preserving experience was a marked alternative to the communities of the surrounding world in ways that "do justice, seek kindness, and walk humbly with God" (Micah 6:8).

Similar dynamics were present in the early church, as we see in Acts. The collective experience of the resurrected Jesus and the giving of the Spirit led to very practical questions: How do we now embody the intense reality of the living Christ among us in our day-to-day life together? What will we do with our goods, our houses, our land? How will we organize fellowship with one another, locally and across great distances? What should be our form of governance and how do we recognize our leaders? How will worship be conducted? How will the rituals, rites, and festivals of our former life be treated? What shall we now say to Caesar, now that "Jesus is our King" (Acts 17:7); and what should we do about service in the emperor's army? How do the relationships of parents and children, of husband and wife, of slave and slaveholder change now? How should transgressors be treated? How should we treat those who take offense at the new gospel and persecute us?

Like the Sinai responses, these efforts eventually bore all the marks

---

36. Fuller discussions of this process of the formation of alternative community in Israel as well as the tensions in maintaining such community can be found in Brueggemann, *Prophetic Imagination*, 2nd ed., esp. chs. 1 and 2; Bruce C. Birch, *What Does the Lord Require? The Old Testament Call to Social Witness* (Philadelphia: Westminster, 1985), esp. chs. 3 and 4; Paul Hanson, *The People Called: The Growth of Community in the Bible* (San Francisco: Harper & Row, 1986); and Norman K. Gottwald, *The Tribes of Yahweh: A Sociology of the Religion of Liberated Israel 1250–1050 B.C.E.* (Maryknoll, NY: Orbis, 1979).

of limited human vision and limited cooperation. Factions formed and proliferated. Nonetheless, lives were transformed in new communities that cannot be understood apart from the empowering experience of Jesus and his Way, vindicated by God in the resurrection and vivified in the Spirit. This early church was, in many ways, deeply Jewish; it was initially an alternative community within Judaism but later diverged from its Jewish origins in that it turned on "following Jesus" (the language of the Gospels) or "putting on Christ" (Pauline language). Upon closer inspection, however, we see that this was the way the Christian communities spoke of their experience of God, and this was their form of the Hebrew moral pattern; that is, a community ethic is inferred from the character of the divine presence they experienced—in Jesus and the Spirit.

CANON AS SHAPER OF MORAL COMMUNITY

At many points in the discussion above, we made reference to the canon of Scripture. A "canon" is a collection of books judged by Christian and Jewish communities to be authoritative as a foundation for the community's beliefs, life, and witness. In complex processes, over a longer period of time for the OT than the NT, the communities of ancient Israel and the early church passed on to future generations the texts they believed most faithfully reflected and witnessed to their experience of God and Jesus Christ. What was experienced as direct encounter with the transforming power of God in Israel's story is preserved, edited, and passed on so that future generations might be transformed by living into that very same story. "Not with our ancestors . . . but with us, who are all here alive today" (Deut 5:3). "Remember you were a slave" (Deut 15:15). In three different segments (Law, Prophets, and Writings), stretching from the fifth century BCE to the start of the second century CE, a settled collection of authoritative texts has been handed down virtually unchanged to the present.

Likewise, as eyewitnesses who knew and experienced the life, death, and resurrection of Jesus of Nazareth began to die off, there was a need for their experience and witness to take written form. "Since many have undertaken to set down an orderly account of the events that have been fulfilled among us, just as they were handed on to us by those who from the beginning were eyewitnesses and servants of the word, I too decided, after investigating everything carefully from the very first, to write an orderly account for you, most excellent Theophilus, so that you may know the truth concerning the things about which you have been instructed" (Luke 1:1–4). The letters of early apostles such as Paul were valued, preserved, and organized into collections. Once again, through a complex process, a collection of texts was agreed upon and became the NT canon of the church.

In chapter 4, we will offer a more thorough discussion of the canon of Scripture and the important role it plays in using the Bible as a resource for Christian ethics. We bring attention to the canonical collections of the OT and NT here because it is the culmination of the community witness that gave rise to the texts of the Bible in the first place. The Bible is both formed in the context of community and made available to future generations through the processes of preserving, editing, organizing, and passing on those texts. The Bible is the product of the community of faith through the generations.

Since the canon developed in the context of actual faith communities, it reflects all the gifts *and* failures of those communities. For example, the NT contains not only witness to the ethic of coequal discipleship rooted in the ministry of Jesus but also the household codes (*Haustafeln*) of Colossians 3 and Ephesians 5, in which that ethic was subverted due to pressure toward cultural acceptability (e.g., advising slaves to submit to masters and wives to husbands).[37]

A canon that reflects the realities of actual community experience with God is necessarily pluralistic.[38] The canon does not speak with a single voice. This is both a witness to the variety of experience with God and a corrective to warn us against absolutizing any selection of the voices through which Scripture speaks. That the biblical communities themselves can be seen judging, reinterpreting, and measuring the tradition against their own experience of God can be read as support for similar activity on our part.

This will, of course, necessitate attention to every level of witness preserved within the text, as well as to the final form of the text as

---

37. Elisabeth Schüssler Fiorenza, "Discipleship and Patriarchy: Early Christian Ethos and Christian Ethics in a Feminist Theological Perspective," *Annual of the Society of Christian Ethics* 2 (1982): 131–72.

38. See a brief but very helpful discussion by James A. Sanders, "The Bible as Canon," *The Christian Century* 98, no. 39 (December 2, 1981): 1250–55.

the ultimate shape given to the text by the biblical communities. The canon is a record not only of a destination but of the journey as well.

The witnesses and arrangements of the texts in the canon of both the OT and NT do not seem related so much to historical realities (e.g., the history of tribal or royal Israel or the actual historical Jesus) so much as to the need to make the story of Israel and the early church, as it has been synthesized by the community, available to future generations. We may be interested in and seek historical and social realities behind the texts, and this may enrich our understanding, but such knowledge, due to the nature of textual resources, will only be partially available in any case. "Thus, the task of [biblical] ethics is to recognize that the canon is a theological construct that does not directly relate to an historical Israel" or early church.[39]

In the next two chapters, we address perspectives on how the authority of Scripture has been and can be understood in relation to the Bible as a moral resource, and to issues and practices that might be helpful in actually claiming and using the Bible as a resource for Christian ethics.

---

39. Birch, "Ethics in the OT," 341, citing the more detailed work along these lines in B. Childs, *Biblical Theology*.

3.

Biblical Authority

No one who wants to talk about the Bible and ethics can avoid talking about biblical authority. In fact, no one who reads the Bible at all can avoid the sticky question of biblical authority, although many try, pretending that the Bible's authority is self-evident when it is not. But when it comes to relating the Bible to ethics, questions about the Bible's authority become even more complex. This chapter will explore some of that complexity.

The Bible's role in ethics is both formative and normative; it shapes the people of God and functions as a resource in discerning how to live faithfully before God. The Bible's authority rests not in the book itself but in its power to enable life-giving encounter with the living God, the self, others, and all of creation. The Bible is authoritative to the extent that it allows people to "know" God as God has been active through cosmic history, and also as God is today creating, saving, and sustaining. That is, Scripture is authoritative in enabling us to recognize the saving and creating work of God in our midst today and to discern the ways of doing and being that enable us to participate in God's activity in the world. The Bible authorizes us to follow in those ways, in forming character consistent with those ways, and in nurturing relationship and conversation within the communities across the ages that have sought to live as people of this God. One could say the Bible is authoritative as it leads people to hear and be led by the Spirit of the Triune God.

THE NATURE OF BIBLICAL AUTHORITY

Two things can be said about the role of the Bible in ethical reflection: (1) it is not the *only* source of ethical reflection for Christians, but (2) it does have a unique role in that reflection. We want to examine each of these claims in turn. Reading the Bible for Christian ethics does not mean expounding the ethics of ancient Israel or those implicit in NT texts. Rather, it means that Christians are wrestling with the deep ethical questions that emerge from their reading of the Scriptures, OT and NT.

What do we mean when we talk about the authority of Scripture? The word "authority" refers to that which an individual or a community acknowledges as a source of decisive influence in its life. *An authority may be a document or a body of material* (e.g., the Magna Carta), a person, or a community. Strictly speaking, an authority is what authorizes or empowers us. The matter of authority focuses not on some inherent quality in a source of authority but on the process of authorization that takes place as we, as individuals and communities, interact with that source.

The question of the authority of the Bible has long vexed Christianity. The Christian faith has had, and continues to have, many and varied expressions throughout the world over time, in part because of diverse understandings of the nature of biblical authority. All Christian traditions take the Bible, understood as Scripture, to be normative for Christian life and practice, but how that normative character is understood varies across the spectrum of Christian faith. Furthermore, how Scripture as an authority is understood in its relation to other authorities (tradition, experience, reason) also varies.

THE BIBLE AS "WORD OF GOD"

The "word of God," according to Martin Luther, as well as other Reformers such as John Calvin, is not the Bible per se.[1] Luther insisted that the "word of God" is first and foremost Christ present with, in, and for creation. The Bible is the word of God in a secondary sense as it points to Jesus Christ. We turn to the Bible in order to know the

1. For a discussion of the Reformers' understanding of the authority of Scripture, see Michael Joseph Brown, "Hearing the Master's Voice," in *Engaging Biblical Authority: Perspectives on the Bible as Scripture*, ed. William P. Brown (Louisville: Westminster John Knox, 2007), 13–15.

living Christ so intimately that we might discern what it means to live according to Christ's ways. As taught by Luther, the faithful are to wrestle with Scripture, guided by the Holy Spirit, and are to use faith, study, reason, and good judgment to discern how the voice of God speaks in particular texts to us in our time and place. Our interpretation of the Bible is to be guided by one norm: the Gospel of Jesus Christ, the living word of God for us, with us, and in us.

The Bible's authority is thus not a property inherent in the Bible itself. That authority derives from God, from the recognition of the Christian community over centuries of experience that Scripture is a primary source of empowerment for its life in the world. Authority derives from acknowledgment of a source's power to influence us, not from an absolute power that operates apart from the affirmation of the community. While some consider the actual pages of a Bible sacred, the Bible's authority does not lie in the paper or the book itself. Rather, the Bible gestures beyond itself to faith communities' experience with the character and activity of God, and the Bible's authority lies in its function as a unique witness to that activity. God called Israel and the church into covenantal relationships in the past, as attested in the Scriptures, and that same God continues to be graciously active and present in those relationships today.

THE DIVERSITY OF THE BIBLICAL WITNESS

Whether we choose to recognize it or not, our lives, including our moral lives, are shaped by many sources of authority. Our identities, both as individuals and within communities, have been shaped and guided by a complex matrix of authoritative influences, including family, education (both formal and informal), religious background, socioeconomic location, gender experience, nationality, ethnic identities, and significant life events, among others. Yet, if we are engaged in Christian ethics, we will see the Bible as normative in some way; otherwise the ethics we are talking about are not Christian ethics. With that said, the Bible is never the sole source of authority (despite claims to the contrary), though it has a unique authoritative function. The authoritative role of the Bible in Christian ethics binds all Christians together, through time and space, in a common tradition of seeking the word of God through Scripture.

The Bible is, of course, not one book but a library of books: a collection of texts written over hundreds of years in various contexts. Who we are as the people of God today is tied to the witness of the communities responsible for the authoring and reception of these texts. Within that diverse witness, the story of Jesus, told in the distinct voices of the four Gospels, stands out as centrally important. Yet, Jesus's story also looks back to Israel's story, as told in the Hebrew Scriptures, and forward to the story told in the early church. Pondering that larger biblical story helps us to discern God's presence and activity in our own stories.

It is worth pausing a moment to reflect on how stories are connected to ethical reflection. How do our minds and hearts encounter the Bible and the living God in it? How does the Bible open doors to these life-giving relationships and power? Human minds work, in part, through storytelling. We order the flood of data in the right hemispheres of our brains via the stories we tell. In moral matters, we cross the gap from "is" to "ought," from what is to what might and should be, by appealing to stories. Their insights and "lessons" help say where we ought to go from here and how we are to get there. So much of moral argument, including deep disagreement as well as agreement, is grounded in the narratives we live by. And much moral ambiguity is grounded in the fact that we internalize competing stories.

Because the biblical materials are themselves diverse, it necessarily follows that the ways in which those materials function as authoritative are also necessarily diverse. One of Paul's letters, written for a specific occasion to a specific group of people, is perhaps not authoritative in the same way that a poem from the psalter or one of Jesus's parables is. Genre is of critical importance when thinking about authority: how stories shape us morally is different from the way we engage the Ten Commandments, for example. This important point is often overlooked, for the different materials in the Bible are not, nor can they be, authoritative in one single way. One might rightly posit a moral imperative, a *normative* imperative, to care for those who have become impoverished based on one's exegesis of legal material, much of the prophetic corpus, or the teachings of Jesus, in contemporary ethical discussions of how to respond to poverty. The counterargument of the so-called "prosperity gospel," on the other hand, is not biblically tenable. One of the most important problems with using the Bible to support a gospel of prosperity is that in those biblical texts where God wills the "prosperity" of the people, the meaning of "prosperity" is not exclusively or even predominantly about material wealth but rather is about God willing the *shalom*, the wholeness, the flourishing of the community. Such wholeness entails much more than financial prosperity. In fact, God's *shalom* for the community is put at risk when the community possesses too much wealth. For example, the prophet Amos argues that the people's accrual of wealth has caused them to thwart justice and care of the impoverished. In the NT, Jesus's attention to the economically and socially marginal and his criticism of acquiring and hoarding wealth are apparent throughout the Gospels.

The authority of Scripture lies partly in how the Bible attests to the way that those who wrote and first received the Scriptures discerned and responded to the presence and activity of God. But it is more than this, for this process of discernment in turn invites our own discernment: we read the Scriptures in order to reflect on the presence and activity of God in our time. There is a dynamic relationship here between the content of Scripture (some of which raises concerns, e.g., slavery, the status of women) and the process of discernment. We will take up this complex dynamic in more detail below.

Yet, the most important authority that Scripture has for us is not its normative force in telling us to do this or not to do that but in the way that it shapes us as people and communities of faith, as it forms our very being. As Luke Timothy Johnson says, "[Scripture] reveals a world that is created, sustained, saved, and sanctified by the living God, and invites humans to enter the world that Scripture imagines and make it real in the empirical world through the way they live."[2] For Scripture to shape us in this deeply powerful way, for it to reach our very bones so that we might enact the world it imagines in *our* world, we have to read and interpret the Bible as a whole, and regularly. This must be done in our homes, with our children (Deut 6:7), but also corporately in our communities of faith (Neh 8:1–3).

2. Luke Timothy Johnson, "The Bible's Authority for and in the Church" in *Engaging Biblical Authority: Perspectives on the Bible as Scripture*, ed. William P. Brown (Louisville: Westminster John Knox, 2007), 69.

COLLAPSE OF TRADITIONAL VIEWS
OF BIBLICAL AUTHORITY

Traditionally, biblical authority has been associated with the concept of inspiration. This began as early as the fixing of the written Torah during the period following the Babylonian exile. For Jews, the text itself became the locus of divine revelation, and within that text, in all of its variety and detail, could be found a divine word and guidance applicable to present and future generations. In the early church, as new documents appeared and became influential in the life of the church (e.g., the letters of Paul, Gospels), these texts also came to be regarded as divinely inspired. Using texts such as 2 Timothy 3:16, "All scripture is inspired by God," and 2 Peter 1:21, "men and women moved by the Holy Spirit spoke from God," Christians elaborated a concept of divine authorship through inspiration.

This way of thinking about the authority of Scripture as a "unique deposit of divine revelation" held sway in both Protestant and Catholic traditions until the Enlightenment,[3] when its inherent weaknesses rose to the surface. One difficulty with this view of inspiration is that there is no agreement on what it means. It can range from inerrancy (see our critique below), to limited notions of inspired infallibility in matters of faith and practice, communicated through socially conditioned contexts, to locating inspiration in the authors or communities that gave us the biblical texts but regarding the texts themselves as human products (and, in fact, we will offer a more robust version of something like this ourselves below). "Inspiration" is too much of a Rorschach blot to be a meaningful category for discussion.

A second difficulty with inspiration as it has traditionally been understood (in its inerrancy formulas or inspiration-as-divine-deposit), is that it tends to invest undue authority in the text of the Bible, and thus advocates that Christians place their faith in a book and not in the God to whom the Bible witnesses. This has been a greater danger in Protestantism than in Roman Catholicism, where notions of inspiration have expanded to include church tradition as well. Such a sacralizing of the text tends to reduce the biblical authors

---

3. Edward Farley and Peter C. Hodgson, "Scripture and Tradition," in *Christian Theology: An Introduction to Its Traditions and Tasks*, ed. Peter C. Hodgson and Robert H. King (Philadelphia: Fortress Press, 1985), 62.

and communities to the role of mere conduits and to obscure what we might learn from the Bible about genuine relationship to God.

A third problem emerges in that views that connect inspiration to authority tend, in practice, and in spite of all theory to the contrary, to elevate portions of Scripture to positions of authority that imply they are more inspired than the rest. This has often been the case with regard to the NT in relation to the OT, and even regarding the Gospels within the NT. Some of this may seem like commonsense observation: "You shall not sow your vineyard with a second kind of seed" (Deut 22:9) does not have the same status as the Ten Commandments. But if the authority of Scripture is rooted in inspiration-as-divine-deposit, then one is forced to come to the conclusion that God was more inspiring on some occasions than on others. A modified version of the inspiration model is recoverable (see our discussion of the role of the Holy Spirit in chapter 4), but this inspiration-as-divine-deposit is not workable.

CHALLENGES TO THE TRADITIONAL VIEW

The first major challenge to the traditional view of inspiration-as-divine-deposit came from the rise of historical critical methods of studying the Bible. Beginning with the Enlightenment, but coming to full fruition in the nineteenth and twentieth centuries, methods of critical study were applied to the Bible, including text criticism, that sought to establish the most ancient and "authentic" text from among the many versions and manuscripts available. Of course, this had the effect of relativizing the text. If authority lay inherent in an "inspired" text, which textual tradition was the "inspired" and thus authoritative one? Or did authority only lie in some original, unrecoverable text? (That would be very problematic since one could not recover it.)[4]

Next came literary, or more aptly, source criticism,[5] with its

4. Some fundamentalists distinguish between "original autographs" and "the original text" of the Bible. The former, some acknowledge, are not accessible, but they claim that "the original text" is nonetheless available to us because "even though a single surviving manuscript might not contain (all of) the original text, the original text could be accessible to us across a wide range of manuscripts" (Michael Kruger, "The Difference Between Original Autographs and Original Texts," The Gospel Coalition, May 14, 2013, http://tinyurl.com/ycgr37fv). But no reputable scholar has offered any credible criteria by which one might assess such "originality" as elements dispersed across multiple manuscripts; indeed, the proposal necessarily recognizes that textual variation has made the identification of a single "original" text impossible.

5. The use of the term "literary criticism" for "source criticism" has led to some confusion because the same terminology is used in more recent decades to talk about approaches

concerns for authorship and sources (as the name "source criticism" implies), closely followed by tradition history and its interest in tracing the development of traditions through generations of the biblical communities and their institutions. Careful study of Deuteronomy shows, for example, that it was not written all at once, but seems to have a core of material to which other sections were appended over time. Studies such as these made readily apparent that biblical materials were not the product of some momentary activity of divine deposit. They were the result of complex literary and historical development within the life of the biblical communities of faith as they witnessed to their experiences in relation to God. Stories were told and retold, combined and edited, preserved and embellished. Most inspiration models focus on the text itself, but critical study shifted some of that focus and attention to the processes behind the text and the communities where those processes unfolded.

Newer methods of literary criticism, borrowed from other disciplines in the humanities (literary theories of narrative, metaphor, semiotics, linguistics, narrative, and poetic ethics), have illumined biblical texts in new and exciting ways, showing that meaning lies not statically in the text itself but in the dynamic process of reading, a process that is always moving from behind the text (the context of production, the writers' context in all its complexity) through the text itself (the words) to what is in front of the text (the context of the reader in all its complexity). This is not a linear movement but a dynamic back-and-forth movement that is going on all the time in the reading process.

Implied in this complex reading process are the social locations of both writers and readers, and the significant attention given to these aspects in the last several decades further undermines most models of inspiration. Real people in particular communities both wrote these texts and currently read them, and this shapes both what is contained in the texts and how they are read today. In the case of the production of the texts, the Bible is still the story of God's graceful initiative, but the actual shaping of the biblical witness to that grace seems more clearly located in and affected by the human communities of biblical times than inspiration views of authority suggest. In the case of how

to reading Scripture that utilize the kinds of methods one uses when reading other kinds of literature (e.g., theories about metaphor, characterization, use of time). Especially in older scholarly publications on the Bible, "literary criticism" usually is equivalent to "source criticism"; only later does it take on the more commonly understood meaning as related to literary studies.

we read them now, there is a powerful sense that different readings are possible based on the social location of the ones doing the reading today.

Three hermeneutical orientations, and the theological frameworks from which they come, have been particularly significant in making the social location of readers (and, to a certain extent, also the writers of the Bible, esp. in the case of feminist and postcolonial hermeneutics) a factor that cannot be ignored in the interpretation of the Bible: liberation, feminist/womanist, and most recently, postcolonial thought.[6] These theologies and ways of thinking, from the perspective of marginalized peoples, have challenged the prevailing modes of Western, Anglo, male, unconsciously colonialist biblical interpretation as ideologically biased. They see clearly that biblical authority does not reside abstractly in texts. It only functions as texts are interpreted and used. When texts are interpreted predominantly from the social locations of the powerful, the rich, the white, the colonizing (and those who benefit from past colonization), and the male culture, then biblical authority is invoked, consciously or unconsciously, to authorize and empower that reigning cultural ideology.

BIBLICAL AUTHORITY: FOCUS AND LOCUS

If we have indeed experienced the collapse of biblical authority, as it has often been understood, then how are we to understand it? A beginning response suggests that questions of biblical authority properly focus not on the Bible itself (qualities inherent in the book) but on the presence and activity of God. The Scriptures themselves attest that it is the transformative power of God, not the text itself, that is to be the focus of our faith.

In the Gospel stories, Jesus speaks "with authority" (*exousia*), which

6. Representative works on liberation theology with attention to biblical hermeneutics include Juan Luís Segundo, *Liberation of Theology*, trans. John Drury (Maryknoll, NY: Orbis, 1976); J. Severino Croatto, *Exodus: A Hermeneutics of Freedom*, trans. Salvator Attanasio (Maryknoll, NY: Orbis, 1981); and bridging from liberation theology to postcolonial criticism, Fernando F. Segovia, *Decolonizing Biblical Studies: A View from the Margins* (Maryknoll, NY: Orbis, 2000). From a feminist perspective, see Carol A. Newsom, Sharon Ringe, and Jacqueline Lapsley, eds., *A Women's Bible Commentary*, 3rd ed. (Louisville: Westminster John Knox, 2012). Womanist biblical interpretation is represented by the excellent work of Nyasha Junior, *An Introduction to Womanist Biblical Interpretation* (Louisville: Westminster John Knox, 2015). For postcolonial criticism, a major figure in biblical studies has been R. S. Sugirtharajah, *Exploring Postcolonial Biblical Criticism: History, Method, Practice* (Chichester: Wiley-Blackwell, 2012).

meant that he was speaking "out of his being," evoking a power based on his experience, on who he was. The point here is that the Bible is, as a book, not the authority. It is Jesus who spoke with authority. *Through* the Scriptures, Jesus might yet speak with authority, but that does not substitute the Bible for Jesus. In fact, both Jesus and the Bible point to the Triune God, in whom we live and move and have our being, as the final source where both Jesus's power and our own rests. The Bible is the unique and authoritative witness to the God of Jesus Christ, who is graciously active in the world and whose will is disclosed to people in and through that activity.

Exegesis, literally "drawing out" meaning from a biblical text, is the "practiced art" of interpreting a biblical passage with due respect for both the ancient context of production (writing) and the modern context of reading.[7] The text records God's self-disclosure to the communities of Israel and the early church in such a way that it illumines the church's understanding of God's activity and the revealing of the divine will for the present-day Christian community. Christian ethics, faced with questions of how Christians are to understand and conduct themselves in a complex and changing world, seeks to read the signs of God's activity and to discern the divine will for the present, and in so doing calls on the resources of the historic Christian faith, including, in primary position, the Scriptures and their history of interpretation in the church. (The history of interpretation of Scripture is often rightly called the "history of consequences."[8]) Exegesis begins with the text and ancient context but must consider present context as well. Christian ethics begins with a present demand to be and do but draws on the ancient texts. Both endeavors are the necessary activities of the same community, the church. As such, it is a travesty that the work of biblical study and that of ethics have been, and continue to be, so often compartmentalized from each other in the life of the church.

Theologically, the problem with locating biblical authority in a narrow concept of inspiration is the equally narrow view of God that results. It is as if God ceased to be active after the closing of the canon. The tendency is to speak as if God's disclosure of the divine will is limited to the distant past, and as if it is only in the written record of

---

7. William P. Brown, *A Handbook to Old Testament Exegesis* (Louisville: Westminster John Knox, 2017), x.

8. On the significance of this change in terminology, see Choon-Leong Seow, *Job 1–21: Interpretation and Commentary*, Illuminations (Grand Rapids: Eerdmans, 2013), 110.

that past that God's presence and will can be known. At stake here is the freedom of God. It has always been the tendency of religious communities to attempt to limit and control the graceful activity of the God who says, "I will be merciful to whom I will be merciful" (Exod 33:19, cf. Rom 9:15). This dynamic was certainly already present in the biblical communities themselves. When the prophet of the exile announced Cyrus as God's Messiah, the instrument of God's deliverance for Israel (Isa 45:1), the people rejected the notion because for them Cyrus, a foreigner, was not a proper source of God's grace; this in turn called forth the prophet's rebuke (Isa 45:9–13).

God was not only active in relationship to Israel and the early church communities. God has continued to make the divine will known to the church in all succeeding ages, and is still present, disclosing the divine will for the church and the world. The job of Christian ethics, nurtured by disciplined yet artful exegesis of the biblical witness, is to aid the church in discerning that will. This wider understanding of God's activity greatly opens the range of possibilities for theological and ethical sources of insight. The history of the church and its understandings of the faith, secular ideologies, the course of contemporary events, data from nontheological disciplines such as the social and the natural sciences—all these and many more become possible avenues through which God may confront us or inspire us with knowledge of the divine will for all creation. Indeed, creation itself, understood as the very environment in which everything must coexist, is a witness both to God's originating activity and God's sustaining and revealing presence in all that surrounds us. In sum, then, a strict view of inspiration leaves no room for the ongoing activity of God and the possibility that God might be revealed through sources other than the Bible.

THE ROLE OF THE CHURCH

In what sense is the Bible primary but not self-sufficient with regard to ethical matters? First of all, it is the document that establishes the particular identity of the historic community called the church. The Bible is the record of the origins of the church and of the faith tradition it bears. It is the only full witness to the person and work of Jesus Christ, who stands as the focusing center for the Christian faith and for the Christian moral life. But these are not the most important reasons for the Bible's primary authority in the life of the church. For it is also the church's experience that the Bible continues to be a source of empowerment in every generation. That this has taken different forms and emphases does not negate the importance of the consistent testimony to the Bible as a source of such authority (*exousia*). Christian ethics is free to choose among the many sources of ethical wisdom available, but it is not free to ignore the Bible unless it wishes to end the continuity of historic identity in which the church stands.[9]

Second, not only does the Bible serve to establish the historic identity of the church, it also provides a chief influence in shaping the perception and action of the church on current moral issues. One of the most significant issues, for example, upon which the Bible reflects again and again in law, prophetic exhortation, story, and the teachings of Jesus, is the plight of those who are impoverished; the consistent emphasis on this matter in the biblical witness does and should inform the church's moral witness. Through the liturgy, proclamation, and teaching of the church, the Bible influences the way in which the Christian community discerns God's will in the world and acts on it. The Bible is already present and functioning to shape Christian moral agency in the life of the church. Only as the church comes to know God in its own historic traditions can the work of discerning the divine activity in the present be completed.

Thus, the Bible's unique relationship to the church makes it the constant source to which the church refers in the shaping of moral character and in the making of moral decisions. When Scripture has shaped us so powerfully because we have drunk so deeply of it that it has reached our very bones, then its shaping power is hardly noticeable to us anymore—the ways in which it shapes the moral character of the church and of ourselves as individuals may not be entirely visible to us, but they are no less powerful and effective at creating ethos in us and in our communities.[10] For Christians, no other source of moral wisdom can claim this kind of shaping power. The primacy

---

9. Similarly, if a person or a group chooses to open the Christian canon to admit other texts as canonical, one is free to do so, but one ceases to be in continuity with historic Christianity. One chooses a new, non-Christian identity in the way, for example, the Mormons did in the nineteenth century.

10. According to Brent Strawn's (*The Old Testament Is Dying: A Diagnosis and Recommended Treatment* [Grand Rapids: Baker Academic, 2017]) analysis, the church now faces serious consequences because, in fact, Christians no longer read or understand the OT (and the NT is likely not far behind).

of the Bible as an authority for Christian ethics indicates its position as the single necessary reference point. It is to be taken seriously in all ethical reflection within the church.

OTHER SOURCES OF ETHICAL REFLECTION

Although the Bible may be the primary authority, it alone is not a sufficiently broad base of authority for Christian ethics in the modern church. While a necessary source, the Bible must be in constant dialogue with the many other sources of knowledge and insight through which God might be disclosed. Such nonbiblical sources are, first of all, necessary simply for data in understanding the issues of modern times and our lives in such times. Many issues could not be foreseen at all in the biblical communities, while others have form, complexity, and context that were not anticipated.

One may well ask what the relationship of biblical authority is to the authority of nonbiblical sources within Christian ethics. While it would be a mistake to attempt a hierarchical ordering of authorities among sources, biblical and nonbiblical, it is possible to suggest that the relationship among sources is dynamic and dialogical.[11] Most views of biblical authority, traditional in orientation, have been too rigid to allow this kind of relationship. Such traditional views have collapsed in the face of developments in modern theology and biblical studies, and this collapse creates a new context in which questions of authority must be raised.

Biblical authority may, however, function to help us claim the authority of nonbiblical sources. It is from the Bible that we have drawn models of the transforming power of encounter with God. As we come to understand the images, symbols, and metaphors used to describe that encounter in the biblical communities, we become sensitized to the possibilities for such encounters with God and their transforming power in our own world. It is our knowledge of God mediated through Scripture that helps us to discern God acting in the present. Since our God is radically free, divine presence and action will not be limited to official understanding, describing, and proclaiming of divine activity. The presence and power of God is potentially discernible everywhere. The Bible authorizes our efforts

11. The idea of relationality in biblical authority can be traced to James Barr, *The Bible in the Modern World* (New York: Harper & Row, 1973).

to couple biblical insight with insight drawn from our own time and place to create models appropriate to proclaim God's "new thing" (Isa 42:9) in continuity with God's graceful presence in our past.

It is precisely the Bible itself that anticipates and makes this point. It has become clear that in the growth of the biblical material, Israel and the early church did not hesitate to draw on sources already in existence outside their communities of faith if those materials served to communicate more clearly their understanding of the relationship to God and the divine will for the people of God. The early parts of Genesis show many affinities with texts and traditions from other ancient Near Eastern cultures, but they are carefully shaped by Israel's theological concerns: Genesis highlights the power and sovereignty of Israel's God, Yahweh, over the cosmos, in contrast to the depiction of the gods in many of the similar ancient Near Eastern materials. Many elements of Israelite law and covenant seem to rely on well-known international legal traditions. It has been known for decades, for example, that the basic form for the covenant between God and Israel found in the Pentateuch has predecessors in ancient Near Eastern treaty formulations. Yet Israel adapted these treaties with considerable theological creativity to suit their theological ends, their experience of God in their community. Wisdom literature is now widely understood as a secular genre characteristic of royal courts in the ancient Near East that Israel borrowed and used to its own purposes. This is clear in Proverbs but also in the affinity between Job and other similar accounts of innocent sufferers found in other ancient Near Eastern cultures. The author of the Gospel of John used a whole range of philosophical categories current in the Hellenistic world of his day to present his unique witness to the life of Jesus. The list could easily be extended. It is sufficient to say that the Bible itself makes clear that the sources of theological and ethical insight are not narrowly limited to those materials that arise only from within the community of faith itself. The community is constantly "finding" God in its wider world and appropriating materials from that world to express faith.

This has continued to be true throughout the history of the church. Saint Augustine's theology and ethics were profoundly influenced by Neoplatonism, and Saint Thomas Aquinas utilized the "pagan" philosophy of Aristotle. It is no less true for our present day. The church cannot do ethics on the basis of the Bible alone. If the Bible is not the only source of ethical reflection for Christians, what are the other sources? We suggest there are two: The first is tradition, understood broadly as the traditions of the church, moral and theological, which includes the history of the interpretation of Scripture. The second is experience, which may be understood broadly to include knowledge of the sociopolitical and cultural contexts in which the church seeks to shape moral character and discharge its mission to the world, and knowledge of the world that comes from secular disciplines (and its attendant categories of discourse for communicating the church's moral concerns to the secular world).[12] There are more specific categories of "experience" available to the church as potential sources in its exercise of ethical judgment than we could list here, but below, we will give a few concrete examples by way of illustration.

TRADITION, INCLUDING THE HISTORY OF INTERPRETATION OF THE BIBLE

Protestants, in particular, are sometimes tempted to believe interpreting Scripture is simply a matter of a believer sitting down to read the Bible, and that whatever emerges from that individual encounter is authoritative. In reality, the Bible has been interpreted for over two millennia within faithful communities, and to ignore that long history of interpretation is both theological malpractice and also impossible. No one sits down to read not having been shaped by certain streams of interpretation. Instead, the history of the Bible's interpretation and the early creeds of the church serve as important sources of authority alongside our present engagement with biblical texts. Luke Timothy Johnson offers a helpful definition of tradition as encompassing

> all the authentic realizations of Christian life based in Scripture and all the profound interpretations of Christian life by theologians grounded in the interpretation of Scripture. And, in the most proper sense, tradition ought to include as well all the saints through the ages whose lives have embodied the vision of God found in Scripture.[13]

12. "Experience," on this formulation, encompasses the "reason" and "experience" categories of the traditional Wesleyan formulation of Scripture, tradition, reason, experience. Likewise, "experience" here encompasses the version of the formulation that will be discussed in chapter 7 in which "reason" is articulated as "other bodies of knowledge."

13. L. T. Johnson, "Bible's Authority," 65–66.

What constitutes "authentic realizations of Christian life" and "profound interpretations of Christian life" may be a matter of some debate, but the underlying idea is sound for Protestants as well as Roman Catholics and Orthodox: the Christian tradition is an important resource for moral and ethical reflection.

An illustrative example comes from the history of interpretation of the Ten Commandments. Many prominent interpreters within Judaism and Christianity have understood the Ten Commandments as a summation of the moral law. As early as the first century CE, the Jewish interpreter Philo of Alexandria understood the Torah, that is, all the laws in the Jewish Scriptures, to be an elaboration of the Ten Commandments. In the Christian tradition, both Martin Luther and John Calvin understood the commandments broadly, interpreting the "negative" commandments positively. Thus, the commandment against killing, for example, is appropriately understood as a command to promote the neighbor's well-being. Calvin observes that the commandment "contains . . . the requirements that we give our neighbor's life all the help we can."[14] More recently, Patrick Miller has extended this Reformation idea by suggesting that a moral "trajectory" emerges from each commandment, thus indicating the broad swath of the moral life that the commandments encompass.[15]

Yet, the history of biblical interpretation has not all been salutary, and this painful history is also important for ethical reflection. The history of anti-Semitic readings of biblical texts, as well as interpretations that have been used to oppress women, people of color, people with disabilities, LGBTQ people, and others who did or do not conform to certain conventional social norms, is painfully long. These elements in the history of Christian interpretation alert us to the dangers of ways of reading that impede the flourishing of others.

EXPERIENCE

The role of experience may seem obvious but needs to be stated. In general, when we speak of experience as an authority for Christian ethics, we do not mean personal, private experience, but the corporate, shared experience of how God seems to be at work in human

---

14. Patrick D. Miller, *The Ten Commandments* (Interpretation: Resources for the Use of Scripture in the Church; Louisville: Westminster John Knox, 2009), 264.
15. Ibid., 4–9.

lives in particular times and places. We say "seems to be at work" because discerning God's work in the world is a task that must be approached with the utmost humility, recognizing that one's judgments are always subject to correction. Yet, that discernment is a necessary task for Christian ethics and should be approached with humble reliance upon God's grace, for God will have God's way with the world in the end.

Two examples make the case more clearly. Long, painful experience has ended chattel slavery (though other forms of slavery are actively practiced today all over the world, such as sex trafficking), and the status of women has changed dramatically over the last one hundred years alone. As a result, many Christians read the Bible in ways starkly different from the way they did even seventy-five to a hundred years ago, to say nothing of the early church period. The significance of Genesis 1:26 ("Then God said, 'Let us make humankind in our image, according to our likeness'") and Galatians 3:28 ("There is no longer . . . slave or free, . . . no longer male and female; for all of you are one in Christ Jesus") come to the foreground, and other texts that had been used to oppress women and minorities are pushed to the background, or are interpreted with new eyes.

In these cases, it is possible to see human experience—the horrors of chattel slavery, the oppression of women—as giving rise to new biblical interpretations, and to see that God was at work in the stirrings of conscience that led to these new interpretations. But experience is not always a positive shaping force in biblical interpretation. Consider Augustine, the great fourth- and fifth-century theologian of the church, who decided in his reading of the garden story in Genesis 3 that the purpose of sexuality must be purely for procreation. Why? For Augustine, had the purpose of sexuality been for companionship, God would certainly have given Adam a *man* as a partner because he thought men were much better company![16] In Augustine's world, in which women were not thought worth educating and so were largely uneducated, it was, not surprisingly, difficult for him to imagine a companionate marriage with a woman with whom he could converse on quasi-equal terms.

What is important to recognize is that we are always making

16. See Kristen E. Kvam, Linda S. Schearing, and Valarie H. Ziegler, eds., *Eve and Adam: Jewish, Christian, and Muslim Readings on Genesis and Gender* (Bloomington: Indiana University Press, 2009), 150–52.

our corporate experience a source of authority in Christian ethics, whether we know it or not. It is, in fact, impossible to interpret Scripture (or any text) without drawing on one's experience. And this is not inherently to be lamented; on the contrary, there is much to be gained. The key is to make conscious how our experience influences our interpretation of Scripture, so we are not blind to the shaping power of that experience in the way we read, and to be alert in our discernment process to how God is at work. Is the Holy Spirit at work in our corporate experience, leading us to new insights about ourselves and the world? Or does our experience pinch us and narrow our view of what is around us, so that our view of God's world and ourselves is constricted and confined? Does our corporate experience lead us to readings of Scripture that help all of creation and humanity to flourish?

We now have considerable knowledge of the world that previous generations did not have when interpreting Scripture—for example, knowledge that comes from advances in science. If God is the God of all truth (and surely that is the case), then God is the God of scientific truth as well. And science that has been subject to the rigors of the scientific method and peer review is worth our acceptance (albeit provisionally, due to its evolving nature) alongside other truths. Science tells us about how the Earth and the universe were formed (4.5 billion years ago in some kind of "big bang"), and science is beginning to tell us about human sexual identities, about the connections between morality and neuroscience, and about how human activity is damaging our climate, and so the health of our planet. The activity of God is not confined to Scripture but is all around us, including in the intellectual tasks of understanding our world.

Accepting science as one voice of experience and allowing it to enter into our ethical deliberations with Scripture and the Holy Spirit does not mean we allow the latest specific scientific theory to guide our thinking without due deliberation, including rigorous peer review; all hypotheses must provide reproducible results according to the scientific method. So, time and discernment are required when reflecting on the role that experience should play in making ethical judgments. Nor does it mean that the Bible is subordinate to science in any overarching way; we are not to submit ourselves, or Scripture, to an uncritical embrace of the Enlightenment project of rationality. On the contrary, there has been a historical temptation to deify the outcomes of science, with disastrous results—this is a hubris that neither humanity nor the rest of creation can afford. But the truths of scientific inquiry, as one voice of experience with Scripture and the Holy Spirit (see chapter 4), can be revelatory of what God is doing in the world.

Dennis Olson, a biblical theologian and pastor, has observed: "Good science and good theology both share a certain epistemological humility, a confession of ignorance that drives our questions and motivates a blend of creativity and rigor as we face unresolved problems."[17] Careful, thoughtful scientists recognize the vital role of consciousness of ignorance in scientific inquiry, as Stuart Firestein, chair of the biological sciences department at Columbia University, has argued. He notes that science is not, at its core,

> the *Scientific Method*, an immutable set of precepts for devising experiments that churn out the cold hard facts. . . . [Science is] not facts and rules. It's black cats in dark rooms. As the Princeton mathematician Andrew Wiles describes it: It's groping and probing and poking, and some bumbling and bungling, and then a switch is discovered, often by accident, and the light is lit, and everyone says, "Oh, wow, so that's how it looks," and then it's off into the next dark room, looking for the next mysterious feline.[18]

Olson suggests that theology, when done well, also acknowledges the role of ignorance in its endeavors. Both seek God's truth, in different ways and according to the methodologies of their respective disciplines. The postulates of rigorous scientific inquiry, as one voice of experience, with Scripture and the Holy Spirit, can be revelatory of what God is doing in the world.

DON'T OTHER SOURCES RELATIVIZE THE BIBLE?

One may well ask whether, in stressing the universal activity of God in all realms of life, one runs the danger of relativizing the Bible by accepting the authority of other sources. There are, indeed, those who regard the Bible as just one among many expressions of religious experience in the human community: all are to be regarded as

17. Dennis Olson, "Revenge, Forgiveness, and Sibling Rivalry: A Theological Dialogue between Scripture and Science," *Ex Auditu* 28 (2012): 96.

18. Stuart Firestein, *Ignorance: How It Drives Science* (New York: Oxford University Press, 2012), 2, cited in Olson, "Revenge, Forgiveness," 96.

authoritative in the same sense. Such a view takes seriously the ongoing activity of God but does not take seriously the uniqueness of the
Bible's witness to that God. We argue here that this uniqueness is not
inherent in the Bible, as one piece amidst the corpus of the world's literature. Rather, its uniqueness appears only when the location for the
shaping of moral character and conduct is the church. It is the faith
community that claims a special place for the Bible as part of the confession of its own identity. And that means that the church claims a
role for the Holy Spirit in working with and among tradition, experience, reason, and the uniquely authoritative role of Scripture in shaping and forming the church's identity (more on the role of the Holy
Spirit in chapter 4). We may say that the Bible has a unique and primary role in ethical matters, but it is not self-sufficient for ethical discernment.

The authority of the Bible for Christian ethics rests as much in
its modeling of process as in its mediation of content. The Bible is
composed of the collected testimony of persons and communities to
the transforming and redemptive activity of God. To be called by
God through the text to the remembrance of this testimony is not for
the sake of the ancient events in themselves. That is the interest of
the historian of antiquity. God calls us to remember for the sake of
our own redemption, to enable us to discern the redemptive activity of God in the events of our lives. Attention to biblical authority as it mediates a process does not mean there is no continuity of
biblical content to be claimed.[19] Our identity as the church is obviously shaped by images, concepts, and metaphors that are part of
the Bible's content and not just its witness to a process. But these
cannot be regarded as revelatory deposits functioning as divinely
sanctioned doctrine. The content must constantly be tested by the
process. Which stories and images continue to manifest the redeeming power of God for us in our particular contexts?

Some matters of content are reassessed by the church, such as the
biblical acceptance of slavery or the Pauline admonition for women
to keep silent in church. Some matters of content are reasserted, such
as God's preferential option for persons who have become impoverished and those who are oppressed. Some matters of content remain
central although our interactions with them may change, such as the

19. See Sallie McFague, *Models of God: Theology for an Ecological, Nuclear Age* (Philadelphia:
Fortress Press, 1987), for an example of constructive theology that works with both process and
content.

Gospel story of the life, death, and resurrection of Jesus. In all cases, one's particular reading context plays a crucial role. A seminary class, for example, was discussing the biblical image of "God the Warrior" (found, e.g., in Exod 15:3) and most of the American students were expressing discomfort with this violent image of God, but one student from Latin America observed that this image was incredibly important in her home church, which was subject to state-supported violence. As she put it, "For us, if God does not fight for us, then who will?" Some texts may seem irredeemable in one context, but in another context they can speak a word of hope. A posture of humility about our own limited perspective serves us well as we read and interpret Scripture, even as we are bold to claim our convictions on core matters, such as God's desire that all parts of creation, including all people, flourish.

Even as we bring our own questions and concerns to the Bible, the Bible must be allowed to speak back into our contexts. On what grounds may a person declare one moral model or mandate wrong but another binding? The most apparent criterion—if it seems outdated or wrong, then it must not apply to our lives—may be appealing, but it is dangerous. This criterion allows us to pick and choose among biblical themes and texts, adopting what confirms our standing assumptions and tossing out what does not. Disarmed is the Bible's power to challenge the normative behavior and assumptions of a society or a person. This criterion betrays Jesus's startling proclivity to challenge commonsense assumptions about what actions cohere with the reign of God.

Finally, as we will explore more fully in the next chapter, any view of biblical authority adequate for Christian ethics must be cognizant of the diversity within the biblical tradition. As noted earlier, different genres require different types of interpretation, to say nothing of different approaches to ethical engagement. The problem with some discussions of biblical authority is that they seem to imply a monolithic view of the Bible and its use. There is no single way in which the Bible is authoritative in ethical matters. We suggest that biblical authority operates differently depending on the nature of the biblical materials that speak to a given issue and the contexts in which they are read. Further, we wish to argue that such a multifaceted view of biblical authority is necessary if the totality of the Bible's resources is to be made available to Christian ethics. It is a narrow definition of authority, implying a prescriptive use of inspired materials, that has led to a narrowing of the biblical resources available to Christian ethics so that only passages explicitly addressing moral matters are often consulted.

Our treatment of biblical authority as primary is intended to allow for a more flexible and functional view of biblical authority and, at the same time, to stress the necessary biblical frame of reference within which ethical inquiry must take place if it is to be Christian. It remains next to discuss the actual processes involved in making available and interpreting the biblical witness for the Christian moral life.

4.

Interpreting the Biblical Witness

Paradox inhibits the effort to take the Bible seriously in the moral life. On the one hand, as we have said at the outset, the church in its many forms claims the Bible as its Scripture; that is, the Bible bears some form of authority for how we are to live our lives, and for most Protestant churches, the Bible is claimed as the "primary" source. On the other hand, many factors make appealing to the Bible as an authoritative source of moral wisdom very difficult. Those factors include:

- Contradictory messages across biblical texts (the Gospels, for example, give differing accounts of Jesus's actions and words)
- Obvious offensiveness of some texts (texts that seem to condone slavery, rape, or the silencing of women are some examples)
- Irrelevance of some texts on a surface level (e.g., "You shall not round off the hair on your temples or mar the edges of your beard," Lev 19:27)
- The fact that many issues faced by contemporary people are not explicitly addressed in the Bible (e.g., the ethics of drone warfare)

Two responses to this double bind are common. One is to use the Bible ritually (read it in worship, etc.) but functionally ignore it when it comes to ethical decision-making. The other response is to use the

Bible selectively, appealing to texts that agree with what one already thinks but dismissing those that challenge one's conclusions.

Both responses are, of course, untenable. What, then, are we to do, given the significant problems? How do we take seriously for moral decision-making Scriptures that seem to demand harsh penalties for small things like wearing clothing of mixed fibers, call for women's silence in church, instruct slaves to return to their masters, preclude divorce, and seem to condone rape and brutal warfare?

Before moving to some constructive reading strategies, consider for a moment what is at stake and what kind of authority the Bible ought to hold for Christian ethics. The stakes are high. How the Bible functions in ethical decision-making shapes what it means to be faithful and how to follow Jesus. The stakes are also great in terms of the consequences of particular decisions. For some LGBTQ people in the world today, for example, judgments regarding homosexuality based on biblical passages may determine life and death.

So, then, *how* is the Bible authoritative? That is, *how* are we to read it as Christians?

In the previous chapter, we reflected on the status of the Bible's authority for Christians, on the nature of its authority for Christian communities. The question now is, How might Christians *read* Scripture in order to engage it ethically? Should one read it as a rule-book and apply its laws, precepts, exhortations, and prohibitions one-to-one (as best we can) to our own contexts? Let us examine this widely held position before examining other approaches.

THE INADEQUACY OF LITERALISM

One would be hard-pressed to use the Bible as an ethical rule book, in no small part because the ethical prescriptions sometimes contradict each other. Proverbs offers one of the most obvious examples:

> Do not answer fools according to their folly,
>   or you will be a fool yourself.
> Answer fools according to their folly,
>   or they will be wise in their own eyes. (Prov 26:4–5)

But apparent contradictions are just the most obvious problem.

Another equally pressing issue is the chasm between the contexts in which the Bible was written and our own.

Whether we live in Indonesia or Zimbabwe or the United States, our contexts are completely different from those in which the biblical texts were written. It is impossible to follow the Bible's precepts literally because we live in social, historical, and cultural contexts far removed from those in which the texts were written.

If you are male, you have probably shaved your beard at one time or another (unless, for example, you belong to a particular Jewish sect, in which case you might not be reading this book) and have therefore violated Leviticus 19:27. Likewise, if you have had the unfortunate experience of having a rebellious teenage son, you should have brought him to the elders of the town to have him stoned to death, according to Deuteronomy 21:18–21. Or, to take a NT example, many Christians have been successful in *not* taking Jesus literally when he says, "it is easier for a camel to go through the eye of a needle than for someone who is rich to enter the kingdom of God" (Matt 19:24; cf. Mark 10:25; Luke 18:25).

So the Bible, both OT and NT, permits or assumes some practices that most moderns do not permit (e.g., slavery, stoning rebellious teenagers). Also, most Western Christians engage in certain practices that some texts in the Bible prohibit (mixing two kinds of material into a piece of clothing, or mixing seeds in a field, just to name *one verse* in Leviticus [19:19]). There are many examples such as these, without even mentioning the controversial laws on same-sex activities that are nestled among these same laws in Leviticus (we will address these below). Many more examples could be adduced because we do not live in an agrarian society in ancient Palestine with the particular worldviews of the biblical authors. Furthermore, appealing to Jesus's interpretation does not solve the problem, because although he came to fulfill the law, he did not come to abolish it (Matt 5:17).

We can see that something other than a slavish literalism is called for in thinking about how to read the Bible. The evangelical writer Rachel Held Evans makes the point forcibly: she spent a year living as a "biblical woman," that is, following as literally as possible the laws and admonitions pertaining to women in the Bible.[1] Her grand

---

1. Rachel Held Evans, *A Year of Biblical Womanhood: How a Liberated Woman Found Herself Sitting on Her Roof, Covering Her Head, and Calling Her Husband "Master"* (Nashville: Thomas Nelson, 2012). Her work was inspired by the earlier work of A. J. Jacobs, *The Year of Living*

experiment helpfully demonstrates in a humorous and engaging way that it is neither desirable nor possible as a twenty-first-century woman to be a "biblical woman" if this means following the biblical precepts literally.[2] What she demonstrates instead is that everyone, including those who claim to read Scripture "literally," is engaged in hermeneutics—the complex practice of interpreting the Bible.

It follows, then, that the Bible cannot be used as a rulebook for Christian ethics—it cannot be read literally, or anything approaching literally. In the first place, it is not possible to fix on one Hebrew (or Aramaic) or Greek text from the ancient world (the old quest for an "autograph" manuscript or even an "original" manuscript tradition is doomed from the start).[3] Instead, we have multiple manuscript traditions. Second, even if we had one fixed text, without any dispute as to what each letter was and how it should be punctuated, we would still have the problem that Evans encountered. Inerrancy, infallibility—these are impossible. If literalism is not possible as a starting point for thinking about the Bible and Christian ethics, how can we engage these together? How should we read?

SCRIPTURAL PRECEDENT FOR ENGAGING THE BIBLE FOR CHRISTIAN ETHICS

If one cannot read literally, both because it is impossible and because even the attempt is not very enriching as a path for ethical engagement, how might one proceed? There is not one way to proceed but many paths, each with strengths and weaknesses. Or, to put it more accurately, each way of proceeding may be found particularly appropriate for certain occasions and contexts.

Let's return to Proverbs 26:4–5 for a moment. In setting these apparently contradictory proverbs side-by-side, Proverbs highlights the extent to which context is crucial to interpretation. In some circumstances, the first maxim may apply, but in others, the second

Biblically: One Man's Humble Quest to Follow the Bible as Literally as Possible (New York: Simon & Schuster, 2007).

2. Indeed, Rachel Held Evans is right to caution against "biblical" being used as an adjective (e.g., biblical faith, etc.). These are code words for insupportable arguments for literalism.

3. For the OT, the standard authority on textual criticism is Emmanuel Tov, *Textual Criticism of the Hebrew Bible*, 3rd ed. (Minneapolis: Fortress Press, 2011). For the NT, see David C. Parker, *Textual Scholarship and the Making of the NT* (Oxford: Oxford University Press, 2012), esp. 5–64.

maxim will be truer. It depends on the context, and the interpretive decision about which proverb is appropriate for which context rests with the interpreter. That is true for ancient contexts and for modern ones.

The authority to interpret the Bible for new situations is not something imposed on it at a later time, after canonization, but is authorized by the Scriptures themselves. This can be seen most obviously in the way the NT Scriptures interpret the Hebrew Scriptures, the church's first Scriptures. But it is already evident in many and varied ways throughout the OT itself. In the story of the daughters of Zelophehad, for example, told in Numbers 27, the daughters present their situation to Moses (their father has died, leaving them with no way to inherit under the current law), who seeks an interpretative word from YHWH in this case. A new interpretation of the law is offered to meet the needs arising from their circumstances (daughters can inherit property, Num 27:8; the law is later reinterpreted again to restrict their marriages to within the tribe, 36:6–7).

Dennis Olson extrapolates from the situation at the end of Numbers in thinking about Israel's life with God as depicted in the rest of the Hebrew Scriptures: "This new generation on the edge of the promised land functions as a paradigm for each succeeding generation of the future, honoring the past but renegotiating its traditions in the face of new realities."[4] This is only one example of the way in which Scripture itself authorizes scriptural reinterpretation for new contexts—it is what is required for life to go on and for the community to flourish.[5]

REQUIRED READING STRATEGIES FOR ENGAGING THE BIBLE AND ETHICS

As discussed above, the Bible assumes a world that we do not inhabit. Given the chasm that separates our worlds, how might we approach reading the many and varied texts within it? Below, we will offer several possible reading strategies, but before we discuss those options, two other elements essential for Christians to read Scripture must be

4. Dennis T. Olson, "'Oh LORD God, How Am I to Know?': The Pentateuch and Contemporary Understandings of Truth," *Princeton Seminary Bulletin* 23 (2002): 94.

5. In addition to Olson (cited above), see also Michael Fishbane, *Biblical Interpretation in Ancient Israel* (Oxford: Clarendon, 1985).

named: the role of the Holy Spirit and the need for an overarching hermeneutic.

THE ROLE OF THE HOLY SPIRIT AND THE NEED FOR AN OVERARCHING HERMENEUTIC

In both the traditions and experience of Christians, the role of the Holy Spirit is often assumed but not widely discussed. The role of the Spirit in interpretation is akin to the role of the Spirit in the writing and reception of the Scriptures themselves: The Holy Spirit was active at the time of the writing of the Scriptures and among the first hearers of each of its texts, as well as within every subsequent community of faith who has heard them and passed them down to the next generation. Likewise, the Spirit is present as the church, understood in its broadest sense, seeks to discern what role its traditions and experience should play in the reading of Scripture. The Spirit is always seeking to shape the church into a body that fulfills God's purposes, and the church must engage in careful discernment of its sources of authority—Scripture, tradition, experience, and reason (see discussion in ch. 7)—in order to better sense the contours of those purposes.

How might one discern the working of the Holy Spirit, when push comes to shove and one confronts a difficult biblical text or is wrestling with a difficult issue in light of Scripture? There are no simple answers to this question, but some guidelines may prove useful:

1. This is, first of all, always a question to be discerned within community and within a community of communities in which differences are present.

2. Each voice is allowed its say, even if it does not have the final say.

3. It is important to submit one's interpretation of particular texts to one's understanding of the overarching trajectory of all of Scripture. That is, what one thinks the whole of Scripture is fundamentally about will influence how one reads any given part of it, will shape the hermeneutical orientation one brings to the text.

In any given instance, interpreting Scripture for Christian ethics involves a dynamic process; it is not a linear movement from step one to step two to step three. Many of the earliest Christian interpreters formulated an overarching hermeneutic for their interpretation of Scripture; Augustine is a premier example. Augustine finds the key to interpreting any part of the Scriptures in the love commandments: "Those who think they have understood the divine scriptures—or any part of them—but cannot by their understanding build up the two-fold love of God and neighbor, have not yet succeeded in under-standing them."[6]

Augustine helps us to see that we never interpret a biblical text in isolation from other biblical texts, and in fact it is neither possible nor desirable to do so. Consider a verse from Ezekiel 5, one of the most terrifying verses in all of Scripture, in which God announces judgment on Judah in the midst of the exile: "Surely, parents shall eat their children in your midst, and children shall eat their parents; I will execute judgments on you, and any of you who survive I will scatter to every wind" (Ezek 5:10). It is crucial, first of all, to face the terror of this judgment speech squarely and ask what motivates Ezekiel to include it (and other graphic and equally terrifying passages) in the book. Certainly an *imitatio Dei* (imitation of God, on which more below) approach to interpretation is appallingly inappropriate, but as with many texts in Ezekiel one is left to wonder whether the book has much in the way of ethical import for the church today?

Yet, one might argue that within the larger context of the book, Ezekiel has important things to say about the degraded state of human beings (and the land), the impossibility of humans to help themselves, and the need for their total reliance on God. He has much to say about human moral agency and unilateral divine action to save humanity from its impossible situation: human beings are both responsible for their actions and incapable of acting rightly. The prophet believes that the only way the people can hear this message in their current state is through these appalling images. But if we were to interpret this passage in chapter 5 alone, without the context of other passages (esp. the second half of the book) and without some hermeneutic for understanding the larger purposes of God as Ezekiel expresses them in the book as a whole and as they are expressed in Scripture as a whole, we would be quite lost theologically.

6. Augustine, *De doctrina christiana* 1.86 (trans. Green, 1997, alt.)

For us, the overall trajectory of Scripture, and a faithful hermeneutic by which to read, is that God desires the flourishing of all creation
and all humanity. God's desire for the flourishing of all creation and
humanity is the drumbeat of Scripture that can be heard throughout
the Bible; it begins in Genesis 1 and it continues through Revelation. As Christian readers of the OT and NT, we understand this God
who seeks the flourishing of all creation to be Trinitarian: Creator,
Redeemer, and Sustainer. So when we read Ezekiel 5, or any other
difficult text, we must take it very seriously in all its particularity,
which includes an understanding of those verses of judgment within
the context of the book in which it appears. Here, we observe that
often Christians do well to take Scripture seriously by reading more
of it, even the parts that make us uncomfortable (though most texts
are easier than Ezekiel 5). But even as we seek to understand the particularity of each text in its context, we should also seek to understand
each text within the overall purposes of God, which is ultimately for
a flourishing creation.

READING SLOWLY AND CAREFULLY: EXEGESIS

A second required reading strategy for faithful interpretation of
Scripture is to exegete the text. The idea of exegesis has been unnecessarily baffling to those who would read Scripture faithfully. To be
clear, exegesis for ethical engagement does not mean reading the
Bible simply to understand what its own ethical norms were (this
would be a history of the ethics of ancient Israel and of the first- and
second-century CE world that produced the NT writings), though
understanding these norms is an important first step.[7] Exegesis, as
mentioned in the previous chapter, is literally to "draw out" meaning from a biblical text; it is the "practiced art, a learned craft" of
interpreting a biblical passage with due respect for both the ancient
context of production (writing) and the modern contexts of reading.[8]
This does not mean saying what a text "meant" in the past and then
saying what it "means" in the present. As Stephen Fowl and Gregory
Jones argue, a much more dynamic and mutually dependent relationship is required. "We have to work analogically and dialectically

---

7. For a careful account of the ethics of ancient Israel, see John Barton, *Ethics in Ancient Israel*
(Oxford: Oxford University Press, 2014).

8. W. Brown, *Handbook to Old Testament Exegesis*, x.

between the past and the present to seek to find ways of appropriately connecting the patterns of human action."[9]

In the discussion of possible reading strategies below, we always assume that one is reading with a clearly articulated hermeneutic—an understanding of what the overarching trajectory of the whole of Scripture is—and that one is doing careful exegetical work, which is an important sign of respect for the text, as well as necessary for faithful interpretation.

POSSIBLE READING STRATEGIES FOR ENGAGING THE BIBLE AND ETHICS

The reading strategies offered in the previous section are necessary whenever we read Scripture. We must have an explicit, overarching hermeneutic (because we have one, whether we know it or not, so it is best to be clear about it), and we must do exegesis, a way of reading that is careful, disciplined, historically informed, and self-aware. But other reading strategies are appropriate for some texts and not for others. In this section we discuss some of these strategies, and the types of texts and contexts in which they are most, and least, helpful. Most of these reading strategies can be engaged simultaneously with other strategies; they are not mutually exclusive.

BECAUSE GOD SAYS SO: OBEDIENCE TO GOD'S WILL

In the history of engagement between ethics and the Bible, obedience to the revealed will of God has played an important role (see also ch. 2 on this topic). Some texts lend themselves to this approach. Consider Micah 6:8:

> He has told you, O mortal, what is good;
>> and what does the Lord require of you
> but to do justice, and to love kindness,
>> and to walk humbly with your God?

Or Deuteronomy 6:5, which is echoed in the synoptic Gospels (Matt 22:37, Mark 12:30, Luke 10:27):

9. Stephen E. Fowl and L. Gregory Jones, *Reading in Communion: Scripture and Ethics in Christian Life* (Grand Rapids: Eerdmans, 1991), 58.

You shall love the Lord your God with all your heart, and with all your soul, and with all your might.

Or Leviticus 19:18, also echoed many times in the NT (Matt 19:19, Matt 22:39, Mark 12:31, Gal 5:14, Jas 2:8):

You shall love your neighbor as yourself.

Many other texts could be added to this list. One can immediately see that the "obedience to divine command" is a rich and significant way of approaching certain texts.

The question for us as interpreters is not whether to obey these commands, but what it looks like to obey them. What does love look like in reference to these texts? What is meant by justice, kindness, and humility? Who counts as my neighbor? (Though Lev 19:34 goes on to command love for the immigrant as well, so it seems that pretty much everyone is included one way or the other.) Of course, the need for interpretive judgment is not eliminated just because a passage appears in a command form. In fact, many commandments are not open to easy appropriation via the divine obedience model of ethics. Leviticus 19:19, to take but one example, commands that one not "put on a garment made of two different materials." Most Christians believe that this and other commandments like it (including all the food laws) have been rendered moot (see Acts 15), but in practice, this strategy is performed unsystematically and selectively, according to criteria derived from outside the Bible. Since not all biblical commandments hold weight in each new time and place, method is needed for discerning whether and how a command in the Bible is valid for believers in varied contemporary contexts. Clarifying that method and enabling that discernment is part of our purpose in this chapter.

Obedience to the divine will works well for some texts, but of course, most of the Bible does not present itself as commands. On the contrary, the genres of the Bible are diverse, with commands being only one type. We will need additional strategies for engaging the Bible and ethics.

IMITATIO DEI AND *IMITATIO CHRISTI*

One way of engaging the Bible for Christian ethics, a way of reading that also has a long history, is to consider "imitation of God" and "imitation of Christ" as an approach to engaging the Bible and ethics (also discussed in ch. 2).

Some texts lend themselves to this approach. Consider this text from the Hebrew Scriptures:

> For the Lord your God is God of gods and Lord of lords, the great God, mighty and awesome, who is not partial and takes no bribe, who executes justice for the orphan and the widow, and who loves the strangers, providing them food and clothing. You shall also love the stranger, for you were strangers in the land of Egypt. (Deut 10:17–19)

Or the famous exhortation from Leviticus 19:2:

> You shall be holy, for I the Lord your God am holy.

Or this one, one of many from the NT that exhorts hearers to imitate Jesus:

> Then Jesus told his disciples, "If any want to become my followers, let them deny themselves and take up their cross and follow me." (Matt 16:24)

Clearly some texts lend themselves to the *imitatio* approach, and there is much to be gained by approaching them in this way.[10]

A weakness of the *imitatio* approach, however, is that most biblical passages were not written to offer models for imitation, nor are they usefully approached in this way. To take an obvious example, the narrative texts depicting rape in Genesis 34, Judges 19, and 2 Samuel 13 are not exhorting readers to "go and do likewise." Yet, these stories (and other violent texts) are useful for ethical reflection in other ways. In the case of the three "rape narratives," consider that they all have the same structure: a rape is committed, men who feel they have been dishonored by the rape react with violence, and as a result of that violence, significant social disintegration ensues that negatively affects

---

10. For a more extended treatment of both the obedience to divine command and *imitatio* approaches in the OT, see John Barton, *Understanding Old Testament Ethics: Approaches and Explorations* (Louisville: Westminster John Knox, 2003), 47–54.

the community as a whole.[11] Because the effects on the community in each case are so harmful, the structure of these texts offers an implicit critique of the honor/shame dynamic that fuels escalating violence in the face of sexual violation. The Bible offers us much to engage our ethical consideration in these stories, and not only because that same honor/shame dynamic fuels similar patterns of violence and disintegration in many parts of the world today. But the approach to reading texts like these requires something other than *imitation*.

Biblical texts can serve as both a norm (so *imitatio Dei/Christi*) and also a mirror. In the case of the rape stories, and many other biblical texts, thinking of the texts as a kind of mirror is a more helpful way of approaching them. Even as we acknowledge the many and varied differences that separate our own contexts from those of the biblical world, biblical texts can helpfully reveal to us significant truths about who we are, who God is, and how we might live so that all may flourish.

UNDERLYING PRINCIPLES: LEVITICUS 18 AND 20, AS EXAMPLE

Another approach to engaging the Bible in ethical reflection is to consider the underlying principles in the laws, precepts, exhortations, and prohibitions. Might one apply the principles upon which a law or exhortation is predicated to one's own context, if applying the law itself is impossible or unfaithful due to differences in context?

An example may illustrate how Scripture, experience, and a hermeneutic that takes underlying principles seriously might work in thinking ethically with Scripture. Two biblical texts disapprove of male same-sex *behaviors* (the Bible does not speak about homosexual *identity*, or any other kind of sexual or gender identity).[12] So how might one interpret Leviticus 18:22 and 20:13, the texts that prohibit

11. See Frank M. Yamada, *Configurations of Rape in the Hebrew Bible: A Literary Analysis of Three Rape Narratives*, Studies in Biblical Literature 109 (New York: Peter Lang, 2008).

12. This is clear in Lev 18:22, 20:13; Rom 1:27; and Jude 7. Gen 19:1–9 contains an allusion to male rape, but it is actually a story about the violation of hospitality (cf. Judges 19 and Ezek 16:49). Though the Hebrew Scriptures largely seem to assume heteronormativity, that is not the case in other parts of the ancient Near East or in the Greco-Roman world; in some of those contexts there was wide gender and sexual diversity. Indeed, scholars are increasingly recognizing that multiple constructions of masculinities appear in the Hebrew Scriptures; see, e.g., Marti Nissinen, "Biblical Masculinities: Musings on Theory and Agenda," in *Biblical Masculinities Foregrounded*, ed. Ovidiu Creangă and Peter-Ben Smit (Sheffield: Sheffield Phoenix, 2014),

male same-sex behavior, for today's contexts? On the one hand, corporate experience and well-regarded science attest that some people have homosexual identities and orientations.[13] Sexual minorities have been populating and enriching the church and society since biblical times, yet it is only recently that they have been allowed to speak with their full voices and identities. On the one hand, one must allow the experience of people who are not heterosexual to speak fully and to resist those who interpret the biblical texts in ways that create obstacles to the full flourishing of others. On the other hand, one does not want to throw the text out as irrelevant, for that would destroy the delicate balance that we are trying to preserve: allowing our own experience to speak, yet also allowing Scripture to offer its own word; genuine conversation requires both voices. Do these difficult texts still have anything to say to us about ethics? We believe they do.

The great Leviticus scholar Jacob Milgrom considers Leviticus 18 and 20 in great detail and observes that the one principle that unifies all the laws in these two chapters (incest prohibitions, prohibitions against child sacrifice, no sex with women during their menstrual period, no adultery, no sex with other males, and no sex with animals) is the threat to procreation and the appropriate use—that is, the placement—of Israel's seed.[14] No seed should be spilled except what will produce legitimate children within the family. The theological exhortation articulated in Genesis 1:28 ("Be fruitful and multiply and fill the earth") expresses one of the core convictions of the priestly tradition, which also produced Leviticus: for people to flourish, the population needs to grow. The goal of these laws in Leviticus 18 and 20 is thus to preserve the stability of the family, and ultimately the community. Within the context of ancient Israel, with its subsistence agrarian economy, it was necessary to produce many children in order to

271–85. On the effects of this diversity on the NT, see Brittany E. Wilson, *Unmanly Men: Refigurations of Masculinity in the New Testament* (New York: Oxford University Press, 2015).

13. It has become increasingly clear, at least since Alfred Kinsey's groundbreaking work, that sexual identities are more diverse than the binaries "heterosexual" and "homosexual" suggest. It is now better understood that sexual orientation intersects with biological sex, gender identity, and gender expression in complex ways. See Clive M. Davis, William L. Yarber, Robert Bauserman, George Schreer, and Sandra L. Davis, eds., *Handbook of Sexuality-Related Measures* (Thousand Oaks, CA: Sage, 2000), 137; also, the Medical University of Vienna, "Networks of the Brain Reflect the Individual Gender Identity," *Science Daily*, January 7, 2015, http://tinyurl.com/y8eykhmt. Despite our understanding of gender and sexual diversity beyond the binaries of "homosexual" and "heterosexual," we will focus on the category of male same-sex behavior because the biblical texts in question seem to address it.

14. Jacob Milgrom, *Leviticus 17–22: A New Translation and Commentary*, Anchor Bible 3A (New York: Doubleday, 2000), 1567.

survive and flourish (since many would not survive to adulthood), so this whole set of laws makes sense in that context.

Milgrom, an observant Jew himself, suggests that observant Jewish gay or lesbian people can fulfill the *intent* of this law by adopting children.[15] Christians can make a similar interpretive move (without necessarily requiring adoption): the stability of the family, and ultimately the community, is the larger principle, the larger good, at stake here, and should be taken seriously. How can the intent to help families and communities thrive be honored in our modern context where *over*population, not *under*population, is the presenting problem?[16] Milgrom's insight is key: God desires the flourishing of the family and the community, so what does that look like in a twenty-first-century world? For one thing, the evidence, both scientific and anecdotal, supports the claim that gay and lesbian people contribute to flourishing families, churches, and communities. Gay and lesbian parents are no worse, and are often better, at raising happy, well-adjusted children, who become productive, flourishing adults.[17] The underlying ethical principles of Leviticus 18 and 20 are being upheld when people contribute to, and participate in, the flourishing of families and communities.

ENGAGING THE MORAL IMAGINATION

Searching for underlying principles can work well in interpreting the legal material in Scripture, but what about the rest of the Bible, the majority, in fact, that is not law or exhortation? What about stories and poetry? What kind of ethical value do they have? Let's take the book of Job, for example. Carol Newsom observes that the different genres in Job offer a dialogue of moral imaginations. Genre is "a mode of perception," a way of seeing the world, and thus the contrasting genres within the book of Job reveal contrasting views of the world.[18] The simplicity of the prose tale in Job 1–2, and its beautiful language, suggests a world that values order, coherency, and whole-

15. Ibid., 1787.

16. George Gao, "Scientists More Worried Than Public About World's Growing Population," Pew Research Center, June 8, 2015, http://tinyurl.com/y7bdj9f5.

17. American Psychological Association, "Sexual Orientation, Parents, and Children," July 2004, http://tinyurl.com/y7aktk3m.

18. Carol A. Newsom, *The Book of Job: A Contest of Moral Imaginations* (New York: Oxford University Press, 2003), 13.

ness.[19] The poetic dialogues that begin in Job 3, by contrast, privilege "dissidence, as [they let] unmediated perspectives speak to and against one another. . . . Whereas the prose tale's sense of wholeness is unbreakable, the wisdom dialogue is fascinated with unmendable brokenness."[20] Neither of these worldviews has a corner on truth; on the contrary, one might argue that both perspectives are necessary. Indeed, the placement of these two genres side by side in Job suggests a profound valuing of dialogical truth, truth that can only be gained through the process of hearing differing perspectives and voices. And it is the juxtaposition of these different genres that conveys this truth. Genre itself is thus a form of thought, one that communicates particular desires and values about the world, and these have ethical implications.

THE MORAL IMAGINATION OF GENESIS 1 AND 2

How might we engage the moral imagination of Genesis 1, the first account of the creation of the world? Might such an engagement inform the way we think about how we relate to our world? Genesis 1 is clearly not a modern scientific account, so what is its genre? Knowing its genre will help us to know what kinds of questions to ask. The evidence suggests that Genesis 1 is a liturgical poem about God's creation of the world. This foundational poem tells us who God is, how God relates to creation and humanity (and how they are to relate to one another), and the importance of sacred time and space. We learn here that God declares *all* of creation very good (Gen 1:31), God gives co-creative functions to parts of the created order (Gen 1:16, 1:28), and that it is not humanity that is the pinnacle of creation but the Sabbath, created on the seventh day, that reigns as the crown of creation. Key theological claims are made in this text that have significant ethical implications; if they were taken seriously today, they could address many of our present ecological and moral predicaments, not because they offer practical "solutions" or are scientific in the modern sense, but because they offer a saner, healthier, cosmos-affirming worldview with God at the center. Scientific and theological knowledge are compatible, however biblical texts yield

19. Ibid., 51–65.
20. Ibid., 89.

not to scientific questions but to our deepest theological questions about who God is and who we are.

The way in which "dominion" in Genesis 1:26–28 has been interpreted has had enormous ethical consequences for our world. "Dominion" has meant that human beings could do whatever they wanted to creation, which has meant, practically, extracting "resources" at will. This view of dominion came to dominance in the Enlightenment period when, for example, Francis Bacon articulated the virtue of conquering nature through scientific progress: "I am come," he says, "in very truth leading you [humanity] to Nature with all her children to bind her to your service and make her your slave."[21] We in the twenty-first century are heirs of Bacon's way of thinking about the natural world.

But that is not the meaning of "dominion" in Genesis 1. In the ancient Near East, "dominion" refers to the relationship between a sovereign and his (it was usually, though not always, "his") people. It is not a despotic vision of dominion, but a *protective* one. Because human beings are made in the image and likeness of God, human beings are to rule as God rules: as those who protect, not those who exploit. God wills that all God's creatures should thrive in the world God has made. Having "dominion" means exercising tender, life-giving care so that all may flourish. "Dominion" is the antithesis of domination.

Ellen Davis connects the "dominion" language to what follows in Genesis 1:29–30: "And to every beast of the earth, and to every bird of the air, and to everything that creeps on the earth, everything that has the breath of life, I have given every green plant for food." God gives food to everything that lives—other creatures as well as human beings. Davis links this gift to the preceding command to human beings to have dominion (v. 28). She says, "the most essential activity befitting humans created in the image of God is to secure the food system that God gives to sustain all creatures."[22] Only human beings have the ability and expertise to dramatically alter the environment. It is not incidental that the first vocational task of human beings in the Bible is to use that ability and expertise to ensure that God's gift of

21. Francis Bacon, *The Masculine Birth of Time*, cited in Richard Bauckham, *Living with Other Creatures: Green Exegesis and Theology* (Waco, TX: Baylor University Press, 2011), 49.
22. Ellen Davis, *Scripture, Culture, and Agriculture: An Agrarian Reading of the Bible* (New York: Cambridge University Press, 2009), 58.

the food system to all creation—to all living creatures—be sustained, not disrupted.

In the second creation story in Genesis 2, God makes human beings "to serve and preserve" the garden (Gen 2:15). The Hebrew word "serve" (*'abad*) is usually translated in Genesis 2:15 as "to till," but that is not its usual meaning. It means, literally, to serve; sometimes it even means "to worship." "Serve" is thus a suitable translation. The purpose, the vocation, of the human being is to serve the Earth where we and all other creatures live, not the other way around. Genesis 2 shows us God making a garden and then making a human being to care for the garden. John Calvin, writing in the sixteenth century, observes that

> the custody of the garden was given in charge to Adam, to show that we possess the things which God has committed to our hands on the condition that being content with a frugal and moderate use of them we should take care of what shall remain. . . . [L]et every one regard himself as the steward of God in all things which he possesses. Then he will neither conduct himself dissolutely nor corrupt by abuse those things which God requires to be preserved.[23]

Calvin is not usually associated with nontraditional interpretations of Scripture, but in our current situation, his reading of Genesis 2:15 puts him at odds with the dominant attitude that sees Earth's resources as objects to be exploited instead of God's beloved creation to be cherished.

The environmental scientist and activist Gus Speth used to think that environmental problems could be solved by science, but then he realized that the "top environmental problems are selfishness, greed and apathy, and to deal with these we need a cultural and spiritual transformation. And we scientists don't know how to do that."[24] Christian faith requires Christians to proclaim to the world the love of God for the whole world God has made. What is needed is a new way of seeing the world, of being united with it by "bonds of affection," as Pope Francis has said; we need to see the world not as something made for our use but as God's beloved creation.[25]

23. John Calvin, *Commentary on Genesis* (Grand Rapids: Baker, 1989), 125.

24. Cynthia Woo, "Religion Rejuvenates Environmentalism," *Miami Herald*, February 18, 2010, http://tinyurl.com/y7mqtzzn.

25. Francis, *Laudato Si'*, para. 11.

THE ROLE OF CANON IN ETHICAL REFLECTION

Earlier in this chapter we talked about the importance of being self-aware about the overarching hermeneutic we hold when reading Scripture, that is, what do we think the Bible as a whole is about? We noted that our hermeneutic is that God desires the flourishing of all creation and all humanity, and this understanding of the whole of Scripture informs how we interpret any given scriptural passage. Another way of talking about this framework is to think about the role of the canon in ethical engagement with the Bible. The task of exegesis is not completed until a text and its themes have been considered within the full range of the Christian canon (see also the discussion of canon in ch. 2).

The word "canon" is used in the Christian tradition to refer to that collection of books judged by the church to be authoritative for Christian life and doctrine. The word itself seems to come from a Semitic root meaning "rod" and, derivatively, "a measure." Thus, the biblical canon is a theological measure in the ongoing tradition of the church. Several basic observations about the nature of the Christian canon shape our understanding:

1. Christian communities understand that the Christian canon is composed of both the Old Testament (sometimes called the First Testament or Hebrew Bible) and the New Testament (sometimes called the Second Testament). Together they form the Scripture of the Christian church. Historically, many in the church have tended to regard the OT as possessing lesser authority than the NT, a position that is sometimes theologically articulated (as with Marcion in the second century CE) but is more often simply practical, the result of consistent neglect (e.g., in many churches, OT texts are seldom if ever preached).[26] Exclusive focus on the NT has truncated the traditional witness of the church that the whole Scripture is the word of God. The negative effects are manifold: First, it leaves the NT cut off from much of its rootage and thus impossible to be fully understood. Second, the full theological witness of the OT is suppressed, along with the range of available resources for ethical reflection, creating a false and narrow context for understanding the rest. Finally, suppressing the OT witness, whether in principle or in practice, participates in the great evil of supersessionism (the idea that God has abandoned

---

26. For compelling, sustained reflection on this topic, see Strawn, *Old Testament Is Dying*.

the Jewish people in favor of Christians) and its foul offspring, anti-Semitism. Concern for the canon as the total framework for our biblical reflection acts as a corrective to the arbitrary suppression of the OT that characterizes much Christian theology and practice.

Here we may observe that, although for Christians Jesus Christ is the focusing center for faith and ethics, there is no single understanding of his life and work that can give a simple, monolithic standard of moral judgment. Indeed, it is increasingly clear that to understand Jesus requires not only the diverse witnesses of the NT to his life and work but also the rich heritage of the OT, which provided foundation and content for Jesus's own understanding and proclamation of the good news that God had acted to redeem the world. The church has preserved the canon not as mere historical documentation but as necessary to the full understanding of its faith centered in the God who is revealed in the OT as well as in the NT, in the person of Jesus Christ. The unity of the two Testaments is theological: in the words of the great OT scholar Patrick D. Miller, "Nothing new about the character of God is revealed in the New Testament that has not already been revealed in the Old Testament."[27]

2. The Christian canon should not be regarded as books that the church chose and granted authority. The church has always stressed that the complex process of canon formation represented only the recognition by the church of authority from God already established in the life of the church. In other words, authority accrued to certain writings over time through their use: they circulated in ancient Jewish, and later, Christian, faith communities, and those communities perceived that these writings testified to the God who had called them into new being and was present and at work in them. Authority lay not in the texts themselves but in the experience of the faith communities with those texts. And so the canonical texts are understood to continue to testify to God and God's activity in succeeding faith communities in every generation into the present and future.

The canonization process is thus understood as an acknowledgment of divine authority that already exists, not the creation of that authority. This perspective provides a safeguard against the notion that the church, having made the canon, can therefore redo it, leaving out those portions that some regard as outdated or irrelevant. In the

---

27. The idea here, if not the exact words, are attributable to Patrick D. Miller, from his introductory lectures over many years in Orientation to Old Testament Studies at Princeton Theological Seminary.

principle of the canon, the church acknowledges all of the OT and NT as possessing the authority of God's word. In matters of ethics, this means that we are not free to disregard the totality of Scripture as in some way authoritative for the Christian moral life.

3. As was noted in chapter 2, the biblical texts were produced and circulated in actual faith communities, which means that they reflect both the gifts and the failures, the grace and the brokenness (to use Christian theological terms) of real communities and persons. Thus, Scripture attests to the depth and breadth of God's love for the whole world (and especially the vulnerable) and desire that justice prevail on Earth (e.g., Psalm 82) but also contains genocidal statements advocating the eradication of entire peoples (e.g., Deut 20:16–18). Scripture attests to the character and activity of a God who seeks the welfare of all people and of creation, but also holds up a mirror to us, revealing both the greatness of which we humans are capable (e.g., the heroism of Esther) but also some of the worst sides of the human condition (e.g., the genocidal impulse).

The canon does not speak in a single voice. This may seem a limitation, or a frustration, to some, but it is a blessing. Within the canon are a multiplicity of diverse voices offering a wide variety of perspectives. Since we modern readers are also diverse, have a variety of perspectives, and live complex lives, the scriptural diversity constitutes a welcome richness. But the scriptural diversity also warns against declaring any particular scriptural voice as absolute. It is more faithful to view the scriptural witness as constituting a conversation, with many voices, about our deepest concerns—what it means to live a full and flourishing life before God and in community.

4. To claim that the word of God speaks to us through the Scripture is not to claim the cultural character of the biblical communities as automatically normative. The word of God is sometimes communicated to us in spite of the social and political bias, the narrow vision, and the participation in the brokenness of sin that we see in the biblical communities alongside their witness to God's grace. Recognizing the intricate ways in which all of this is entangled together helps us realize the ways in which we too are enmeshed in brokenness even as we testify to God's grace.

The importance of the canon in the Christian tradition means that any person who seeks to do exegesis within and for the church must do it in the context of the total canon. The understanding gained in study and reflection on any given passage must be brought into conversation with the full range of materials in the Christian canon, OT and NT. Are there other, related passages or places where similar language is used, and if so, how do those passages talk about the matter in question? When the full range of pertinent material is before us, we can then seek to understand the dynamic relationships among all the biblical materials. A passage seen by itself might appear quite different in meaning and significance from how it is seen alongside a much wider range of related biblical material.

Implications for Christian ethics are obvious. One cannot with integrity enter into dialogue with the Scripture over ethical issues if the biblical warrants appealed to are narrow selections that have not been tested against the totality of the biblical witness. Of course, to do exegesis in the context of the canon runs the risk of discovering tensions and contradictions in the biblical material rather than a uniform moral witness. One can no longer cite only that pole of the tension most compatible with a position reached on other grounds. The canon often forces those who come to the Bible for moral guidance to face these tensions directly as a part of the moral struggle. We suggest that often these tensions prove to be present in the contemporary ethical situation and need to be faced there as well.

TWO BRIEF EXAMPLES OF THE IMPORTANCE
OF CANON

Two examples, one from the OT, and one from the NT, will illustrate the above points.

One concern in the OT is whether foreign women pose a threat to the community or constitute a blessing to the community. Foreign women are sometimes thought to represent a threat to the community because they are perceived as tempting the Israelites to worship foreign gods (Exodus 34; Numbers 25; 1 Kings 11; Ezra 10; cf. Nehemiah 13). Other texts suggest a more positive role for foreign women (e.g., Rahab in Joshua 2 and 6) or are indifferent to them (1 Chr 4:21–22).

Many scholars believe that Ruth was written about the same time as Ezra and Nehemiah (and possibly also around the same time as the editing of Numbers and Kings). In Ruth, a foreign woman (a Moabite, like the Moabite women who are dangerous in Numbers

25) becomes the channel of blessing for Israel as a whole and the great-grandmother to the greatest king of Israel, David. There appears to be an intra-biblical conversation taking place about whether foreign women are a threat or a blessing to the community. This conversation is part of a larger intra-biblical concern about criteria for inclusion in the community of faith: does the community benefit from open borders, or is it harmed? Good arguments can be made on both sides: When the boundaries of a community are too porous, the identity of the community becomes too undefined, and assimilation is a threat. But when the boundaries are too strictly policed, the community becomes too insular, too incestuous, and cut off from the creativity and energy that newcomers bring. Engaging the Bible around these ethical issues involves exploring all the biblical texts that wrestle with these questions, hearing the conversation they are already having, and then entering into that conversation with the questions we bring from our own contexts.

An example from the NT occurs in Matthew 26:6–13 (cf. Mark 14:3–9; John 12:1–8). A woman pours a jar of expensive ointment on Jesus's head, which scandalizes the disciples. They complain that the money spent on ointment could better have been given to the poor. Jesus replies: "Why do you trouble the woman? For she has done a beautiful thing to me. For you always have the poor with you, but you will not always have me." He goes on to treat the anointing as a foreshadowing of his preparation for burial.

Jesus's statement, "For you always have the poor with you," has been a constant nemesis to those in the church who have tried to arouse the conscience of Christians to the harsh realities of poverty in our society and elsewhere in the world. Those who have defined the gospel solely in terms of individual and "internal" salvation use this text to justify a total lack of concern for the victims of poverty and the establishment of a just social order. They maintain that this text proclaims the futility of seeking to relieve the condition of the poor and focuses attention instead on the person of Jesus.

Indeed, if our exegesis is limited narrowly to this text, we might well come to this point of view. Jesus *does* rebuke the disciples in their desire to give to the poor. He *does* turn attention to his own person. But does Jesus intend that we should not be concerned with the material needs of those who suffer? Is attention to Jesus's own person a turning to "spiritual" matters? When we move to a wider canonical context, our understanding of this passage begins to alter.

The first move is naturally to the wider description of Jesus's ministry in the Gospels. From the very beginning, Jesus identified his ministry with the poor and the oppressed. In Luke 4:16–19, at the inauguration of his public ministry, Jesus preaches at Nazareth and chooses as his text Isaiah 61:1–2 ("The Spirit of the Lord is upon me, because he has anointed me to preach good news to the poor . . . "). Jesus associated himself with the poor and with society's outcasts and was criticized for it (Matt 11:19; Luke 7:34). In his preaching, Jesus spoke with great concern for the poor (e.g., Luke 6:20–21). Perhaps most striking is the passage on the great judgment in Matthew 25:31–46:

> I was hungry and you gave me food, I was thirsty and you gave me drink, I was a stranger and you welcomed me, I was naked and you clothed me, I was sick and you visited me, I was in prison and you came to me.

Acceptance of Jesus is equated with ministering to the needs of the vulnerable: "Truly, I say to you, as you did it to one of the least of these my brethren, you did it to me" (Matt 25:40).

In light of the strong witness elsewhere in the Gospels to Jesus's concern with the material needs of the poor, we surely cannot understand Jesus's statement in Matthew 26:11 to be a repudiation of his own ministry. Jesus is focusing attention in this passage on his own passion but is not urging that we ignore the needs of the poor and needy.

Moving more widely in the canon, we find in Deuteronomy 15:4–11 a text with a statement so similar to that of Jesus that it raises the probability that Jesus is directly referring to it. This passage is a part of the Law, the Torah, which was central to the faith of Jesus and the Jews of his time. The passage is making clear that concern for the poor is obligatory in the community of faith. It begins with the assertion that "there will be no one in need among you . . . if you obey the commandments of the Lord" (Deut 15:4–5). It then continues:

> If there is among you anyone in need . . . do not be hard-hearted or tight-fisted toward your needy neighbor. You should rather open your hand, willingly lending enough to meet the need, whatever it may be. . . . Give liberally and be ungrudging when you do so. . . . *Since there*

will never cease to be some in need on the earth, I therefore command you, "Open your hand to the poor and needy neighbor in your land." (Deut 15:7–11)[28]

This passage suggests that if the demands of the covenant were fully embodied, there would be no poverty, but since Israel, like all human communities, is a "stiff-necked people," some of its inhabitants will inevitably be poor. Therefore, God's people are commanded to care for them. This task is part of what it means to be the people of God; it is not an optional activity.

This greatly alters our consideration of Matthew 26:6–13. Jesus is responding not to the disciples' desire to give to the poor but to their rebuke of the woman. He is reminding them that the existence of the poor is a constant judgment against the whole covenant community. The woman is not to be self-righteously singled out; the poor are a corporate responsibility. By calling attention to the constant presence of the poor, Jesus is not urging us to forget their needs. He is directly referring to God's command that we care for the poor, and their constant presence is an indictment pointing to our failure as the covenant community. It is because they are always present that we do have a responsibility to them. The parallel passage in Mark includes an addition that points in this direction: "For you always have the poor with you, *and whenever you will, you can do good to them*" (Mark 14:7). Jesus then goes on to use the woman's gift to focus attention on his own passion, his own ultimate involvement in human suffering.

A wider canonical context completely alters our view of this passage. If we had searched more broadly, we would have found even more texts relating the people of God to the welfare of the people (the prophets, Paul). Far from allowing anyone to narrowly interpret Matthew 26:6–13 as elevating spiritual over material needs, an exegesis in the context of the whole Scripture overwhelms us with the power of the moral imperative regarding the poor and needy.

CANON AS FRAMEWORK OF CONTROL

We may summarize the above discussion of canon by noting the several important ways in which the canon functions as a framework of interpretive control:

28. NRSV, with italics added.

1. The canon underscores the crucial role of the community of faith in appropriating biblical resources. The canon grew out of the life experience of Israel and the early church in discerning the will of God, and the church's recognition of the whole canon as authoritative implies the continuity of those communities. Thus, the Bible cannot be interpreted with integrity by individuals in isolation from the wider community of faith.

2. The canon reminds us of the ongoing activity of God. When we must relate to the whole sweep of Scripture, we see God revealed in ever-new ways within the Bible itself. Although this portion speaks with authority of God's presence as it was apprehended in a particular time and place, it is clear that no one word is the final word concerning God's self-revelation. The Scripture points beyond itself to the reality of God. Faith understands that same God as active in our present. Thus, the canon encourages a dialogic use of Scripture, not to discover God enshrined in the past, but to assist us in discerning God's activity and will in our own day.

3. As a corollary to the previous point, the canon rules out "bibliolatry," that is, the worshiping of the biblical words themselves, instead of the God to whom they witness.

4. The canon discourages "selective engagement," where texts are understood to be ethically important only when they confirm the presuppositions of the interpreter. Even when it presents us with difficult tensions and contradictions, attention to the canon requires that the totality of the biblical witness be weighed in reaching moral judgments. To do Christian ethics is to enter into dialogue with the whole of the Christian canon, recognized as Scripture throughout the history of the church.

5. Finally, emphasis on the canon avoids "atomizing" Scripture, the reductionistic tendency to focus on individual parts without reference to the whole. Concern for the canon constantly calls the interpreter back to the dynamic interrelationship of the whole Scripture. Critical methods are essential in the interpretation of individual passages, but those individual texts must then be put into the framework of the broader canon, in order to discern the address of the word.

If the Bible is made available through understanding its character, and through careful exegesis of its passages in the context of the whole canon, then it can become a rich resource for the Christian moral life.

CONCLUSION: SHAPED BY SCRIPTURE
IN COMMUNITY

As we have argued, exegesis, the artful practice of the disciplined reading of Scripture, which involves slow reading and takes the contexts of both ancient and modern communities seriously, is necessary for faithful interpretation. But as Fowl and Jones, among others, have argued, as important as good reading practices is the *character* of the one reading. "Wise readings" are made possible because readers are already immersed in "Christian communities that are given their shape and form by the Triune God."[29] Fowl and Jones emphasize that the rehabilitation of Christian practices within Christian communities is required before faithful reading of Scripture can happen. In other words, engaging ethics and Scripture is not simply a matter of the question, "What shall we do?" but "Who are we to be?"

Scripture itself is a primary shaper of Christian identity within Christian communities. Where the faith-shaping practices of those communities are healthy and faithful, where Christians are nurtured in a dynamic, life-giving relationship with God, faithful reading of Scripture will ensue. No one comes to the Bible alone, that is, not having already been shaped, for good or ill, by the communities out of which they came. When those communities are nourished by a life-giving relationship with the God of Jesus Christ, and thus seek the flourishing of all God's creatures and creation, then their reading of Scripture will reflect those values and practices. We recognize, and even affirm, the circular nature of this process: formation in faithful Christian communities makes it possible for people to become faithful readers of Scripture.

We have discussed a number of reading strategies in this chapter, some required and some that will be useful with particular texts. We close this chapter with a few practical guidelines for engaging the Bible in ethical reflection.

---

29. Fowl and Jones, *Reading in Communion*, 49.

PRACTICAL GUIDELINES FOR USE OF BIBLE
IN MORAL DISCERNMENT

1. Be aware of what you bring to the text, personally and culturally
    (worldview, analysis, biases, longings, fears, etc.) and how this
    will affect your interpretation.

2. Hold in mind and account for the historical context, that is, what
    concerns underlie the text in its context? To whom was the text
    directed in its original context? Bear in mind the "otherness" of
    the people, social systems, and worldviews present in the text.
    Do not read your modern or postmodern assumptions into the
    text.

3. As part of attention to the historical "otherness" of the text, look
    for and acknowledge uncertainties in translation.

4. Listen for the unnamed and the hidden voices, especially of
    women and others who have been historically marginalized.

5. Hold in mind and account for the systems of oppression that
    have shaped particular texts and interpretations of them
    throughout history. Are those structured oppressions consistent
    with what we now hold to be good and true in light of the
    gospel?

6. Become familiar with the entire canon. The Bible contains
    many voices, with tensions arising sometimes from the diversity
    of those voices. The diversity and tensions can be productive
    for ethical and theological reflection, but the conflicts must be
    acknowledged and addressed. (Avoid "false harmonization.")

7. Seek to read the Bible in community, especially one in which
    difference is present and honored, power differentials are
    acknowledged and challenged, and voices of the underside are
    heard.

8. Be intentional and aware about the purpose of turning to Scrip-
    ture (that is, be aware of what kind of authority you ascribe to
    the Bible). Consider it not primarily as a source of concrete rules
    but rather as testimony to God's desire that humanity, and all
    creation, might flourish.

PART II

Elements of the Moral Life

5.

What Are Morality, Ethics, and Christian Ethics?

How are we to perceive the world and live in it? How do we do so in view of God's boundless love for creation and presence within it, especially as God is revealed in the biblical witness and experienced in the lives of believers throughout time? How Christian communities respond to these questions is the story of Christian ethics and provides the structure of the Christian moral life. This chapter and the following two are an excursion into these questions.

ETHICS AND MORALITY

"Morality" and "ethics" are commonly used interchangeably. But in the discipline of ethics and in this volume, they are not. Morality refers to the lived dimension of life pertaining to doing and being—for individuals and groups—in ways that are good, right, and fitting. That simple statement cloaks a world of complexity, controversy, and intrigue. This chapter and the following two pursue that intrigue. At stake is life on Earth.

Ethics, on the other hand, is disciplined inquiry into morality. Ethics brings self-consciousness, method, intentionality, and sensitivity to the process of discerning what is good and right for any given situation and context. This dimension of ethics, known as moral decision-making or moral discernment, entails three interfacing tasks each with an accompanying question. A simple chart tells the tale:

Tasks of Moral Discernment	Accompanying Questions
Descriptive	What is?
Constructive	What could be?
Normative	What ought to be?

Moral decision-making or discernment is central to ethics. Yet, if understood as the entirety of ethics, it is dangerously limited. It ignores two other aspects of morality.

One is the question of moral-spiritual power to do and be what we ought. Human history and individual lives are shaped not only by people discerning what is right and then doing it but by people discerning what is right and then *not* doing it. Many people are certain, for example, that it is not moral to drive a car to work many times a week, given the tons of carbon emitted by driving and the dire impact of climate change on the world's most vulnerable people. Yet, at this point, many continue driving to work. Ethics, as inquiry into morality, must include the questions of moral-spiritual power.

The second missing piece if ethics is limited to moral discernment is moral formation. Morality includes the formation of individuals and societies into people and groups who know and choose the good, and malformation toward the opposite. Ethics, therefore, must address the dynamics of moral formation and malformation.

The tasks and questions of moral deliberation expand, then, to become the tasks and questions of ethics as a whole.

Tasks of Ethics	Accompanying Questions
Descriptive	What is?
Constructive	What could be?
Normative	What ought to be?
Formative	What morally forms and malforms us? What disables and enables the moral-spiritual power to do and be what we discern that we ought?
Practical	To what actions do these questions point?

We have arrived at a fuller understanding of ethics. It brings self-consciousness, method, intentionality, and sensitivity to (1) discerning what is good and right for any given situation, (2) discovering what forms individuals and society toward the good and what malforms us away from it, and (3) uncovering and cultivating the moral-spiritual power to act toward the good.

Part 2 of this volume considers all three dimensions of the moral life—moral formation, moral discernment or deliberation, and moral agency—devoting chapter 6 to moral formation and chapter 7 to moral action and deliberation. In reality, however, the three are not separate. They are inseparably intertwined, forming and informing each other.

ETHICS AS CHRISTIAN ETHICS

Our primary concern in this book is not ethics, per se, but Christian ethics. Christian ethics is done from the perspective of what God is doing in the world as revealed in and by Jesus Christ and by the Holy Spirit working throughout creation, with human society a crucial dimension of it. Christian ethics considers moral discernment, formation, and agency in light of God's love for the world and presence in, with, and for it.

Christian ethics is the disciplined art of coming to know ever more fully both the mystery that is God and the historical realities of life on Earth. But ethics does more; it holds these two in one breath, so that people may shape ways of life consistent with and empowered by God being with, in, among, and for creation. "Knowing" here refers not merely to "knowledge of" but to "being in relationship with."

This is consistent with the meaning of the biblical Hebrew verb *yada'*. It means "to know" not in the sense of cognitive knowledge but in the sense of entering into and experiencing that which is known. A most notable example is God's statement to Moses, "I know their suffering" (Exod 3:7), implying divine relationship to human suffering (i.e., divine vulnerability).

Where vision and knowledge of God and of life's realities are obscured, a task of Christian ethics is to know and see more truthfully. Where dominant forces distort historical realities by describing them falsely, ethics must "redescribe the world."

"Holding in one breath," God and the historical realities of life bridges chasms that are characteristic of modernity yet are contrary to the biblical witness. They include the separation of sacred from secular, of faith life from political life, of personal relationship with God from relationship with structures of society, of Jesus's life and ministry from his execution, and of Christ from the ordinary world.

This notion of Christian ethics implies a purpose. It is not simply to iterate or reproduce past Christian ethical convictions. That is, the purpose is not to learn what our traditions say is right and good and then simply repeat it. Rather, Christian ethics is in the service of making Christian communities into living moral communities that can draw critically upon the traditions of the churches, put themselves in dialogue with other sources of moral wisdom, and read contemporary and historical circumstances clearly in order to craft ways of living consistent with faith in the God revealed in Jesus and the Spirit. By "ways of living," we mean everything from personal lifestyle to influencing public policy and social structures. (In chapter 7, we work with the crucial distinction between reproducing moral traditions and drawing critically upon them.)

But that is not all. The purpose of Christian ethics is also to offer the resources of Christian traditions to efforts in the broader public to address the moral issues of our day. Given the rampant misuse of religion in the public sphere, the criteria for appropriate and valid use of religious resources is a vital question of Christian ethics. We consider that matter more fully at a later point. Suffice it here to note that Christian ethics does not negate other religious ethics and secular ethics, or claim to be superior to them. To the contrary, in addressing the life-and-death issues facing humanity today, Earth's people must call upon all of the great faith traditions—and place them in conversation with each other and with other wisdom traditions—in order to plumb their depths for moral wisdom, guidance, and power to forge just and sustainable ways of life.

Christian ethical inquiry, then, draws upon the Bible, Christian historical traditions, and other sources of knowledge and moral wisdom to respond to the question noted above:

"How are we to perceive the world and live in it?" How do we do so in view of God's boundless love for creation and presence within it, especially as God is revealed in the biblical witness and experienced in the lives of believers throughout time? Christian ethical inquiry holds together (1) the mystery of God's unquenchable love for each and every one of us and for all of creation, and (2) the complex realities of life on Earth, including our daily lives.

WHY BE MORAL?

There is yet another dimension of ethical inquiry. Called "metaethics," it asks and answers the question, Why be moral? Metaethics seeks to discover people's most basic assumptions about right and wrong, good and evil. What do we regard as their origin or cause? Where, in the end, do we ground our own stands on moral matters? What is the final, bottom-line reason we give for what we seek to be and do? In a word, metaethics pushes us to disclose the sources of our morality and ethics.

For Christian ethics, metaethics rests in essential theological convictions. Consider, for example, Joseph Sittler's remarks:

> Before the church is the company of them that love God, it is the communion of them who acknowledge, and in that acknowledgment have their lives given a new center in One who loved them. The passive verb dominates the New Testament story! I love because I am loved; I know because I am known. I am the church, the body of Christ, because this body became my body.[1]

For teachers of ethics, few questions are more revealing of students' basic orientation to God and to life than the metaethical question, Why be moral? A surprising number of students respond that being moral is the pathway to life in heaven after death. This is a problematic response, and one that has been the response by some Christian traditions throughout time.

Others have said quite the opposite. Good works do not earn our salvation. God's love saves us, and the human choice to live rightly—summarized as loving as God loves—is a response to God's gracious gift of unconditional love for us. Some articulate that response as one of gratitude, others as the living Christ dwelling within the believer, others as the work of the Holy Spirit. Regardless, the point is important in the work of ethics: before we are called to love others, we are beloved by God. Traditionally, the Great Commandment ("You shall love the Lord your God with all your heart,

1. Joseph Sittler, *The Structure of Christian Ethics* (Louisville: Westminster John Knox, 1998), 11.

and with all your soul, and with all your mind. . . . You shall love your neighbor as yourself" Matt 22:37–39) is seen as generating two moral norms for human life—loving God and loving neighbor. But we argue there is a third—caring for creation—with a fourth norm that precedes them all: receiving and trusting the gracious love of God. (This is the metaethical level and the level this volume assumes.)

In short, we find four overarching norms for Christian ethics and metaethics:

- Acknowledging and trusting God's gracious love
- Loving God with heart, soul, mind, and strength
- Loving "neighbor" with self-honoring and justice-making love
- Caring for creation

METHOD MATTERS

A quick look at history and at the church today reveals astounding —perhaps infinite—variety in response to ethical questions by communities of people who have sought to follow Jesus and the Spirit. This is crucial: Christian ethics does not assure specific unalterable answers to moral questions. Nor does it assure singular pathways for reaching answers. This variety may be seen as moral relativism, but it is not. It flows from the fact that God is a living and loving God, ever-creating, ever present to the changing needs and circumstances of human existence.

The diversity in ethical perspective and method stems also from the cultural conditioning that shapes and limits our perception and thinking, even without our awareness of these processes. E. F. Schumacher distinguished "thinking with" from "thinking about." When we think, we do not just think, we think with concepts, ideas, images, metaphors, similes, and analogies. All of them join one thing with another to create a thought, express a feeling, or offer a point of view. Cumulatively, these "think withs" form a dynamic "mindset." They form the mind-set through which we view, interpret, and experience our world.[2]

"Thinking with" begins very early on, with our first relationships,

2. E. F. Schumacher, *Small Is Beautiful: Economics as if People Mattered* (New York: Harper Perennial, 2010).

our first words, and our first environment. As infants and toddlers, we learn an initial world through which we explore other worlds as we grow and move beyond our first circles of intimacy into other communities (school, for example).

We use "think withs" to think "about" anything and everything, big or small. What do we plan to do with our "one wild and precious life" (Mary Oliver)?[3] Should our town sponsor Syrian refugees? What should the next meal be? Was my stand in the recent election the right one? What do I most want to make of the time I have left?

Differently said, "think withs" are the instruments of our thinking, the preexisting notions we bring to any given circumstance or issue as we think about things. They filter, interpret, and respond to whatever has our attention.

How does this distinction help explain moral and ethical method?

The word itself is telling. "Method" is from the Greek words *meta* and *hodos*. *Meta* means "inclusive of," "taking the full range of," "gathering in the whole." *Hodos* is short for "the way." "Method" is the way we take in the whole. It's the framework and infrastructure of our mind-set, together with other tools and processes we use.

Everyone has a mind-set that takes in the world and responds to it. Thus, everyone has a method to make sense of things and decide what to do. While few of us are self-conscious of our method, and even fewer subject it to critical reflection and analysis, it is always at work as we make choices and live them out.

Yet, this does not say enough. It does not distinguish moral method from ethical method. (Recall the earlier distinction of ethics from morality, with ethics the disciplined inquiry into morality.)

We all have a *moral* method. It's the way we frame, structure, and engage our moral universe in all the choices we make. Our preexisting "think withs" do the work, largely on autopilot. In contrast, *ethical* method is our moral method used self-consciously. Ethical method is the disciplined way we mindfully, consciously answer those basic questions of ethical deliberation—what is, what could be, what ought to be—and knowingly carry out the corresponding tasks of ethics—the descriptive, the constructive, and the normative. Ethical method x-rays our moral mind-set and works with what it finds. It does the same for the collective mind-set of others, including whole cultures, societies, and traditions.

3. Mary Oliver, "The Summer Day," in *House of Light* (Boston: Beacon, 1990), 60.

There is more. For Christian ethics, method has an additional qual-ifier. It is how Christians go about the work of ethics as people for whom their faith matters. The substance of their morality, as well as their moral and ethical examination of their world and the world of others, is qualitatively modified by "Christian."

Yet method, understood as the way we "gather in the whole," can be misleading. The word does not tell us that every mind-set is inher-ently limited and views the world at a slant ("on the bias"). The whole is never wholly gathered in. Our "think withs" take in only some of what is before us, never all. They filter and interpret, meaning they also filter out and exclude. They pay keen attention to some mat-ters while overlooking, dismissing, or ignoring others. They mark and rank priorities for our response, thereby granting higher status to some actions and ends over others. They value some people and groups over others. And this goes on largely beneath our awareness.

The mind-set through which we perceive, interpret, and respond to the world is shaped by largely unspoken and unacknowledged assumptions of the dominant culture. They are assumptions about what is natural, normal, inevitable, or divinely ordained. For exam-ple, morally weighted decisions in the United States since its incep-tion have been influenced by an unacknowledged assumption of white superiority. As a result, voting rights and arrangements, the criminal justice system, education systems, and more have privileged white interests over the well-being of black and brown people. This we discuss more fully in chapter 6, understanding this dynamic as crucial to moral formation and malformation.

Christian ethical method is limited in the same way all human knowing is. Paul's description holds: "For we know only in part, and we prophesy only in part . . . we see in a mirror [only] dimly." We do not yet know "as we are known" [by God] and we do not yet see "face to face" (1 Cor 13:9, 12).

Given the preinclined and partial nature of our mind-set and method, it is hardly a surprise that the Christian life is never a singular path on the same line of sight. It is always conditioned by time, place, culture, circumstance, and in particular, the dynamics of power and privilege. Endless nuance marks what people of an ancient faith choose as the course of their discipleship.

For Christian ethical method, this creates a standing question of location and variety. What matters of time, space, circumstance, power, and privilege shape our perceptions, interpretation, and assessment of the world, of our experience, and of moral matters within them? As a part of what histories and traditions do we do ethics?

In sum, Christians, over two millennia, have "done ethics" in many modes and have used different "think withs" to do so.

These dynamics highlight the importance of method. Not only does method always matter, it matters decisively. It determines what counts as a serious moral question just as it determines the direction ethical reflection will take. It precipitates our first responses and puts in place our initial range of choices. Even what strikes us as moral or immoral about an issue is a consequence of method. It determines whose suffering counts and whose does not, whose good counts and whose does not.

Consider, for example, your response to issues such as these: police use of deadly force, civil disobedience, capital punishment, drilling for oil, the location of waste sites, capitalism, socialism, abortion, regressive or progressive taxation, the proposed city budget, what memorials and statues should be placed where, the use of alcohol, striking children, slavery, foreign trade bills, warfare, buying a luxury item, driving a car to work, whether or not to have children, or assisted suicide. Indeed, how decisions are made about these matters and what mind-set determines how they are made have consequences, even life-and-death consequences. Method in ethics matters.

Method in ethics includes more than the overarching mind-set shaping perception and thinking. Method in Christian ethics also includes theories of moral decision-making, sources of moral wisdom (including the Bible), how those sources are prioritized, whose voices count, the starting point of ethics, theological grounding—understandings of God, salvation, Jesus Christ, sin, the nature of the human—and more.

This book is an inquiry into one contested and vital domain of ethical method—the role of the Bible in ethics. To discuss that, however, we must set the stage by considering these other aspects of method.

We consider here two initial methodological concerns that have emerged with the increasing urbanization and globalization of life and of the ecological impact of human moral choices. The two are (1) an expanded moral universe, and (2) the dual subject of morality. They are crucial for a valid and adequate method in ethics in the twenty-first century. Both are introduced here and treated more fully in subsequent chapters.

THE MORAL UNIVERSE EXPANDING

Ethics worthy of the name in the twenty-first century must address not only the human dimension of life on Earth but Earth's entire web of life and its support systems. The scope of ethics has become planetary. Caring for other-than-human creation joins caring for human neighbors as a fundamental norm of Christian life.

Recall a sentence from the introduction and the questions that followed: On a dramatically changing planet, what is required of us is a new era of enhanced human responsibility. What dialogue of Bible and ethics helps shape the contours of moral imagination and human responsibility when no terrain goes untouched by both human goodness and human molestation, and everything turns on our actions and choices? What dialogue facilitates human character and conduct when, as never before, our collective reach is "exercised cumulatively across generational time, aggregately through ecological systems, and nonintentionally over evolutionary futures?"[4] What biblical and contemporary understandings of ourselves help generate a capacity to take responsibility not only for present and future generations of humankind but for the community of life as a whole, including its generative elements of earth, air, fire, and water? Don't these parental elements of life—earth, air, fire, and water—make moral claims upon us, rather than only we upon them? What kind of Bible and ethics exchange helps retrieve, renew, even create Christian practices for living the faith amidst Anthropocene powers? What manner of living chooses "life and blessing" over "death and curses" so that our "descendants may live" (Deut 30:19)?

These are the kinds of questions Christian ethical analysis asks. They are also questions that ask whether "new occasions teach new duties" and inherited "think withs" need to change. In this case, the basic change is an expanded moral universe, a universe with a further reach in time and a broader reach in space than the one that has reigned since the Industrial Revolution. The scope and focus of "industrial world" morality has been almost exclusively human-to-

4. Jenkins, *Future of Ethics*, 1.

human, with scant moral attention to the planetary systems upon which all life depends and, for that matter, scant attention to the needs of distant generations, human and other-than-human. Moral citizenship in this world sidelines other-than-human life and the parental elements of creation upon which all life depends—earth (soil), air, fire (energy), and water. Its mind-set has filtered them out or interpreted them as without moral value or standing (except as resources or capital). They are material means to human ends, not ends in themselves.

The contrast of modern industrial world morality, including most modern Christian morality, with the enhanced human responsibility now required of us, can be graphed as two figures. For both, the outer circle represents life on the planet. Both also show a circle of moral responsibility. Likewise, for both, that responsibility includes the elements that belong to any and every human morality: moral character, the consequences of our actions, and what we are duty bound to do (or not do). But it matters immensely which circle of responsibility is yours.

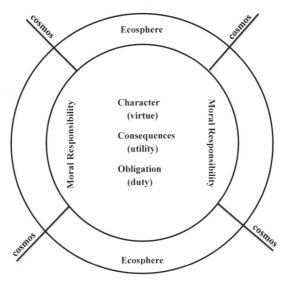

Figure 5.

In the first diagram, within the planetary circle, the moral universe rests within a smaller inner circle, the circle of human society. Here, human-to-human relationships and well-being comprise the moral universe and its boundaries. Yet, while human society is necessarily nested within the planet's life, much of the ecosphere and its future sits outside the circle of lived moral attention.

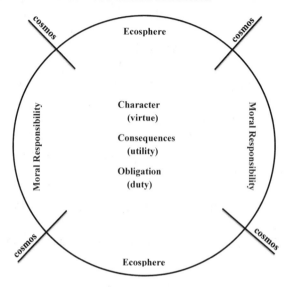

Figure 6.

In the second figure, the boundaries of human moral responsibility are coterminous with planetary boundaries. The ecosphere as a whole, both presently and for future generations, is home to moral responsibility. This is the expanded terrain of responsibility for current and foreseeable life that comes about because all natural systems are either embedded in human systems or profoundly affected by them, whether in the atmosphere, in the oceans, or across landmasses. The moral universe aligns to match the ecosphere.

With this altered alignment, the basic ethical questions surface anew. What crucial content of individual and collective character and conduct belong to this wider circle? What choices, actions, policies, and systems effect the consequences we need for a big human world on a small planet? What are we duty bound to do, or refrain from doing, as the moral bottom lines of a viable way of life? What yields a durable future?

These are all questions of ethical method. Answering them answers the basic questions of ethics: What is? What could be? What ought to be? They are also questions of content, with answers that carry life-and-death consequences.

In both figures, justice is rendering what is due. In figure 5.1, the basic moral relationships are human-to-human. Human society is the domain of moral responsibility and justice is essentially social justice, rendering what is required for human flourishing. In figure 5.2, the basic moral relationships include human-to-human and expand to human-to-life, or to the community of life and its requirements for surviving and flourishing, including the welfare of earth (soil), air, water, and fire (energy). Justice is creation justice, rendering what the community of life is due for its well-being, including human well-being. (Social justice thus is no less important than in figure 5.1 and belongs part and parcel to creation justice, but creation justice is broader and more inclusive.)

The Hebrew Bible especially is permeated with creation justice as our moral responsibility. The entire Hebrew canon opens with two complementary testimonies to creation, emphasizing in the first its origins in God's word and its goodness, and in the second, creation's interrelatedness (soil, plants, animals, humans) and the responsibility that comes with the gift of creation. The covenant with Noah highlights God's commitment to the ongoing reliability of creation in spite of human sin. God's deliverance of Israel from Egypt includes revealing a divine name that ties God the deliverer to God the creator and source of all being. The covenant on Sinai includes commandments calling for care for the land and its creatures with observance of Sabbath and Jubilee. Prophetic judgment and promise include the suffering of creation and human society from sin and God's desire to redeem and restore all of creation (e.g., the peaceable kingdom described in Isaiah 11).

Creation justice is less overtly expressed in the New Testament, but even before the writing of the Gospels, the apostle Paul had proclaimed Jesus as new creation and implied not only that the brokenness of sin affects human experience but that "the whole creation has been groaning" (Rom 8:22). The Gospel of John, closely influenced by Genesis 1, announces Jesus as the Word present with God in the beginning of all things. Revelation ends with a vision of New Jerusalem that is also new creation.

THE DUAL SUBJECT OF MORALITY:
PERSONS AND SYSTEMS

Self and society are twinborn. We could not, and do not, exist apart from our highly specific worlds. We also co-create those worlds. Our world forms us, and we contribute to forming it. We are always in society and society is always in us, even though society and the natural world in which it is embedded always constitutes more than our individual lives alone.

The dynamic relationship of self and society bears close attention. Our lives touch others not only through face-to-face actions but through the actions (or inactions) of social systems or social structures of which we are a part. Because human beings are inherently social—we are born to belonging—we establish patterns of interaction. "Social structure" and "social system" are terms used by sociologists to refer to these patterns, power arrangements within them, and belief systems rationalizing them. Social structures may be as small as families and as large as global networks. Included are the larger patterns and systems that make up the material environment: the economic order (local, regional, national, international); the governance system and wielding of political power; and the cultural system of social communication, with its major sectors in education, the mass media, and social media, together with the numerous informal ways interaction happens within families and between friends and neighbors. Such are the social systems or social structures we are part of. (We will use these terms—social systems and structures—interchangeably.)

In a world in which systems of everyday life connect people across town and across the planet, nearly every act of life bears consequences for other people far and near. A person may be morally upright and responsible in personal relationships, yet at the same time participate knowingly or unknowingly in systems of society that render tremendous and unnecessary suffering for some people while benefitting others. Those systems may be health care systems, educational systems, economic systems, or political systems, for example.

Because we do not actually see or encounter most of the people we touch with our "systemic hands," it is easy to let these people and the consequences of our actions slip from our moral consciousness. "Out of sight, out of mind." It is easy not to see or think, for example, about the millions of people who have lost their homes and livelihoods due to the climate change for which our consumptive lifestyles are profoundly responsible. Christian morality, however, must include social systems precisely because they are so powerful in determining well-being and suffering. People who are called to love neighbor cannot ignore where the neighbor is being trampled by unjust social systems.

In short, social systems as well as individuals are moral actors. That is, societies (and other groups) act, and those actions may be morally good or evil, or more likely a mixture of both. In what ways are social systems moral actors?

One is by doing particular things. After devastating storms struck Haiti, the Philippines, and other highly vulnerable lands, for example, many nations and groups from around the world responded. Hurricanes, typhoons, and massive fires tend to elicit societal or communal moral responses of aid. These acts pertain to morality. How long that action lasts and the nature of it—whose interests it serves—is also a matter of morality.

Public policies and budgets are yet more far-reaching forms of societal moral (or immoral) action. They determine which communities will be protected from natural disasters and who will have access to health care, adequate food, quality education, defense in the court system, and more. Public policy determines who will have toxic waste dumped in their neighborhoods, nuclear weapons tested near their lands, and bombs dropped on their homes. Public policy in the form of trade policy and economic policy influences who will starve and who will have food. A law, a regulation or deregulation, a declaration of war, a state budget, and a foreign trade agreement are examples of societal actions that have tremendous impact on who will thrive and who will not. Many of the homeless women served by our churches, for example, would not be homeless if corporate wage and benefits structures or public policy regarding health care had been different. Discussing and passing a public policy or budget are morally weighted acts.

Societies are moral actors in a yet more subtle way. They establish moral norms and an overarching moral code. That is, societies determine what will be considered good and what will be considered evil, right and wrong. This function is essential for human communities' flourishing.

Yet, this form of action has shadow sides. Ethical norms and processes in any society are established by dominant sectors to reflect their sense of morality and to uphold the power arrangements that maintain their dominance. Thus, the established moral code rationalizes itself and is ill equipped to assess itself. That is, socially constructed moral values and norms perpetuate, through moral sanctioning, a prevailing order that might be considered unjust according to another moral vision. In colonial North America, for example, moral norms were established by Northern European men who owned property. Slavery, therefore, was seen by slaveholding society as moral, and primary sources of moral authority such as the Bible were regarded as sanctioning it. The focus of ethics too easily becomes what is ethical according to the prevailing moral code, rather than challenging the rightness of that moral framework itself.

That socially constructed moral norms are established by dominant sectors has yet another shadow side—their relative invisibility to those who are advantaged by them. The norm of white privilege in contemporary society is an excellent example. White people in white dominant societies, such as the United States, tend not to realize that whiteness is "normalized" and receives privileges. Thus, notes one of our authors, my young white son could play with a toy gun in the park and not be in danger of being shot by police who think he is a dangerous criminal, whereas my black friend cannot allow her son to play with a toy gun in the park; he may be shot as a perceived gun-wielding criminal.

Christian ethics, therefore, to live up to its charge of enabling healing and liberation as manifestations of God's love, must reveal uncritically held assumptions regarding what is morally good that sanctions "the way things are." Method in ethics—how we do ethics, including how we use the Bible in ethics—is a primary determinant of whether ethics reinforces or questions prevailing moral assumptions and social relations. This book aims at elaborating an approach to the use of the Bible in ethics that enables seeing these dynamics more clearly and acting faithfully in response to them.

So, we see many ways in which social systems are moral actors. Social systems have immense impact on people's lives. Jesus's call to love neighbor—that is, to serve the neighbor's well-being—means that Christian ethics must address systems precisely because they impact people's well-being and the well-being of the entire ecosphere, for better or for worse. Christian ethics thus addresses not only the private and interpersonal aspects of morality but also the social-structural. The role of the Bible (the Scripture of a particular religious tradition, Christianity) in matters of public morality in a religiously pluralistic society is no small question!

We move now to consider in more depth the dynamics of moral formation (ch. 6) and of moral deliberation and action (ch. 7).

6.

Moral Formation

How do we become people and societies who seek to know what is good and right and then choose to live accordingly? Human beings have pursued this question for millennia. It is the question of moral formation.

The question takes a specific form for Christians. If what is moral is what most closely reflects the love of God—as revealed in creation, covenant, Jesus, and the Spirit—then the question becomes, "How do we become people and communities who seek to discern which ways of living best reflect God's love," and then dare to act in that direction?

While this question is a solid guide, Christian ethics—to respond fully—must acknowledge the complexities. We must unearth the layers that render this question both elusive and crucial. In the process, the question will shift and become more powerful as a doorway into moral formation for faithful living.

Christian traditions claim that human beings are called to love one another in response to God's love. Jesus's invitation/commandment to "love neighbor as self" may also be understood as "love others as God loves you" (John 13:34). The vocation of the human is to receive and trust this love and then breathe it into the world, not as a mere feeling but as the guiding norm for all that we say and do. Our lifework is to receive love and to love. The question of moral formation becomes, "How do we become people who trust God's love, discern what coheres with it, and then act upon it?"

Humans were given a related vocation even before the calling to love. The second creation story teaches that God put humans on Earth with a summons and a duty: to "serve and preserve" God's garden, Earth (Gen 2:15). God brings the animals to 'ădām (the human) to name them, an act of taking responsibility for their well-being (Gen 2:19). Once again it is the question of moral formation: How do we become people who trust God's love and live it into the world, where this includes serving, preserving, and seeking well-being for God's good creation?

Finally, ethics cannot tend to moral formation without acknowledging what gets in its way. Let us call this moral malformation. Every moment of our lives, while blessed with the presence of God and the goodness of the world and the life that God has given, is also subject to monumental forces that betray God's love and tempt human beings to serve other gods—be they gods of wealth, reputation, power, addiction, comfort, self-denigration, or other. Equally problematic for the moral life are social structures that weave oppression into our lives, even while we try to live morally in our personal lives.

Climate change illustrates: we (this book's authors and readers) may seek to live in ways that serve other people's well-being, yet—for most of us—our lives as middle-strata US citizens produce multiple times the greenhouse gasses that are produced by many of Earth's people. Thus, our lives play a role in the displacement and death of countless victims of climate change. White privilege similarly illustrates moral malformation. A white person in the United States may seek to dismantle the white racism that is so present in our society. Yet at the same time, white people continue to be shaped unconsciously to associate white with good and black with evil or inferiority, reap the "advantages" of being white, and remain oblivious to the dangers of being black or brown. We note this not to cast blame or shame but rather to highlight the complexity of moral formation. Moral formation includes developing the capacities to uncover social dynamics that oppress, exploit, or otherwise damage some groups of people while benefitting others, even while those dynamics remain invisible to those who receive some benefits from them.

We arrive now at a question worthy of pursuit in the quest to understand moral formation: How do we become people and communities who trust God's love, discern ways of living that reflect it (while recognizing forces that work against it), and then act in those ways?

A complete response, of course, would take us into many fields of human endeavor and knowledge. One particular thread of the response is the focus for the readers and writers of this book. What is the role of the Bible in forming people and societies? Before honing in on the role of the Bible, we consider more fully the dynamics of moral formation itself and in particular the morally formative interplay between moral selves and groups.

MORAL CHARACTER: SELVES AND SOCIETIES

Previously, we said that morality has two subjects: individuals and social systems. Moral being—or moral character—as well as moral doing pertain not only to individuals but to groups, communities, societies. The good society is as much a concern of ethics as is the good individual.

Individual character formation and its impact on moral behavior is impossible to consider apart from the character of the groups in which we become who we are. Those groups range from families and other communities of initial intimacy to entire societies. Societal structures, actions, norms, and the worldviews and values that accompany them all comprise the moral character of a society. Individuals' character formation and these societal factors go hand in hand. The moral nature of a society and its subgroups influence the morality of individuals within them. Likewise the people who comprise a group or society shape its moral character. To consider moral formation—how we become people who live the love of God into the world—we must attend to the intertwining of individual and societal moral character.

This chapter considers two of the following four touchpoints in the dynamics of moral life, the two that deal with the formation of moral character:

- Who we are as moral beings (moral character)
- What we do as moral beings (moral doing)
- Who we are as societies (moral character)
- What we do as societies (moral doing)

Although the issues of moral doing will be fully discussed in chapter 7, it is necessary to keep in mind that all four shape and are shaped by the others. The flow among them is constant.

To understand that flow more fully, the following sections discuss two dynamics of moral formation.

- Societies and other groups shape moral character.

- People who are morally good in private life participate—consciously and not—in societal good and in societal sin or evil as participants in social systems.

From there we explore the crucial role of moral vision. Finally, we examine the role of the Bible in moral formation.

SOCIETY AND OTHER GROUPS SHAPE
MORAL CHARACTER

Here we note two matters: the role of community and other social groups in moral formation, and the essential beginnings of moral formation in our first communities of intimacy, the family above all.

Moral formation is ensemble work. Because we are social creatures by nature, born to belonging and relational by desire and habit, the bulk of moral formation is through the influence of communities and other societal forces. Even something so much a part of the inner life as individual conscience betrays this. "Conscience" derives from "*con*" and "*scientia*"—"knowing together," "knowing in relation to," or simply "joint awareness." Conscience is the expression of personal moral character. Character is formed in community and by the "messaging" of the broader society. Conscience is nurtured with materials initially provided by communities, both explicitly and through implicit transmission of values and assumptions. Moral "knowing," all moral knowing, is grounded in "knowing together." This includes our inner guidance systems.

Religions have long assumed that communities are essential to the life of faith and morality. Jewish and early Christian communities are emphatic about this. Few realities are so apparent as the strong sense of peoplehood in Judaism and the early church. "A people of the Way" describes the continuity across centuries of a group identity that includes a moral identity. The immediate point, however, is that, in the scriptural accounts, these communities are the matrix of moral formation.

The role of biblical communities acknowledged, we turn to the more general place of community in moral formation. Specifically, we ask about the place of childhood and youth in the moral life, those early character-forming and conscience-forming years. What might be said about the very beginnings of moral formation?

Our discussion of morality and ethics would be misleading if it cast morality and ethics chiefly as a matter of rational discussion among adults. The moral life does not begin with the reasoning of adults. It begins well before we ourselves make any significant moral choices and even before we show evidence of moral consciousness at all, much less moral reflection. The examined life, the only kind Socrates thought worth living, is a long trail into the future from the onset of the moral life. That onset is with infants and toddlers. Granted, we have few, if any, conscious memories of that. Nonetheless, the outlines of moral identity occur when the first contours of personality and temperament are set down, well before we said our first sentence or knew which part of the book was the "front." It begins with the texture of life presented to us by our very first companions. Even a basic disposition toward the world—whether life is itself trustworthy or not—is largely determined in the parent-infant bond. As infancy moves into toddlerhood, learning is principally imitation, including moral imitation. The rudiments of right and wrong—acceptable and unacceptable behavior—are communicated in the small circles of childhood. Even the basic social graces (too tepid a term for learning how to treat one another) are first acquired in a hundred small ways, spread across any given week, at home and in daycare. All of which is to say that our most basic moral learning is prior to the "reason" with which we might eventually question, clarify, and extend it; communities of intimate others first do this crucial moral work. This is where the world itself is first transmitted and the ways of culture originally learned. It is here character is initially fashioned and the first spoken and unspoken catechisms are inculcated. (Tellingly "character" is from the Greek *charaktēr*, meaning the impression left by an engraving tool and, by extension, the marks made by the engraving tool.) Here, when people are most tender, is when and where moral formation, including malformation, happens. "God lays souls into the lap of married people" is Luther's comment,[1] to which we add, of the unmarried, too. All companions of children, in fact.

Understanding the moral personhood of children, then, is not best gained by interrogating their own limited moral vocabulary or by studying them as individuals. These budding moral persons are best understood by looking to the moral quality of their limited communities and the practices and conditions of these communities in the midst of the larger society bearing down on them. They are best understood by looking to the quality of the child's primary world, dimensions of race, class, gender, and culture included. Later, the child's world will expand. New relationships will multiply quickly and older ones evolve significantly. The moral life will then take on other hues as children learn to enter and live amid expanded relationships and their environments. But in all of these, moral formation is ensemble work. None of us traffics in universal behaviors expressive of universal reason; we traffic in the unavoidably particular cultures of communities present to us in concrete ways and specific places. And the first of these, chronologically and by virtue of life significance, are initial caregivers, above all, families in all of their varied forms.

Since these communities may be cold and atrocious as well as warm and caring, violent as well as protective, pedestrian as well as convivial, even magical, the occasion of moral formation is also the occasion of moral malformation. The persons who emerge may be loving, hateful, caring, fierce, withdrawn, irascible, responsible, or irresponsible—or any mix of these and other character traits. In any case, our first communities were making us the kind of person we are long before we ever knew.[2] "Home" was a microcosm of how we care for one another, our community, and even our world, including other-than-human parts of it.

Even the very sense of reality that so deeply affects moral development throughout life is inculcated in the patterns of our first communities. As feminists point out so effectively, gender and sexual patterns *as basic social patterns* are learned here, to the point of rendering the culture "natural," that is, treated as simply "the way things are." So, too, a whole range of ways we conceive body and spirit, ourselves, our neighbors, and the rest of nature. Likewise, the lan-

---

1. Herbert Brokering and Roland Bainton, *Luther's Germany* (Minneapolis: Fortress Press, 1985), 45.

2. This section draws heavily on the pages from Rasmussen, *Moral Fragments*, 124–25.

guage through which reality is mediated and ordered is learned in this school, with indelible moral effects. Thought and the ordering of our world emerge with the emergence of language. So, for example, if our God-talk teaches that human subordination is the theologically and morally proper relation both to God and one another, along stipulated lines of authority, then a way of life has been learned as we learn to talk, whatever the age and occasion. And if our nature-talk always puts the other-than-human world outside us and as an object of use to a species that arrogates all mind to itself, then children learn with language itself that the natural world is theirs to exploit. In short, the life-fashioning continuities that run between these close-in schools of morality and people's wider expectations are strong. Home and neighborhood, school and temple and the company we keep are the first schools of justice—and injustice. Justice and injustice begin at home.[3]

Given the formative significance of these years, it comes as no surprise that communities for whom the Bible matters readily use Scripture to morally form the young. Some formation is via teaching—learning bible verses and drawing out their lessons. Perhaps even more common are bible stories, often acted out or drawn and colored, with moral formation happening by way of children stepping into the paradigmatic accounts themselves and identifying with the characters and story line. Songs also imprint messages. In later years, study, instruction, and discussion will be more formal, often with a catechetical rite of passage as the goal and conclusion. These years, too, self-consciously use Scripture for moral formation and discernment.

MORAL SELVES PRACTICE SOCIAL SIN

People who seek to be moral live with a troubling reality. We may dedicate considerable effort to living a morally good life. That may be one of our primary commitments. When we die, we want to be recalled as people who made the world around us a better place, as people of compassion, generosity, and a worthy legacy. And indeed that commitment may shape our interpersonal lives in profound ways. It is not unusual to find people sacrificing tremendously for

---

3. Martha C. Nussbaum, "Justice for Women!," review of *Justice, Gender, and the Family*, by Susan Moller Okin, *New York Review of Books* 39, no. 16 (October 8, 1992): 44.

others, even to the point of giving their lives. No one wants to be remembered for hurting, depriving, or taking from others. In the end, "eulogy" virtues matter even more than "résumé" virtues.[4]

At the same time, and whatever our intent, as members of societies, we participate in ways of being that deprive and damage other people and the natural world. Often, we do not recognize those impacts, at least until we come to know the life stories of those who are victimized or until we look beyond the surface into the systems that channel our behavior. Endless are the examples of ways in which people of strong moral character who live morally good lives on the interpersonal level still participate in social structural sin. Consider three.

Food

A colleague once said that she had sensed for years something terribly wrong about the relative inexpensiveness of many fruits and vegetables in the United States, but had not dared to look into it. When she did, she uncovered the horrors behind the lovely, healthy meals that she so relished for herself and family. She found exploited farm labor (provided mostly by people of color), dangerous pesticides, the carbon footprint of a meal (including shocking levels of greenhouse gas emissions produced by the meat industry), the destruction of lands and water supplies in parts of the world that export food to the United States, and more.

Climate Change

Climate change and its life-threatening, even deadly, impact on vulnerable people—as noted above—provides a second example. Caused overwhelmingly by the world's high-consuming people, climate change is wreaking death and destruction first and foremost on impoverished people, who also are disproportionately people of color. The island nations that will be rendered unsuitable for human habitation by rising sea levels, subsistence farmers whose crops are undermined by climate change, and coastal peoples without resources to protect against and recover from the fury of climate-related weather disaster are not the people largely responsible for greenhouse gas

4. David Brooks, "The Moral Bucket List," *New York Times*, April 11, 2015, http://tinyurl.com/y7von9hw.

emissions. Nor are they, for the most part, white. Should the Gulf Stream and Japanese currents slow down, Europe and North America will be massively impacted. People with financial resources will be most able to relocate, and financial resources in these continents lie disproportionately with white people.

White Privilege

A third example is the "white privilege" that grounds our nation historically and contemporarily, yet is so little recognized by white people. White people of Northern European descent benefit from being white in ways that undermine the well-being of many people of color. To illustrate: A young black man is more likely to be stopped by police officers for walking or jogging in a largely white neighborhood than is a white man. Data shows higher rates of suspension from school of black youth than of white youth as a consequence for the same behavior. A person with a white-sounding name and accent is more likely to be called for a job interview than is a person whose name on the CV sounds black or Latino. The school in a white neighborhood has funds for art and music programs that may be unavailable for schools in black neighborhoods. As has become so painfully evident in the reality that the Black Lives Matter movement has revealed, black people are more likely to be stopped while driving and more likely to be arrested as a result than are white people. Two brief stories speak loudly: A white woman—the friend of one of this book's authors—recently was stopped by a police officer for having run a red light. She was let go without citation after the officer commented, "I will let you off this time. You don't look like a criminal." Would this have been his response had this woman been black? Another friend, who is black, instructs her son with an intensity born of mother love that when stopped by police he must keep his hands on the wheel and not reach toward the glove compartment for the car license because the officer may falsely assume he is reaching for a gun. Black parents teach their sons to "keep your hands at 10 o'clock and 2 o'clock on the wheel." They know that these sons are at risk if they move their hands.

People who are morally good in private life participate in moral wrong as parts of social structures simply by following the paths of behavior and belief laid out for us. Sociologist Alan Johnson refers to this as following the "path of least resistance." "You don't have to be ruthless people," he writes, "in order to follow paths of least resistance that lead to behavior with ruthless consequences."[5] Those consequences may be deadly without our ever being aware of them. Most of us are not aware of the people who will die today due to climate change or the black youth who are funneled into prison with its life destroying consequences or the Indian peasants who must flee, destitute, to the city because their rural water supply is drained by the Coca-Cola plant on their lands.

The purpose here is not to cast blame or shame. Far from it. The purpose is to enable people to respond more fully to God's call to love. For Christians called to love God, self, neighbor, and Earth, passive complicity with structural sin is untenable where moral alternatives exist.

How, then, can we respond faithfully? By understanding more fully how eco-social structural sin operates and how it interfaces with moral character. What is the interaction of character and social structure that permits and institutionalizes morally questionable actions by societies or social groups, actions that may be deadly for "neighbors" we are called to love around the globe?

The notion of "social," or "structural," sin helps us understand the links between moral character and social structures. Societal acts that harm some people unjustly or exploit Earth unnecessarily in order to benefit others are known as social or eco-social sins. Eco-social sin includes not only the policies, power arrangements, and practices that oppress, exploit, or otherwise damage others or the Earth. It includes also the silence or acquiescence of people who comply with those dynamics. In addition, social sin includes the worldviews or ideologies that undergird these dynamics. Three features of social/structural sin help in understanding its power and our "bondage to it."

FEATURES OF SOCIAL STRUCTURAL SIN

First, social/eco-social sin tends to remain invisible to those not suffering from it and especially those who benefit from it.[6] It manages to hide from our conscious awareness.[7] Dietrich Bonhoeffer, reflect-

---

5. Allan G. Johnson, *Privilege, Power, and Difference* (Boston: McGraw-Hill, 2006), 88.

6. This section is taken from Moe-Lobeda, *Resisting Structural Evil.*

7. This is true also of social good. We may remain largely unconscious of the good that we do through taxes, for example: building schools, parks, fire departments, etc.

ing from prison on the widespread complicity with fascism in Hitler's Germany, provides striking insight into the hiddenness of evil. (What Bonhoeffer calls "evil" is another term in this case for social sin.) "The great masquerade of evil has played havoc with all our ethical concepts," he writes. "For evil to appear *disguised as light, charity, historical necessity, or social justice* is quite bewildering to anyone brought up on our traditional ethical concepts, while for the Christian who bases his life on the Bible, it merely confirms the fundamental wickedness of evil."[8] Its ability to "appear disguised"—to hide—confirms its wickedness. That is, the cloaked nature of structural evil or eco-social sin is at its very heart.

Bonhoeffer's words reveal more. They name four masks behind which social sin hides: "light, charity, historical necessity, [and] social justice." That is, we often fail to recognize structural sin because we mistake it for good or charity or justice, or we accept it as necessary. Think of the examples above: how many white people in the United States have accepted as "justice" a system that incarcerates and otherwise penalizes young black men unjustly? For decades, US society has accepted as "the good life," a lifestyle that is rapidly destroying Earth's capacity to sustain life as we know it. Is the ongoing burning of fossil fuels, and thus drilling for oil, fracking, and coal extraction, seen as historical necessity? Where eco-social sin remains unseen by those who benefit from it, they are unlikely to repent and seek freedom from that sin.

Second, social structural sin is transmitted from generation to generation through processes of socialization, as is societal good. Members of a society are socialized toward assuming unconsciously that its social structures and attendant values and worldviews are normal, natural, inevitable, and even divinely ordained. In this process of socialization, cultural, political, economic, and ideological structures that perpetuate injustice tend to be accepted and passed on to the next generations as though they were just "the way things are," maintained by a force akin to nature, rather than products of human decisions and actions.

To illustrate: Parents in our society commonly teach children to make money and make it grow in order to be "successful." Children strive for the material comforts sought by parents and paraded by

8. Dietrich Bonhoeffer, "Ten Years After," in *Letters and Papers from Prison*, ed. Eberhard Bethge, trans. Reginald Fuller (New York: Touchstone, 1997), 4. Emphasis ours.

public idols. Tacit communications teach that poverty or apparent poverty signifies failure. A life of voluntary "downward mobility" in terms of material consumption, if even imagined, would bear the hue of failure. Thus, we are morally formed away from such a choice.

Over time, inherited patterns of human interaction and perceptions become what Marcus Borg refers to as "common wisdom" and Stephen Brookfield as "culturally produced assumptions."[9] Where these patterns are exploitative or oppressive, this structural injustice is passed on. Thus, for example, a black student walking to the dorm from the library late at night is far more likely to be stopped by security personnel asking to see his ID than is a white student. "Conventional wisdom" passed on over time leads the security guard to stop the black student or black jogger or black driver, while the white student, jogger, or driver goes unnoticed. The sobering reality is that what a society assumes to be moral may, in fact, be quite the contrary. At one time, to illustrate, chattel slavery was deemed moral and was sanctioned by theology and interpretations of the Bible. Our food system was—until recently—also assumed to be moral.

However, we may choose to intervene and halt that passage. Doing so requires recognizing the injustice as such. Shortly, we consider this further.

The third feature of structural sin pertains to role morality. We live in highly differentiated societies of interlocking systems and complex organization. Such societies only work if members take on multiple roles. One might be a student in one role, a clerk in another, perhaps an athlete in a third, and a soldier in a fourth, all in addition to the social roles of being a son or daughter, lover, husband or wife, uncle or aunt, brother or sister, and a good friend. The roles are differentiated, with different responsibilities and behaviors expected in different settings.

The roles we inhabit on a daily basis are powerful determinants of the moral life we live. While most people's moral character is formed by early adulthood, their lived morality as adults is usually best understood by noting the roles they play and how they play them. Role morality is a prime form the moral life takes for our adult years.

This shifts attention to the moral content of systems themselves

---

9. Marcus J. Borg, *Meeting Jesus Again for the First Time: The Historical Jesus and the Heart of Contemporary Faith* (San Francisco: HarperOne, 2005), ch. 4; Stephen Brookfield, *Developing Critical Thinkers: Challenging Adults to Explore Alternative Ways of Thinking and Acting* (San Francisco: Jossey-Bass, 1987), 17.

and the roles their functioning create. To oversimplify a bit, good institutions make even bad people do good things while bad institutions make good people do bad things, and both because of roles that channel behavior so as to meet institutional goals. If, say, the doctors conscripted by Nazi Germany for blatantly evil work in the concentration camps and in medical experiments to generate a superior Aryan race had instead all emigrated to New Zealand and Australia in 1930 and practiced medicine there, they would not have done the despicable things they did in Germany. Whatever their individual character, their role as physicians might have bent their practice toward personal and social good.

Consider another example from this time. Kurt Waldheim was the United Nations secretary-general from 1972 to 1981. As such, he was the chief international diplomat for human rights. In June 1986, he became president of his native Austria. Not long before the election, but after his tenure at the UN, evidence came to light about his links to Nazi atrocities in the Balkans during the time he served as a liaison officer in the German Army Group E. Group E was responsible for sending thousands of Jews, civilians, partisans, and Allied commandos to forced labor camps and to concentration camps. An international commission concluded that Waldheim had to have known of the atrocities by his army unit and had done nothing to stop them. Furthermore, he subsequently kept his wartime activities secret when he was being considered for the UN post and the presidency of Austria.

In response to these revelations, what did he do? He admitted that he consistently withheld the truth of his whereabouts in WWII and, in a nationally televised address to the people of Austria, that he was not among "the heroes and martyrs" of the war. He went on to say that he had no intention of resigning the presidency, and should not. He then pointedly asked Austrians to make the definitive (moral) assessment of him and his conduct under the conditions of war and in view of later service:

> You can judge for yourselves whether your President is the young lieutenant—or even the distorted picture of this officer of the Wehrmacht—or whether your President is a man who, for decades of his life, worked for justice, tolerance and peace. I ask you to form your own judgment.[10]

10. Serge Schmemann, "Waldheim Assails 'Slanders,' Vows Not to Step Down," *New York*

Waldheim's posing of the choice as "either/or" forecloses a third possibility, one for which the evidence is strongest. Namely, he was both the lieutenant who, as an army officer doing his duty in the chain of command, actively complied with evil and the diplomat who gave years to international human rights and welfare. What helps explain contrary moral behaviors, during decades when there is little indication that Waldheim's character itself changed, is this: his roles and context were markedly different, requiring different actions on his part. They carried contrasting behavioral pressures with different moral content and outcomes. Our hypothetical emigration of German doctors to New Zealand and Australia before they instead became Nazi doctors has its counterpart in Waldheim's actual move into high-level international diplomacy where guarding and furthering human rights was one of his prime duties.

IMPLICATIONS FOR MORAL FORMATION

These three features of structural sin—its invisibility to those who benefit from it, its transmission through assumed processes of socialization, and its common form as role morality—reveal a great deal about its power in our lives and the paths toward freedom from it. We learn, that is, more about why even people with deep commitments to doing what they believe is right in the eyes of God participate—to a large extent unknowingly—in social sin, and we learn about how to renounce it.

From these features, we may conclude that good character and morality in private life are *necessary* conditions for a good society, but not *sufficient* ones. Virtue ethics, which focuses on the development of moral character, is crucial but does not of itself suffice. Living according to clear conscience is crucial, yet utterly insufficient because—as ethicist Miguel De La Torre explains—a conscience formed to accept oppressive structures as moral will simply reinforce them.[11] A critical mass of morally good people is required but is not adequate for

Times, February 16, 1988, http://tinyurl.com/yc74hahc. We have also drawn information from Serge Schmemann, "Inquiry for Austria Declares Waldheim Knew of War Crimes," *New York Times*, February 9, 1988, http://tinyurl.com/y8t35zzu; David Binder, "Waldheim Linked to Nazi Roundup," *New York Times*, February 18, 1988, http://tinyurl.com/y9fqg3jn; and "Austrians Divided over Waldheim's Nazi Issue," *Nairobi Daily Nation*, January 16, 1988.

11. Miguel A. De La Torre, *Doing Christian Ethics from the Margins* (Maryknoll, NY: Orbis, 2014).

achieving and maintaining a moral life. The good life and the good society require more than virtue and character per se can provide.

What, then—in addition to moral character—is needed for an adequate ethic to undergird the quest for a moral life? Here we note three requisites.

First, moral character must find channels in public policy and social structures designed to meet the demands of morality, including social justice and ecological well-being. That is, morality calls for steadfast commitment to shaping policies, systems, and institutions of society along lines that build the good. They are critical not only to channel the morally good impulses among us but also to "check" or counter the morally bad. Human beings are fallible creatures. The doctrine of human fallibility describes our active and ample capacity for *both* good and evil. Something deep within us, which Christians call "original sin" and Jews "the evil impulse," belies the common conception that the world is made up of good people and bad people.

It is wise to be sober and realistic about human behavior, and acknowledge the evil impulse, while yet refusing to set limits to the good that can be accomplished. A debate at the Constitutional Convention of 1787 makes the point. The debate was over the New Jersey Plan for the contemplated US Congress. That plan proposed a single house, with each state casting one vote. It granted the house considerable power and provided no internal mechanism for checking or balancing that power. James Wilson of Pennsylvania, opposing the plan, commented: "In a single house [there is no check but] the virtue and good sense of those who compose it." And everybody, he went on, "knows that check is an inadequate one." Wilson did not believe that proper structural arrangements would guarantee the social good; they would assure only a "checking and balancing" of power that, if unchecked, would invariably lead to injustice.[12] The doctrine of human fallibility or recognition of the evil impulse means we must attend with the greatest care to the complex interplay of character and social structure so that good character is both cultivated and bears fruit in a moral society.

Yet, as we have already argued and as we see in the development of the US Constitution, even where policies and social structures favor what is considered to be just and check the "evil impulse," a

12. George W. Carey, "James Wilson: Political Thought and the Constitutional Convention—The Imaginative Conservative," The Imaginative Conservative, February 27, 2014, http://tinyurl.com/y8wy6h78.

society may be brutally unjust because dominant sectors have determined self-serving ideas of what is just. Hence, a constitution purported to serve liberty and justice for all, in fact excluded more than half of its people from that liberty and justice. Neither black people nor women could vote.

This points to the second requisite. Effective morality in the context of social/structural sin calls for what we will call moral vision. Moral vision includes a commitment to deepen one's perception of dynamics that damage some people or other parts of creation, and one's perception of God and the good that God intends for life on Earth. In the foregoing example, moral vision would have expanded "liberty and justice for all" so as to include women, people of color, and Native Americans. To moral vision we turn next. But first, we note a third requisite and then recap what is learned from this foray into the features of social/structural sin and their implications for morality.

Third, effective morality requires skills, many of which are quite independent of character. Our classrooms are full of students with a deep desire to create a more just and sustainable world. The mission statements of many universities include the ideal of creating leaders for a more just and sustainable world. Fulfilling that mission means not only nurturing in students this hunger but also equipping them with sophisticated skills. They are the skills to translate hunger for the good into effective action toward it, skills in professional and vocational arenas and in citizenship: public policy advocacy, economic advocacy, analyzing moral implications of budgets and taxation policy, and economic and ecological literacy are a significant few.

In short, given the reality of social sin, moral character is a necessary but insufficient guarantor of the good. Being good is not adequate to achieving it. This gives pause to all hopes that character can be created so as to guarantee a good society. Character formation is one ingredient to be matched with at least three others: social structures as nurturer and conveyor of good and as check upon destructive behavior, moral vision, and skills. The nature and significance of moral vision deserves a fuller discussion.

MORALITY CALLS FOR MORAL VISION

"Are your hearts hardened? Do you have eyes, and fail to see?" (Mark 8:17–18)

"What could be?" and "What ought to be?" are, we noted earlier, two of the basic questions of ethics. "What is?" is the third.

What "could be" and "ought to be" express moral vision. It's the vision of the good we hold. It is sometimes brought to full consciousness and changed by startling or cataclysmic events. More often, it remains as the socialized (or internalized) reflection of the communities within which we move. People are often unaware or only dimly aware of this internalized socially constructed moral vision, but it is effective in our lives nevertheless. Indeed, the most powerful morality is unwritten but culturally inscribed. That raises the question, To what extent and in what ways have we been socialized into a vision of the good that, in fact, rationalizes systems of oppression, exclusion, or exploitation that we do not even see? To what extent have we been socialized to not see the social sin in which we participate?

PERCEPTION AND CRITICAL CONSCIOUSNESS

Even the most ordinary moral cases appear differently to different people. "It all depends, it all depends . . ." we say, and mean that it all depends on your point of view. Yet, we don't always recognize that differences of perspective depend on how viewers are enabled and accustomed to seeing, and with whom.

How *do* people come to see, in moral matters? At birth, each of us enters fresh into moral and social worlds already crowded, complex, and filled with contradictions. The moral legacies of the past live on. They reside in the ways of cultures and their institutions, in power arrangements and systems of exclusion and inclusion, in the habits of heart and mind, memories and hopes, of people. They are expressed in the varied objects and symbols of human love, trust, allegiance, commitment, and fear. They manifest themselves in forms of religious devotion in the choice of cultural heroes and heroines, in the direction of a nation and its people, in its laws and institutional structures, and in people's causes, creeds, and ways of life. All these convey the moral worlds we enter as we engage our social world. Moral legacies, expressed in these varied forms, display what is valued.

They also may betray what the society claims to value. As we have noted, a society or other group may claim to hold particular values and applaud them, while also effectively betraying them. The point is crucial for our consideration of moral formation. It means that people can be morally malformed to perceive as just (or as democratic or equitable) that which in fact is just the opposite. The label of "just" given to something that is profoundly unjust, forms people to become oblivious to that injustice. Justice in the United States illustrates. The United States claims to value justice, while at the same time maintaining a "criminal justice" system that is riddled with injustice in relationship to race and class. Some refer to it as the "criminal injustice" system. Yet, that injustice may be invisible to white people and people of an economic status whose interests may be served by that system.[13]

Jürgen Habermas's idea of "immanent critique" is helpful. Immanent critique uses the claimed values of a particular system to critique that very system. People who strive to expose the racism within the "criminal injustice" system and who appeal to the norm of justice to call for change are practicing immanent critique.

In short, as human beings are socialized in a society, we "breathe in" a worldview.[14] We take on a prevailing set of assumptions about reality that shape our sense of meaning, purpose, identity, and self-interest. They are assumptions about how life should be lived, how power should be organized, and what people and things are inherently more valuable than others. These are enormously influential formative processes. They shape our sense of morality—our presuppositions about what is good, right, and true, our picture of how we are to live. They shape our judgments of other people. Most of these processes go on beneath our consciousness, producing what Stephen Brookfield calls "culturally produced assumptions," "taken-for granted values," "common-sense ideas," and "unquestioned givens" that, to us, have the status of self-evident truth.[15] They

---

13. See Michelle Alexander, *The New Jim Crow: Mass Incarceration in the Age of Colorblindness* (New York: New Press, 2012).

14. William Bean Kennedy, "Integrating Personal and Social Ideologies," in *Fostering Critical Thinking in Adulthood: A Guide to Transformative and Emancipatory Learning*, ed. Jack Mezirow (San Francisco: Jossey-Bass, 1990), 99.

15. Brookfield, *Developing Critical Thinkers*, 16, 44.

include both the overt moral claims of a society and the betrayal of those claims. Both are morally formative.

Yet, the moral and social worlds are varied, and our internalizing of them is selective. We integrate some, but not all, of society's objects of trust, devotion, and fear; some, but not all, of the images, stories, and other carriers of meaning that are present in our world; some, but not all, of the reigning commitments and perspectives.

That selection is shaped by where we are located in a society and in its systems of exclusion and inclusion, of privilege and oppression—our social location(s). White people, to illustrate, whose social world is largely comprised of other white people, will perceive life and society largely with other white people. They are thus not likely to realize that black and brown people are killed daily at the hands of racist social structures. If, as white people, our conversation partners, neighbors, close colleagues, and intimate circles are largely white, then we are not likely to know that black parents are terrified (and justifiably so) that their children will be suspended, expelled, shot, or jailed for the same actions white children will be merely reprimanded for. We are not likely to hear black parents teaching their sons how to convey themselves when stopped by police in order to minimize the chances of being shot or jailed as a result of the encounter. If our close and trusted colleagues are largely white, then as white professors we are not likely to know about the gut-wrenching pain that many faculty and staff of color experience regularly on our university campuses because of microaggressions that white colleagues unknowingly commit. Nor do they acknowledge the white supremacist assumptions that go unrecognized except by people of color.[16] Social location shapes how we perceive the moral world, what aspects of it we internalize, and which of those internalized elements we most honor and act upon.

The results may be internally conflicted and multiple, for we all belong to varied communities and have varied social locations. We are an expression of some communities, but never all, and we carry only some aspects of the communities of which we are part, never all. Moreover, we can choose to challenge and go far beyond the perceptual boundaries that social location constructs.

Which social experiences, *which* images and stories have been

16. Gabriella Gutiérrez y Muhs, Yolanda Flores Niemann, Carmen G. González, and Angela P. Harris, eds., *Presumed Incompetent: The Intersections of Race and Class for Women in Academia* (Boulder: University Press of Colorado, 2012).

internalized and integrated matter immensely for morality. The selective internalizing forms our moral character, and that character then shapes how we act, as individuals and as parts of social systems. It shapes what public policies we support or challenge, which norms of behavior we accept or reject, which people we believe or distrust, and which roles we seek to take on.

The foregoing can be summarized: our selective internalization of society, and our selective integration of its morality, molds the way we see the world, think about it, and respond to it.

It is difficult to exaggerate the significance of perception for the moral life. A Chinese proverb expresses it well: "Ninety percent of what we see lies *behind* our eyes." Perceptions aren't mental photographs, they are highly active images. Perception "defines" our reality and what we define as real is real in its consequences. It helps set the direction and limits of our conduct, generating certain choices and actions rather than others, underlining some issues as more significant than others, and disposing us to some responses rather than others. Why we do one thing and not the other, indeed why we do something rather than nothing at all, depends on our apprehension of things. At the end of specific responses dangles perception.

One crucial task of adult morality is critical consciousness and its analysis of these dynamics. Stephen Brookfield notes two steps in that consciousness.[17] First is becoming ever more self-aware of these formative processes and the assumptions they have produced. Second is assessing those assumptions and determining which are worth retaining, which ought to be revised, and which ought to be exposed and rejected because they obscure what is good and true (or worse yet, reinforce the opposite).

Moral vision and perception can change. History is rife with examples. The divine right of kings entailed a moral vision of the monarchy as having ultimate authority derived from God. A king, therefore, was subject to no earthly authority, constraints, or sanction, and to oppose the king was to oppose God. The day came, first here, then there, and never without conflict, when this view of how human life should be ordered was condemned as inherently immoral. What caught on among enough people was the moral vision of the fundamental equality of "all people" and their right to some form of governance by the people. This example shows also the

17. Brookfield, *Developing Critical Thinkers*, 15–22.

slippery nature of change in moral vision and the deep-seated power of underlying but unacknowledged assumptions. The equality of "all people" did not include *all* people. And the right of powerful people to operate "free" from democratic constraints has erupted in other forms. Nevertheless, the vision of equal rights as a moral good constitutes a shift in moral vision that bears power. It may be that we are in the midst of another shift in moral vision—a vision of equality that would actually include all people and would thereby challenge worldviews and policies that privilege some people over others.

IMPLICATIONS FOR MORAL FORMATION

These observations regarding moral vision bear significant implications for morality and ethics, and specifically for moral formation. Consider six of them.

1. Needed are tools for morally responsible vision, especially of the power dynamics that determine who has the necessities for life with dignity (and, as we will soon discuss, the terms of humans' relationship to the planet). Furthering that morally responsible vision is a primary function of Christian ethics. The "bane of ethics," notes moral theologian Daniel Maguire, is to ignore or "inadequately see reality."[18]

2. One of those reality-exposing tools is critical eco-social analysis. It is an indispensable tool for an adequate Christian ethic. Without it we simply fail to uncover the eco-social moral world. The reason is that our provincial world is often so powerfully present that we effectively identify it as the only real world and act accordingly. We assume that the reigning moral standards of our world are *the* standards, and we treat them as though they were universal rather than parochial. Critical analysis uncovers the "particularity" of morality and exposes its limited dimensions. Assumed moral notions go largely unnoticed until they are challenged.

Critical analysis is needed for another, quite different, reason. A Christian ethic that does not have routine ways of investigating concrete, encultured moral reality will not have credibility when it makes specific moral judgments and offers recommendations. It will be too far from life as it is actually lived, and people will instinctively

18. Daniel Maguire, *Death by Choice* (Garden City, NY: Image, 1984), 65–66.

recognize its irrelevance. In short, social analysis is vital to Christian ethics for both critical and constructive tasks.

3. Critical analysis and, with it, moral vision depend upon the company we keep. Who we listen to and whose perspective we seek out matters. A fundamental tenant of an ethic grounded in Jesus is that moral perception and moral deliberation are deeply flawed unless they seek out and prioritize perspectives from the margins of power and privilege. The life and death import of this commitment is evident in the movement within the United States to face and dismantle America's "original sin" of racism. Until white people dare to see—or at least glimpse—reality as it is experienced by people of color, we are less likely to join that movement.

A caveat is necessary: no person situated in privilege can claim to read reality accurately from the margins. However, a critical perspective holds that one can and must make every effort to do so, always acknowledging the limitations of that effort. That is a central challenge and commitment of Christian ethics done from or addressed to positions of historically accrued privilege.[19]

4. Moral vision for citizens of Earth community will encompass the full Earth community, not only humans. The scope of morality in the modern Western world has been the scope of the human. A moral future calls for profound shifts in moral consciousness. Our vision of the world will be eco-centric and biocentric rather than anthropocentric only. The early Christian moral vision of *oikos* still has relevance, to cite one example. *Oikos* is Greek for "house" and "household" and the root of "ecumenics," "ecology," and "economics." While it referred first of all to the households of faith of early Christians, under Stoic influence it also envisioned Earth itself as the "world house." The *oikoumenē*, whence come "ecumenics" and "ecumenical," was regarded as the whole inhabited Earth, or imperial claims to it. (The Roman Empire referred to itself as the *oikoumenē*.) The emphasis in this use of *oikoumenē* falls on the unity of the household—all belong to the same family—and nurturing this unity across the expanse of inhabited terrain. The householder was the *oikonomos*,

19. This commitment as it pertains to Christian ethics, while launched, per se, in liberation theologies—beginning with Latin American liberation theologies in the 1960s—is firmly grounded in Jewish and Christian Scriptures, and in the notion that the great Mystery referred to as God in these two traditions is a God who (1) worked in and revealed Godself through people and peoples on the underside of power, and (2) resisted relations of oppression and exploitation. Theology knows these ideas respectively as the "epistemological privilege of the poor" and "God's preferential option for the poor."

literally the "economist," the one who knows the house rules (*oikos nomos*, law) and cares for the material well-being of its members. (*Oikonomos* is often translated "steward" or "trustee" even though "economist" is the more exact rendering.) Household dwellers are *oikeioi*. Their task is to build up the community and share the gifts of the Spirit for the common good. Paul's language is classic: "Now there are varieties of gifts, but the same Spirit: and there are varieties of services, but the same Lord; and there are varieties of activities, but it is the same God who activates all of them in everyone. To each is given the manifestation of the Spirit for the common good" (1 Cor 12:4–7). This continual building up of the household for the common good is designated *oikodomē*. Building up the community requires knowing the household's ethos, logic, and laws, which is what "ecology" means (*oikos logos*). Ecology is knowledge of the interrelated relationships that build up and sustain.

The vision of *oikos*, then, is a conception of economics, ecology, and ecumenics as interrelated dimensions of the same world. Though ancient, it accords with the seamlessness, or integrity, of creation in the Hebrew Bible as well as the actual interplay of all these elements in planetary creation today. The ecosphere is a shared home.

5. Moral vision will see beyond the private or interpersonal dimensions of life to the communal and social structural. This means that when we imagine who we are in the relationships that shape our lives, we will perceive the threads that bind us to people and ecosystems we will never actually see and may not know exist: the workers whose low wages produce our inexpensive consumer goods, the farmworkers who pick our food and may be sprayed with chemicals in the process, the indigenous people whose lives are lost or endangered while resisting the invasion of their homelands by the oil companies that supply our homes with heat, the underpaid laborers who make our clothing. Moral vision does not simply see the homeless child in the streets of our cities. Moral vision sees also our functional relationship to that child and sees, in particular, whether or not our way of life and the public policies and corporate actions that make it possible are contributing to her poverty. Moral vision also sees the moral good fostered by structural threads that bind us to people around the world and to other-than-human creatures. Business practices that insist on a living wage and safe working conditions and healthy environments, or public policies protecting people and lands,

are illustrative. In short, moral vision must extend beyond immediate interpersonal relationships to social structural and ecological relationships. The goal, in fact, is to so order our lives that "the flood of life flows freely" through structures that service the common good.

6. The stories of faith communities shape moral vision. Christian communities hold that God as seen in Jesus and experienced in the Holy Spirit and on the Earth itself is the final source of moral goodness and the object of ultimate trust, love, and commitment. This does not mean that God as understood through other faith traditions is a different God or is a less trustworthy ultimate ground of being, but rather that Christians know this God through God's revelation in Jesus, the biblical witness, the Holy Spirit, and Earth's creatures and elements.

Christian communities have the task of forming perception and character in accord with this God. The community is a socializing agent of faith. A major part of this work consists of immersing members in the particular stories, traditions, symbols, and lessons (both positive and negative) of past and present faith communities. These become essential content as the community helps to define moral goodness.

This means that what "story" is told and through whose interpretive narration matters tremendously. One story of Jesus Christ and the salvation he wrought, believed to be deeply true by the Christian communities who held it, justified slavery. Another story justified slavery's abolition. One story of God told by Christian communities taught men to beat their wives; another saw that beating as moral abomination. To this important matter we return in the following section on the Bible and moral formation.

MORAL VISION: FACING REALITY WITH HOPE AND MORAL POWER

We have talked thus far about the moral responsibility to see beneath the surface in order to uncover dynamics that may cause suffering and damage while remaining largely invisible to those not suffering overtly from those dynamics. Grave danger accompanies this courageous moral commitment. People may be overwhelmed by the magnitude and complexity of systemic injustice, by guilt or shame for our role in it, or by a sense of powerlessness to make a difference. The forces of wrong may seem too powerful for human beings to impact. One's efforts may appear futile. A sense of inevitability and hopelessness may suck away at hope and moral agency.

If faith calls us to face reality, including structural sin, how do we address the despair and hopelessness that may attack us when we do? We propose a mode of moral vision that entails seeing three things at once.

The first is seeing "what is," especially social sin where it parades as good or where we are seduced into ignoring or denying it. As we have argued, if eco-social sin continues and goes unconfessed largely because we fail to recognize it, then morality calls for developing deep skills of analysis that get beneath the surface of "the way things are" to uncover the hidden implications of life as we know it. Yet, seeing "what is" is dangerous unless that form of vision is accompanied by a second and a third.

The second is seeing "what could be," that is, alternatives to the structures and practices that exploit or oppress people or Earth. If we are socialized to accept uncritically "the way things are" as "the way things will be," and if role morality seduces us into complicity with structural sin, then keen ability to see alternatives is a lynchpin of morality. These two together—envisioning "what is" and "what could be"—we call "critical seeing." This includes attuning ourselves to the movements, groups, and people—both distant and near—who are working to create more life-giving, healing, just, ecologically healthy alternatives to whatever impediments are at hand. Seeing creative alternatives is vital to critical vision. A Chinese proverb cautions, "Unless we change direction, we will get where we are going." Changing direction requires first recognizing, even dimly, alternative viable destinations.

We might refer to the third mode of vision as "mystical vision." By this, we mean seeing ever more fully the Spirit of God's healing liberating love coursing throughout creation and leading it—despite all evidence to the contrary—into abundant life for all. It's a vision that "in everything there is a hidden wholeness."[20] If feelings of powerlessness accompany the courage to face the pervasive and powerful nature of structural sin, then the capacity to recognize God's life-giving, lifesaving, life-savoring presence at play and at work in the world is necessary food for the moral life.

---

20. Thomas Merton, "Hagia Sophia," in *A Thomas Merton Reader*, ed. Thomas P. McDonnell (Garden City, NY: Image, 1974), 506.

Christian ethics has at its heart the crucial task of holding these three together. Vision of this sort is subversive because "it keeps the present provisional and refuses to absolutize it."[21] Such vision reveals a future in the making and breeds hope for moving into it.

MORAL VISION AS CENTRAL FOR REPENTANCE
AND LAMENT

Why place so much import on "seeing" social sin or structures of injustice? The transformative power of repentance and lament come into play.

Failure to see social injustice or social sin presents a great problem for the moral life. The problem pertains to repentance. Fundamental to virtually all forms of Christianity is the claim that Christians are called to eschew sin, and that freedom from sin begins with repentance. Repentance means ceasing the way of sin and "turning the other direction." *Teshuvah*, the Hebrew word often translated as "repentance," suggests turning from sinful ways and toward the good by means of turning back to God. It is a powerful act of changing direction that can redirect one's entire life. The Greek *metanoia*, translated as "repentance" in the New Testament, means to perceive differently, to have a new mind and consciousness. Repentance then involves a distinct turning away from sin, in both consciousness and action. ("Do not be conformed to this world, but be transformed by the renewing of your minds, so that you may discern what is the will of God—what is good and acceptable and perfect" Rom 12:2.)

Repentance is possible only where sin is acknowledged. If we do not see the structural sin in which we live, we cannot repent of it. Failing to renounce it, we remain captive to it. Failure to see structural sin fosters complicity with it and passes it on to the next generation. The call to renounce sin contains a call to "see" the structural sin of which we are a part, in order that we might repent of it, renounce it, and resist it.[22]

Lament, like repentance, is not possible if we fail to see that for

---

21. Walter Brueggemann, *The Prophetic Imagination* (Philadelphia: Fortress Press, 1978), 44.

22. We are not raising sin as a problem related to personal "salvation" for life after death. That issue is of no concern to us here. We believe that we are forgiven and are assured eternal life after death regardless of the magnitude of sin. Hence, we are free from striving toward the good for the purpose of gaining "heaven" after we die; we are free to seek the good as a matter of loving God, self, neighbor, and Earth.

which we are called to lament. In a powerful sermon on the book of Joel, Christian womanist ethicist Emilie Townes claims that social healing begins with communal lament. Communal lament, she explains, is the assembly crying out in distress to the God in whom it trusts. It is a cry of sorrow by the people gathered, a cry of grief and repentance and a plea for help in the midst of social affliction. Deep and sincere "communal lament . . . names problems, seeks justice, and hopes for God's deliverance." "When Israel used lament as rite and worship on a regular basis, it kept the question of justice visible and legitimate."[23] Lament is integral to social restoration.

If repentance and lament are doorways to social healing, and if they depend upon seeing the wrong that is done, then Christians who benefit from structures of injustice are called to see those structures realistically. In the words of James Baldwin, "Not everything that is faced can be changed, but nothing can be changed until it is faced."[24] Facing social realities entails seeing them. Moral vision is vital to a people called to love as God loves.

MORAL VISION AND AESTHETIC VALUE

"Beauty will save the world," proclaims the main Christlike character in Dostoevsky's brilliant work *The Idiot*. "What is this?" queries Alexander Solzhenitsyn in his 1972 Nobel lecture. "For a long time," he goes on, "it seemed to me simply a phrase. How could this be possible? When in the bloodthirsty process of history did beauty ever save anyone, and from what?" Solzhenitsyn's response to his own inquiry into Dostoevsky's insight is telling: "There is," he responds, "a particular feature in the very essence of beauty. . . . It prevails even over a resisting heart. . . . And then no slip of the tongue but a prophecy would be contained in Dostoyevsky's words: 'Beauty will save the world.'"[25]

A few years ago, following revelations of the horrific long-term suffering and death caused by the US bombing in Iraq coupled with

23. Emilie M. Townes, *Breaking the Fine Rain of Death: African American Health Issues and a Womanist Ethic of Care* (New York: Continuum, 1998), 24.

24. The Baldwin quotation is taken from the interview with Mary Pipher, author of *The Green Boat*. She was interviewed on the media program *Living on Earth*, July 12, 2013, http://tinyurl.com/ybcqa749.

25. Alexander Solzhenitsyn, "Solzhenitsyn Explains 'Beauty Will Save the World,'" *Intercollegiate Review*, Fall 2015, Intercollegiate Studies Institute, http://tinyurl.com/yddkyehy.

the embargo against that nation's people,[26] one of our authors was overcome by a sense of despair at the magnitude of structural injustice and the forces lined up to maintain it. Devoid of hope, she stumbled on the pianist from her congregation rehearsing a stunning piece. The pure beauty of the music flew into her heart and transformed the despair into hope. It was the beauty of the music but also the sense of awe that it had been composed as beauty centuries ago, passed down as beauty, and then re-created through the hands, heart, and diligence of a young Eastern European pianist to rekindle hope in the face of despair. Reborn was a sense of power to move into life's calling.

In *The Cellist of Sarajevo*,[27] a musician in Sarajevo under siege witnesses twenty-two people killed instantly by mortar attack while standing in a breadline. His response, to sit in the line of fire at the site of the deaths daily for twenty-two days playing cello with haunting and captivating beauty, restores a sense of humanity and goodness to the novel's other main figures. All had been ravaged emotionally and materially by months under a siege that was destroying the city and the means of living in it. Their lives are transformed by the music's beauty.

Why is it that the particular blue of the sky just as dusk becomes night can restore one's trust that God's reign of life and love indeed will transform the world? Why does beauty—be it visual art, dance, music, or poetry; the splendor of mountains, trees, flowers, clouds, waters; or the beauty shining in loving eyes—have the power to heal and to impart moral courage?

It may be that the human capacity to create and to be fed by beauty is at the heart of who we are as human and hence also at the heart of morality. Beauty reveals to us the goodness that is possible even in the midst of the terrible. It grips us with a world that could be and ought to be. Moral vision, then, attends deeply to beauty. In this sense, aesthetic value is critical to ethical value.

MORAL VISION: IN SUM

Hebrew Bible scholar Walter Brueggemann writes: "The ones who minister to the imagination, who enable people to see the world dif-

---

26. According to UNICEF (the United Nations Children's Fund), half a million children had died in Iraq by 2000 as a result of the sanctions imposed by the UN Security Council and the destruction by bombing of water systems and other elements of infrastructure.

27. Steven Galloway, *The Cellist of Sarajevo* (New York: Riverhead, 2008).

ferently and to live now in the world they see are fatally dangerous to the establishment."[28] "Poets and artists are silenced because they reveal too much of what must remain hidden."[29]

We have noted the challenge of recognizing and assessing the socially constructed moral vision into which one is socialized, and the implications of that socialization process for moral formation, formation for both good and ill. We have noted the import of seeing not only "what is going on," but also "what could be" and the power and presence of God permeating creation.

Iris Murdoch's call to "pay attention" captures this. Crucial "moral choices" are determined, she asserts, by what one has been giving attention over time. Attention or seeing, Murdoch says, is "the effort to counteract illusion . . . false pictures of the world."[30] "The difficulty is to keep the attention fixed upon the real situation. . . . [T]he background condition of [moral action] is a just mode of vision. . . . It is a task to come to see the world as it is."[31] Ours has been a toolkit for coming "to see the world as it is" as a basis for responding to the world in ways that reflect the love of God for it.

This toolkit is crucial to the central question of ethics with which we began this chapter: "How are we to perceive our world, and live in it, *because of God's boundless and invincible love for creation and presence with and in it?*" If Christian ethics is to hold in one breath two things—the mystery of God's unquenchable love for all, and the complex realities of life on Earth—this toolkit assists in uncovering the latter.

The next chapter takes up the question of moral choices and action. First, however, we spend more time with the last "implication for ethics" noted above—"the stories of the faith community shape moral vision." What is the role of the Bible in the moral formation of faith communities? This inquiry also sheds light on how we are to "perceive . . . the mystery of God's unquenchable love for all." The primary role of the Bible in ethics is to enable human creatures to perceive, know, trust, and embody that love.

28. Loretta Whalen, "Dear Colleague" letter from Church World Service Office on Global Education, October 31, 1998.

29. Walter Brueggemann, address at Fund for Theological Education's Conference on Excellence in Ministry, Vanderbilt University, Summer 2001.

30. Iris Murdoch, *Existentialists and Mystics: Writings on Philosophy and Literature* (New York: Penguin, 1997), 329.

31. Ibid., 375.

THE BIBLE AND MORAL FORMATION, MALFORMATION, RE-FORMATION

Given the crucial nature of moral formation and given the power of the social worlds in which we live to form and malform us, what role does Scripture play?

FORMATIVE STORY

The Bible is a powerful force, forming people and communities who recognize it as Scripture.[32] It sometimes is understood to be formative by establishing a set of "rules for living" perceived as God's rules. This understanding is problematic for reasons that were discussed earlier. The more deeply formative power of Scripture lies elsewhere. It is formative by situating the community in a grand story that tells us who we are.

A young woman speaking on a panel in Seattle regarding religion in the world noted to one of us that she had left the church for years to explore other religious traditions and to experiment with withdrawing from religion all together. After some years, she said, she returned to Christianity. When asked "Why?" she replied after a pause, "Because it offers a different and more life-giving story of who human beings are."

Second-century church leader and martyr Irenaeus of Lyon would have smiled at her account. Irenaeus refuted the gnostic claim that the Hebrew Scriptures (what Christians now call the Old Testament or the First Testament) were not Scripture for Christian communities. He refuted also the resulting conclusion that the God Yahweh was not the God of Jesus. In doing so, he averred that Scripture as a whole—including the sacred texts of the Hebrew people—tells an epic story in which Christians are players with an identity, purpose, and destiny. That epic story begins with creation, includes the history of the ancient Hebrews and their journey to know and live in covenant with God, and continues through life today and on to the eschaton.

This shaping story narrates not only who we are but also who God is, what God desires for life on Earth, and who other people are in relationship to God and to us. It suggests what and whose the other-

---

32. By virtue of its formative influence on the modern world, the Bible also has indirectly "shaped" people who do not hold it as Scripture, but that is not our focus here.

than-human parts of creation are in the eyes of God. This epic tale provokes inquiry into what kinds of human behavior are mistaken and sinful and what kinds of behaviors are good. What constitutes righteousness (right relations) is a central theme. Thus, the story suggests what is to be valued, who is to be served, what is important, what is right and good and true. It invites us to know what is worth living and dying for. The story tells Christian communities how to live and how to be faithful to God, and empowers us for that life.

In these ways, the Bible forms selves and communities. Two points follow.

First, this is only one of many competing stories telling Christian communities who they are and how they ought to live in the twenty-first century. The story of the profit-maximizing market is another. It offers a competing god and a compelling message about what is good and right and true in the eyes of that god. How is the church to be church in ways that enable the story of life with and in the God Jesus loved to be more convincing and formative than the competing stories and their gods?

Second, if the Bible tells a powerfully formative story, then what that story is matters. In other words, biblical interpretation and method matter. What the story says about who God is, what God wills for life on Earth, who we are, and who others are, matters. What we hear when we read the text, matters.

The documentary film *Weapons of the Spirit* tells of a French Huguenot village in Vichy, France that was occupied by Nazi forces at a time when villages all around were turning Jews over to Nazi forces. Yet this village—lead by the Protestant pastor and school-teacher Andre Trocmé—smuggled four thousand Jewish children and adults into freedom. A young Jewish man returning to the village—he had been born there to his refugee parents—sought to understand why the villagers had risked death and worse to rescue Jews. One old woman responded to his query with a puzzled, "What else would we do?"

The movie depicts the profound extent to which these villagers had been shaped by the biblical story as a story that included resistance to whatever demanded the allegiance that they believed was due God alone. They saw themselves as players in that story; it was an ancestral story reaching into their present and their future—a living heritage of resisters who refused to bend to any force that demanded them to betray God and God's love. Their hymns and the illustrations in the hymnal told that story explicitly. It was a biblically grounded story of God and of life in relationship to other people shaped by relationship with God.

Shortly after joining University Lutheran Church in Seattle as its youth and children's pastor, Anne Hall preached: "I could empathize with Paul in prison because last time I was in prison, I too was in solitary confinement." The hush in the congregation, of which one of us was a member, was palpable. "*This* is our new youth and children's minister?" Soon the people learned that Anne—this new gentle Jesus-loving pastor—had been arrested twenty-seven times for protesting the Trident nuclear submarines stationed near Seattle. Over the next years, the youth and children were invited to participate in nonviolent actions at Ground Zero (the locus of protest), to carry the church banner in protest marches and pride parades, to serve homeless people, to learn about conscientious objector status, and more. They did and were joined by adult members. Pastor Anne's civil disobedience and these actions of the congregation were grounded in a story in which they saw themselves as players. It was a story of Jesus and his forebears (such as the Hebrew prophets and the brave midwives who saved Moses from the Pharaoh's deadly hand), who saw obedience to God as more important than compliance with societal norms. It was the biblical story told regularly in the congregation's worship life and educational programs.

Here we pause to consider more closely the role of biblical interpretation in malforming and re-forming society and Christian communities.

MALFORMING: SOCIAL RELATIONS

When slaveholders in colonial America read the Bible, explains Kelly Brown Douglas in *The Black Christ*,[33] they heard a story of what she calls "the white Christ." This Christ justified the enslavement of African people as a moral good. Slaves, on the other hand, reading the same Bible heard an utterly different story. They heard the story of a Jesus who was "in solidarity with them." "He was for the slave a fellow sufferer, a confidant, a provider, and a liberator." Likewise, note other scholars, enslaved Africans read the exodus story as a story

---

33. Kelly Brown Douglas, *The Black Christ* (Maryknoll, NY: Orbis, 1994), 21, 24.

of liberation, affirmed in Jesus. "Their tenacious faith in the liberating Exodus power of God demonstrated through the life, death and resurrection of Jesus of Nazareth was one of the primary sources, if not the primary source, of their endurance and resistance through centuries of wretched dehumanization."[34]

Both the slaveholders' story of the white Christ and enslaved Africans' story of Jesus were profoundly formative. One shaped a people to own and brutalize other human beings and to hold this as a morally good thing sanctioned by God. The other formed a people into lives of infinite hope and courage for a freedom struggle that lasted beyond their lifetimes.

Where the Bible is taken seriously—consciously or unconsciously—what communities and individuals understand the biblical text to say, what grand story it tells, shapes how we understand the way we are to live. What we understand the Bible to say depends in large part upon the lenses through which we read and the ears through which we hear it. Through whose eyes do we read the "story" told in the Bible? Whose version of the Gospel is proclaimed in interpreting the texts?

Until the sixteenth century, when the Bible began to be translated into vernacular languages, its stories were known mainly through the instruction of the church hierarchy, itself largely composed of men representing dominant social sectors. The educated male elite who could read told the people what the Bible "said." Those understandings were passed on by the fabric of Western Christian culture in sermons, music, and art. A trip through the galleries of Rome, Florence, and elsewhere reveals the story that was passed on as the Bible's story. A pale-skinned woman, usually with light eyes, gave birth in a rather pastoral setting to a European-looking baby surrounded by equally light-skinned angels. The Jesus who declared: "He has sent me to proclaim liberty to the captives" and "to set at liberty those who are oppressed" (Luke 4:18) does not frequent the art. We see little to suggest that Jesus was executed by the Roman Empire as a threat to imperial hegemony. The story of a white Christ, born to a white virgin, and crucified for reasons not related to a radical social ministry, was told and retold through the church.

---

34. Brian K. Blount, Cain Hope Felder, Clarice J. Martin, and Emerson B. Powery, introduction to *True to Our Native Land: An African American New Testament Commentary*, ed. Brian K. Blount, Cain Hope Felder, Clarice J. Martin, and Emerson B. Powery (Minneapolis: Fortress Press, 2007), 5.

In modernity, Christians the world over learned the biblical texts as they were interpreted by Europeans and European Americans, who assumed that their interpretations were not culture bound but were objective, universally authoritative, and culturally transcendent truth. Recent decades have uncovered the deception. What posed as universal was in fact highly particular; it was shaped by culture, self-interest, and historical circumstances, and is all interpretation.

The image of Jesus—who he is understood to be—illustrates. As explained by Leticia Guardiola-Saenz and Curtiss Paul DeYoung, in the earliest centuries after he lived, Jesus was depicted as a "beardless young man with a brown complexion. Only under the Byzantine Empire of the fifth and sixth centuries—which often depicted Jesus . . . after the fashion of the byzantine courts, as a monarch, seated on a throne, his hand raised in command—did artists begin to create what has come to be the standard representation of Jesus."[35] Later, Europe developed European-looking images of Jesus for telling the story of Jesus.

> The "European" Christ image was used to support European colonial expansion into Africa, Asia, and the Americas, as well as the genocide of indigenous peoples and the capture and enslavement of black Africans. In effect, a white likeness of Jesus served the purpose of being God's stamp of approval on the actions of conquerors and demonstrated that the white "race" was superior to peoples of color by virtue of the whiteness of Jesus.[36]

We must take into account "a long history of European conquest and colonialism that were intertwined with Christian missionary efforts. It has long been possible for white Christians of European descent to imagine that the Bible was 'theirs' more than it belonged to others. They could read themselves in to the biblical story, spontaneously identifying themselves with the people of God" and with Jesus, Mary, and hosts of angels.[37]

Even today, one may walk into a currently active congregation established by the British in India and see one wall adorned by pictures of a light-skinned Jesus, surrounded by blond, curly-haired angels. The biblical interpretation of the British was universalized.

35. Curtiss Paul DeYoung, ed., *The People's Companion to the Bible* (Minneapolis: Fortress Press, 2010), xxii.
36. Ibid., xxii.
37. DeYoung, *People's Companion*, xiii.

Jesus as they knew him looked like they did. They, it seems, were closer to this Jesus than were the dark-skinned people they colonized.

In short, Eurocentric interpretations were spread throughout the world. Not widely recognized until recent decades is the fact that they are culturally contingent. That is, people did not realize that their understanding of what the Bible said about God and about how they should live in accord with God was actually shaped by the worldview of the Eurocentric Western world. New Testament scholar Vincent Wimbush puts it well. The Bible has been read through "largely unacknowledged interested, inverted, racialized, culture- and ethnic- specific practice of [Eurocentric] biblical interpretation that is part of an even larger pattern of such interpretation of literatures and of history in the West."[38] Thus, slaves were taught a biblical story that justified slavery as God's will.[39] And Latin American peasants learned that their subordination and exploitation should be endured patiently as the cross they had to bear, and that their freedom awaited them in life after death.

Does it matter for the moral life today that the biblical story has been told through Eurocentric lenses? We invite our readers to explore this question. As indicated in Kelly Brown Douglas's account of the white Christ, culturally shaped understandings of what is morally good shape views of what the Bible says and means, even if we are unaware of that influence. In turn, what we understand the Bible to say reinforces what we already perceive to be true about God and God's ways and will. The consequences for moral formation, malformation, and re-formation strike at the heart of Christian discipleship. Consider two compelling consequences.

First, as long as people who benefit materially from structural injustice read the Bible only through the perceptual filters of privilege, our vision of God and of how we ought to live will be dimmed and distorted by those filters. The God we encounter in the Bible will continue to be colored by our vested interests in existing social arrangements. Our reading of the Bible—shaped and experienced through lenses of privilege—inadvertently and despite our best intentions may reinforce that privilege. In 1990, after a particularly bloody aerial bombing of retreating Iraqi soldiers by the United States, an

38. Vincent L. Wimbush, ed., *African Americans and the Bible: Sacred Texts and Social Texture* (New York: Continuum, 2008), 8.

39. White Christians can learn much from reading the theological justifications of slavery—grounded in Scripture—used by Southern slaveholders.

aide to General Norman Schwarzkopf declared publicly that the sound of the bombing was like a chorus of angels. It was a culturally influenced interpretation of what the angels of God would celebrate.

Second, Eurocentric biblical interpretations continue to have morally malformative influence on contemporary Christians by virtue of having silenced or precluded other voices and their interpretations. Silencing the interpretation from other social locations, or preventing those interpretations from arising, deprived the world of God's revelation in the Bible as it would be understood through other cultural lenses. That is, moral formation into knowledge of God and what ways of life cohere with God's love has lost out on knowledge that may have been offered through other cultures. For example, "American Indian peoples are characteristically spatial in their thinking, while Euro-Western folk tend strongly toward being temporal thinkers, emphasizing time as a priority," writes George (Tink) Tinker. This distinctive emphasis renders two very different understandings of the *basileia* (kingdom) of God, he goes on to explain. While the Eurocentric understanding was oriented at a future reign, and theologians speculated "when" the kingdom would come, "In an American Indian reading, the *basileia* has little, if anything, to do with what happens in the future. Rather it is concerned with how one images oneself in the present in relationship to the Creator and to the rest of creation."[40] The implications are breathtaking. How would Christian communities live differently if God's "kingdom" come did not pertain to the future but to the present, if it pertained to place and ways of life rather than to time?

RE-FORMING: SOCIAL RELATIONS

Uncovering the history of cultural colonialism that has shaped reading of the Bible is a priceless invitation for Christians who have read the Bible primarily through that lens. It is the invitation to read the texts, and encounter the living God, through perspectives of people and peoples on the margins of dominant cultures who have been underrepresented in biblical scholarship and, thereby, also underrepresented in basic understandings of what the Bible says.

Two guidelines will help. One is to read and study the biblical texts through interpretive lenses of people whose contexts and expe-

40. DeYoung, *People's Companion*, 49.

rience are highly different from one's own in two senses: culture and power. Ron Moe-Lobeda, a Lutheran pastor who worked for years with homeless women in Washington, DC, and Seattle, once said in a sermon that he had learned more about the Bible from homeless women in Bible study groups than from any other context. Human beings learn more from what is different than we learn from what is similar. But the challenge is to hear the interpretations of people who are not only culturally different but also situated on the under-side of dominant power structures. This is, in part, because the dam-aging impact that power imbalances have on people's lives is known more deeply by those who are on the underside. Christian communi-ties of the dominant culture will seek to hear the interpretive reflec-tions of brothers and sisters in other cultural contexts and especially the voices of marginalized communities. Thus, for example, straight Christians will read biblical interpretations of LGBTQ Christians; Euro-Americans will seek the voices of Indigenous American, Latina, and black Christians; able-bodied Christians will hear how Christians who identify as differently abled read the biblical texts. Christians with houses and cars will study the Bible with people experiencing homelessness or abject poverty. This does not mean that persons from marginalized communities speak *for* their communities or that their interpretations are infallible or necessarily good, only that they are vital.

A second and closely related guideline is to recognize how exten-sively cultural lenses shape what we read in the biblical texts. We might look for images and perceptions that we have assumed to be universal truth that are, in fact, culturally contingent. "In order to appreciate the wealth of meaning in Scripture, it is often necessary to recognize and set aside, at least momentarily, our own culture-bound assumptions so that we can understand the perspectives of other peo-ple . . . from social locations where we have never stood before."[41]

Fortunately, the last two to three decades of biblical scholarship have provided invaluable resources for heeding these two guidelines. The voices interpreting biblical texts are enormously more diverse than were they just thirty years ago. They include scholars and eccle-sial leaders from underrepresented communities in the United States and from Africa, Asia, Latin America, and Oceania. Moreover, post-colonial theory, theology, and biblical studies are exposing the white

41. Ibid., xv.

and Western bias of biblical scholarship and its consequences.[42] Clarity about purpose here is crucial. The purpose of this expanded reading is not because it will provide the correct interpretation. We humans are too limited, and the biblical witness is too full rich, alive, dynamic, and in-Spirited to have a single meaning.

Rather, we do this in order to see more fully the God revealed in Scripture and what God desires for life in the Earth community. We seek, that is, to understand more fully the nature and force of God's love, and what we are to do and be in relationship to God, self, others, and the Earth in order to be faithful to this God. Deeper vision and moral-spiritual power for embodying it are formed when we hear that story through multiple voices, including those of people on the margins of dominant cultures and the underside of history. This expanded hearing has yet a second purpose. It is one concrete means of *metanoia* (repentance), challenging and "turning the other direction" from the ongoing heritage of colonialism that privileges some people over others. In both senses—forming moral vision and power for embodying it, and repentance—the Bible is morally re-formative.

MALFORMING: EARTH-HUMAN RELATIONS

The biblical story as it played out in modernity was primarily—although not singularly—the story of God and humankind. The great drama was the drama of God saving human beings from the condition of sin. The rest of the created world was largely a stage on which the main story played out. The scope of morality was the scope of humankind, and ethics sought to enable the fullness of human life. Humans, in fact, were seen as having a divine mandate to "have dominion" over the rest of creation, to use it for the sake of human flourishing alone. The point here is the formative one. Biblical interpretation contributed to *forming* us into people who saw and experienced the Earth as primarily existing to serve human need. Things not human had instrumental but not intrinsic worth, and certainly had no rights.

The consumptive way of life that is destroying Earth's life systems is grounded in the worldview of Western modernity. Its anthropological and cosmological presuppositions are rooted in a complex,

---

42. The Society of Biblical Literature's section on decolonization, for example, just celebrated its twenty-fifth anniversary.

interactive mix of Neoplatonic philosophy, themes in Jewish and Christian Scriptures, and the human to nature relationship of industrialization and extractive economies. Especially powerful have been interpretations of what the Bible says about the nature, destiny, and purpose of the created world and about human beings in relationship to the rest of creation. Climate change and other aspects of the ecological crisis prove the folly of this human-centered and human-limited biblical "story" and the moral framework flowing from it.

RE-FORMING: EARTH-HUMAN RELATIONS

Bursting forth in the church today is the Bible's morally re-formative power. Faith communities, biblical scholars, ethicists, and others are "rereading" the Bible and allowing it to reshape who we understand ourselves and the Earth to be. The emerging eco-hermeneutical lens finds human flourishing wed explicitly to creation's well-being in the biblical witness. Psalm 104 is a wonderful portrait of interrelated creation in which God's care and concern touch all of its elements, human and nonhuman.[43] Re-formed biblically based cosmologies posit the cosmos itself as locus of God's life-giving, life-saving, life-savoring presence and power. God speaks in the winds and waters. Other-than-human parts of creation are recognized as subjects. (In Deut 30:19, for example, God calls upon Earth to bear witness.) Understandings of who human beings *are* is shifting in biblical scholarship. We are 'ădām (human being)—as are all other creatures—from 'ădāmâ (dust). We are interdependent creatures in God's *oikos* (household) of creation. Our first calling, even before the call to love neighbor as self, is the call to serve and preserve (Gen 2:15) God's good garden. Morality is normed by the flourishing of Earth's life community, not only its human part.

The morally re-formative power of Scripture invites reformed understanding of who we are in God's eyes (theological and moral anthropology); the nature, destiny, and purpose of the created world (theological cosmology); and who and where God is at work and play in our world. Faith communities the world over—drawing upon emerging ecological biblical hermeneutics and Earth ethics—are

---

43. Bruce C. Birch and Larry L. Rasmussen, "These All Look to Thee: A Relational Theology of Nature," in *The Predicament of the Prosperous* (Philadelphia: Westminster, 1978), 118–23.

reforming these fundamental roots of the moral life. The consequences for all aspects of morality are dramatic.

Consider, for example, economic life. A recent article on economic ethics, written for an encyclopedia of Bible and ethics, dedicates fully the first half of its pages to cosmology and to what makes for the flourishing of the Earth. The article's centerpiece is the "vision of '*oikos*'" in early Christianity that we cited earlier. "This vision and [the] integrity [of creation assumed through the Hebrew Bible] frame the understanding and practice of economics and economic ethics in scripture."[44]

Otherwise said, the morally formative biblical narrative to which the author of the article appeals for doing economic ethics is the cosmological narrative. It is a descriptive account of creation that

1. situates the humans as first and foremost creatures of the Earth (crafted of humus), kin with all creatures "by virtue of common origin and shared destiny";[45] and

2. posits "the continuation and flourishing of life [as] of a piece with the flourishing and degradation of the land."[46]

From this descriptive account emerges a normative account, an ethic. The foremost test of morality is "the survival and continuation of flourishing life," human included.[47] The role of economics is "to cultivate and meet the material conditions for the continuation of life," marked by economic justice within the human community.

Can this turn in biblical understanding help to re-form not only Christian communities but the larger society toward ways of life that see humans as highly dependent parts of God's creation, rather than as "lords" over it? Can Christian communities convey newly discovered eco-centric cosmology to the broader public in ways that effectively challenge the anthropocentric and dominion-oriented predecessor stories? This is a powerful moral responsibility of biblically grounded communities today.

44. Larry L. Rasmussen, "Economic Ethics," in *Dictionary of Scripture and Ethics*, ed. Joel B. Green (Grand Rapids: Baker Academic, 2011), 263–64.

45. Rasmussen, "Economic Ethics," 264.

46. Ibid.

47. Ibid., 265.

CLOSING

The moral formation of people and societies is central to morality. Crucial in that formation process are moral vision and the influence of social structures including institutions, ideologies, systems, policies, practices, and more. We have examined these dynamics and the roles of Scripture in moral formation, noting that the most crucial role may be enabling human creatures to perceive, know, trust, and embody God's boundless justice-seeking love. Yet, attention to forming people who will make moral decisions and act on them does not tell us how to make those decisions. To that challenge we turn next.

7.

Moral Discernment and Action

What should I do? How do we proceed? What's right in this case? We face questions and decisions like these every day.

"This case" varies as widely as the circumstances we face. The decision may be an excruciatingly difficult and painful one—whether to instruct the attending physician to withdraw life support systems for a terminally ill parent or child; whether to terminate a pregnancy; whether to enlist in the military if the country is engaged in military operations that you believe are unjust and unwarranted; whether to risk the dangers of commuting by bike and pulling your toddler in a bike trailer in order to lower your carbon footprint; whether to negotiate with people who have taken hostages. Or the case at hand could entail happy choices (but not necessarily easy ones). Your organization has $85,000 to give to the cause or causes of its choice, but which? Or you face the proverbial fork in the road and can choose but one of two careers, as posed by different job opportunities. Both are acceptable, but they force you to ask what you most want to do with your life.

The choice at hand may not be as momentous as any of these: should we sign the petition, buy that book, take a day off to visit a friend, volunteer for the tutoring program, reprove a neighbor about an unsettling remark, look for a different part-time job? These and other plausible examples have one thing in common: decisions. They all press the irrepressible question: What should I, or we, *do?*

Moral discernment is the process of determining, to the extent possible, the more moral course of action for the matter at hand. Moral decision-making, practical moral reasoning, and moral deliberation also describe this process. We use these terms interchangeably. All refer to the manner by which people arrive at moral choices. How Christian faith informs moral choice is the primary concern of this chapter.

For Christians, the answers to these questions are found in another. What course of action coheres best with the ways and will of the God revealed in Jesus? Posed differently, what course of action best enables us to embody in social form God's love for the world, or to participate in God's work in the world? Response to these questions is the stuff of Christian moral discernment.

WHY FOCUS ON MORAL DISCERNMENT?

It is readily apparent that decisions are a critical part of the moral life, but it is not immediately obvious why decision-making merits separate attention. Why not trust that good character and sound social arrangements will result in right decisions? What else needs attention, beyond character formation and the general ways in which our lives are socially ordered? Why do decisions require special consideration?

One answer pertains to the faith claim that what best coheres with the ways, will, and work of God in the world is morally good. How do we know or even come closer to knowing that? In venues from interpersonal to international, how are we to discern what God is doing, through whom, and where, so that we may align ourselves with it? Amidst the complexity and moral ambiguity of life, *how* are we to discern what God is doing in any given situation, let alone how we might most faithfully give social form to it? How do we go about seeing signs of God working amidst the beauty, confusion, and wreckage of history so that we may be the hands, channels, and means through which God works? Responding to these questions is an aspect of moral discernment.

A second answer is inherent in the nature of morality. A person of good moral character, according to the moral assumptions of a given society or subculture, tends to make moral decisions in accord with those assumptions. This leaves no mechanism for testing the actual morality of those assumptions by any standards outside of them. Hence, for example, citizens considered morally upright in the early nineteenth-century southern United States made decisions, considered moral according to the moral code of that subculture, to enslave other human beings. People formed to accept a particular social structure as morally normative are ill equipped to test the morality of that social structure. Some form of moral reasoning capable of that questioning is required. That critical questioning is one requisite of adequate moral deliberation.

And finally, moral decisions entail questions and require information that attention to character and social structure does not supply: What information is important for this particular issue (whatever the issue may be)? What factors weigh most heavily in the decision? What moral criteria should be brought to this decision, and what norms should guide us? What if those norms conflict with one another? Who determines these criteria or what data is necessary? What if there is no moral option? What if all options have harmful results? How should we make the decision, using what process? Who has authority in this matter? What sources do we consult? What if those sources conflict with one another? What options should be considered? What strategy and tactics should we use in order to see our choice realized?

Character, even good character, cannot of itself answer such queries. Qualities of character do not "decide," even when they are vitally important to any and every decision. Social arrangements and roles do not of themselves "decide," either, even though, as we have seen, they are powerful determinants. Processes of moral deliberation must be developed even as we continue to emphasize the indissolubility of "being" and "doing" and even as we lodge a protest against any version of Christian ethics which would reduce ethics to decision making and moral problems only. Ethics as *only* decisions is too reductionist; ethics as *only* character formation is too simplistic. For this reason, too, attention to moral discernment is necessary.

With few exceptions (very young children, or people who are severely mentally incapacitated), everyone engages in moral reasoning. Often it is an exercise so mundane and habitual as to be hardly noticeable. We don't consciously consider whether to hold up the clerk and empty the cash register as we pick up a gallon of milk at the store, or whether we should care about a friend as she faces an important appointment with her physician. Any number of moral judgments have been so internalized that we make them intuitively and quite apart from conscious and prolonged deliberation.

Still, our decisions entail a process of some kind. This is true even for many decisions made reflexively, or intuitively. We may, for example, make a particular decision because others, whom we respect, have so decided. Or we may respond as we did in the past, relying upon the cumulative wisdom of our experience. Or we may choose to act in keeping with a moral maxim on which many of us have been raised: I act in the way I would want others to act toward me.

None of these decisions entails practical moral reasoning in the form of involved argument or weighty deliberation. They are, nonetheless, common ways by which people arrive at moral choices—and they are more complex than their reflexive nature initially signals. They are in fact rudimentary forms of moral reasoning: in the first example, we decide through appeal to *example* as the operative moral authority; in the second, through *tradition and experience* as trustworthy guides; in the third, through a form of the Golden Rule as a *universal principle*. Each is a different escort through decision-making, and each entails a process that is learned.

Intuitive or reflexive moral reasoning is crucial to morality. Much of our morality is habit. We do not constantly have time or opportunity for more complex or systematic reasoning.

However, reflexive moral decision-making has its dangerous face. We alluded to it above in the second reason for giving attention to moral decision-making. Reflexive moral response—grounded in example or tradition—uncritically reinforces reigning moral codes. That is, it reinscribes actions and social arrangements that are assumed by the reigning moral codes to be moral or normal but that may in fact be quite the opposite. For precisely this reason, ethics brings intentionality, self-awareness, and method to the process of moral decision-making.

Beyond its intuitive or reflexive mode, moral discernment takes more complex forms. For difficult decisions, several sources of guidelines are usually drawn upon, many factors are weighed, and various points of view and consequences are considered. An examined decision is made, rather than a reflexive and intuitive one. We move through an intentional process in order to make a decision on the moral issue before us.

Be it reflexive or examined, the choice is never whether to engage in this process; it is only what *form, context, and content* it will have.

This is the stuff of method. And, as we have said, method matters! How people carry out this process determines its outcome, and that can have life-and-death consequences.

THREE TASKS OF MORAL DISCERNMENT

Two common mistakes can have tragic consequences even where intentions were good. First, grave mistakes ensue when decisions about what we ought to do are made without adequate understanding of the situation at hand. For example, the 2003 decision by the United States government to attack Iraq based on the premise that it was developing weapons of mass destruction was grounded in inadequate effort to understand "what was going on" before deciding "what to do." A decision to suspend one child from school for hitting another might be ill-made if it is reached without first investigating the circumstances.

Responding to the question "what should be done?" requires first responding to the question "what is going on?" This is the "descriptive task" in moral discernment. It is a requisite for the "normative task," the question "what should be done?"

The other mistake is the failure to consider and construct all of the possible alternative responses to an ethical dilemma. It is far too easy to assume that only option A or B exists when, in fact, thinking outside the box could uncover other, more life-giving responses. Positing possible options for resolving the dilemma may be seen as the "constructive task" in moral deliberation.

Moral deliberation or discernment, then, involves three interfacing tasks, each with an accompanying question. Recall the chart introduced in chapter 5:

Tasks of Moral Discernment	Accompanying Questions
Descriptive	What is?
Constructive	What could be?
Normative	What ought to be?

THE DESCRIPTIVE TASK IN MORAL DISCERNMENT

We have said that Christian ethics involves coming to know ever more fully both the God Jesus loved and the realities of life on Earth, so that we may respond to the latter in ways that are consistent with and empowered by God's love for the world and presence in and with it. And we noted that where social forces distort or hide what is going on, ethics must know and see more truthfully.

The descriptive task is this effort to perceive clearly and understand deeply the realities of life on Earth in any given situation. It is the effort to ask, "what is going on?" This is perhaps the most important and most controversial question in ethical deliberation. It demands a clear and honest examination of economic, technical, scientific, material, and political realities. Ethical conflict often has more to do with people's accounts of what is going on than with accounts of what should be going on. The killing of black men and youth by white police officers makes this point shockingly clear. What one person describes as murder or manslaughter, another describes as self-defense. These two highly contradictory accounts of what is going on will yield vastly different decisions.

The descriptive task in moral deliberation goes under varied names. Catholic social teaching uses the terms "see," "judge," and "act" to explain the process of moral deliberation and action. In that framework, "seeing" is what we refer to as the descriptive task. Moral theologian Daniel Maguire, in his excellent essay "Ethics: How Do You Do It," refers to this as "setting up the moral object." His paradigm is useful in suggesting a set of questions to enable recognizing and describing "what is going on." They include the simple questions "what, when, why, where, who, and how."[1] Think of this as "getting the facts."

Getting the facts, while necessary, is not adequate for describing what is going on if structures of power and privilege hide relevant factors of oppression or exploitation from the perceptive lenses of people who benefit from them. If one considers only the situation at hand and ignores the deeper factors of the eco-social structures in which it is situated, one misses crucial dimensions of the situation, and moral decision-making is perilously flawed.

---

1. Maguire, *Death by Choice*, ch. 4. Maguire also asks a final question, "what are the alternatives," but we locate that question as a second step, the "constructive task" of moral discernment.

In the Gospel of Mark, Jesus asks his disciples, "Have you not eyes to see and ears to hear?" Daniel Maguire says it another way: the "bane of ethics," he writes, is to ignore or "inadequately see reality."[2] If we do not ask adequate, reality-revealing questions, moral judgments will fall short and possibilities for faithful response will be undermined.

If part of the moral task for Christians is to have "eyes to see" the deep reality—including perceiving the world from beyond the blinders of privilege—then what are the keys to seeing more clearly? What questions enable us to see what is going on, especially when society is structured to obscure systems of injustice from people who are advantaged by them.

It is helpful to pursue the descriptive task as two sets of questions. One set pertains to the particular situation at hand for ethical consideration and uses Maguire's set of questions. The other set pertains to the broader and deeper socio-ecological context and draws upon the following additional set of reality-revealing questions. See them not as comprehensive but as suggestive of the questions to be posed in the effort to understand social realities that pervade our lives but often remain unnoticed by people who benefit from them.

REALITY-REVEALING QUESTIONS

1. Whose voices are not heard? Whose perspectives not accounted for? Whose existence is not seen in considering whatever moral issue is at hand?

2. Who benefits and who loses, and how, from the way things are? What are the long-term consequences?

3. What are the power dynamics at play? For example:

   a. Who has power to make decisions that impact the ecological sustainability of our society and that determine who has the basic necessities for life with dignity, and who does not?

   b. Who has the power to name their own needs and self-interest, in contrast with having them named by someone else?

---

2. Maguire, *Death by Choice*, 65–66.

    c. For whom is dissent dangerous? Who makes it so?

    d. Who is making whom an object?

    e. Who has the power to define what is natural, normal, inevitable, or divinely ordained?

    f. Who has the power to define themselves as normative?

4. What categories of people involved have unearned privilege that disadvantages other groups? What are some of those unearned privileges?

5. What are historical roots of "the way things are?"

6. What are theological underpinnings of "the way things are"?

7. What other belief systems or worldviews underwrite "the way things are"?

8. Relative to the issue(s) at hand, what is presupposed to be inevitable, natural, normal, or divinely ordained that actually is not? In other words, what is seen as "the way things are" when in fact it is a human construct, the result of human decisions and actions, and hence, at least in theory, responsive to human agency?

9. What other questions would you add?

The importance of this deeper seeing for morality in everyday life cannot be overstated. The previous chapter discussed the power of socialization or enculturation to shape perceptions of reality according to the vision of dominant sectors. Where systems of injustice—such as racism, sexism, or classism—benefit those sectors, people are socialized to perceive "the way things are" as normal, inevitable, natural, or God's will.

We discussed, too, the power of privilege to blind its beneficiaries from the reality of that privilege and the suffering it brings. Cynthia makes the point this way:

> When I had young children, I loved taking them frequently to the library, scooping up countless books about children and their lives. As a heterosexual person, it did not occur to me that when the lesbian couple next door took their children to the library, they could not find books depicting happy loving families with two mothers. Day after day, these

children paged through books in which the families portrayed as normal did not look like theirs. My heterosexual privilege obscured their pain and confusion from me. (Note also that, in this sense, a library budget becomes a moral document.) As someone who owns a car and has money for gas, it may not occur to me that Camille, who lives in a shelter for women experiencing homelessness, must travel (without a car or bus fare) to four different sites just to accomplish a single job interview—she must access a computer on which to check job ads, find interview clothing at a day center for women, take a shower and get a free lunch at a church, and interview for the job. My position of privilege obscured her reality from me until hearing her describe it in a homily in my church. Election of city officials and all decisions that lead to or away from homelessness or that impact homeless people are moral decisions.

Moral oblivion happens, too, on a broader scale and is even harder to crack. Theologian Douglas John Hall writes:

> [Western] Christianity in the modern epoch gave itself over to a vision that promised the imminent emergence of a better world within history . . . manifest in daily demonstrations of progress. . . . The non-recognition, minimization, and resolution of evil formed an integral part of this new worldview from its inception. So long as the ideology of progress could seem to be sustained by experience it did not require so great an effort to *close one's eyes to the evils that were present*, always, even at the height of the age of progress. . . . In these decades [the vision of progress] can be maintained only at the expense of *shutting one's eyes* to experience altogether. The non-recognition and minimization of evil, which was part of this enterprise from the outset, has assumed the proportions of a way of life (italics ours).[3]

The descriptive task of moral discernment seeks to understand what is going on in any given situation. The great challenge is to do so in ways that open eyes to see through the moral oblivion born of privilege.

THE CONSTRUCTIVE TASK IN MORAL DISCERNMENT

Moral deliberation falls short where we fail to uncover and consider a full range of possible alternative responses to an ethical dilemma. Often one unthinkingly assumes that only certain options

3. Douglas John Hall, *Lighten Our Darkness: Toward an Indigenous Theology of the Cross* (Philadelphia: Westminster, 1976), 113.

exist—option A or B, or possibly C. While indeed these may be the most obvious and commonly considered options, thinking beyond the obvious could uncover other options that may ultimately be more life-giving, healing, or liberating than A or B or C. Identifying possible options for resolving the moral dilemma may be seen as the "constructive task" in moral deliberation.

The constructive task involves creativity and a willingness to look outside the box. It depends upon collaborative thinking. People thinking together, allowing their ideas to build on one another's insights, often generate a more expansive range of possibilities than does one person thinking alone.

The constructive task well done bears two features. It seeks the insight of people who will be impacted by whatever decision is made, and especially those who stand to lose from any particular resolution to the dilemma. The second feature is a commitment to play out the consequences of the various alternative resolutions identified. What are the long-term and the short-term consequences for various people and—where pertinent—for the other-than-human elements that will be impacted?

The constructive task is apparent in a number of examples cited in this volume, but the reader may wish to consult especially chapter 8, and, within that chapter, the subsections *Laudato Si'*, Civil Rights, and Flor de Manacá.

THE NORMATIVE TASK IN MORAL DISCERNMENT

Having examined a situation or dilemma of morality carefully and critically and having imagined all possible courses of action leads to the next task: assessing those options and seeking to understand which coheres best with the love of God. "Given the situation and given the options, what in fact ought we to do?" This is understood as the normative task of ethics (asking "what ought to be?"). In simple terms, it entails learning from various sources of moral wisdom what guidance they offer, and then putting the findings from that inquiry into dialogue with each other. Those sources, in Christian ethics, commonly have been seen as of four kinds: the Bible, the traditions of the churches throughout the ages, other bodies of human knowledge, and human experience. (Shortly we will note a problem with a problem with this configuration; it relies only on the wisdom of human beings, not on the wisdom of other than human parts of creation. In response to this problem, we will suggest a fifth source of moral wisdom—Earth wisdom.)

COMPLEXITIES ERUPT

With this question—What ought to be or what ought we to do?—complexities erupt. A few illustrations bring them to life.

Jesus's Ambiguous Call to Love Neighbor as Self

A convicted sex offender recently out of prison begins visiting an urban congregation in the Midwest. He decides to join the congregation, which includes full participation in all activities. Will he be allowed to teach Sunday School for the young elementary students? One member argues: "Yes, of course. He has paid the penalty in prison, and Jesus's call to love includes forgiveness. Forgiveness means that the slate is clean. He gets to start over, forgiven and accepted." "Wait a minute," responds another member, "Jesus's call to love includes loving our children and that means protecting them from being alone with a former sex offender!" What should the congregation do?

Jesus's Ambiguous Call to Love Neighbor as Self:
Another Scene

A church council has been asked by its social justice committee to join a coalition of religious groups calling for an end to the use of military drone strikes. The coalition will lead a public protest rally. "Jesus's call to love neighbor as self means that we cannot be killing innocent civilians with drones. We must support this rally," insists one member of the church council. "No, no," argues another, "loving neighbor means that we must protect the innocent from terrorists and if drones are an effective means of doing so, then we would be failing in the call to love if we fail to use the drones!" "Drones are the lesser evil," interjects a woman vet whose horrible memories of service in Iraq convinces her that the use of drones is better than the use of soldiers. "But drones shed blood, and the early Christians insisted that a Christian could not shed the blood of other people for any reason, including warfare," notes a long-time pacifist. "But what of the 'just war theory?'" asks yet another council member. "Christians have a noble history of determining that some warfare is indeed just while other wars are not." What should this church council do?

Competing Moral Obligations

A single mother on the borderline of homelessness must get an A in her class in order to retain her scholarship; a B on tomorrow's exam would yield a C in the class, which would drop her grade point below the scholarship level. She has worked diligently in this course, perhaps harder than most students. The evening before the final take-home exam, her sixteen-year-old sister threatens suicide. She has been "let down" throughout her life by people who are "too busy for her," and this single mother is the one person who seems to be able to reach her. It seems that the single mother's choices are (1) to desert her sister, study, and get the A; (2) give time and attention to her sister at this crucial moment instead of studying, and accept the likelihood of losing the scholarship; or (3) accept a good friend's offer to cheat on her behalf on the take-home exam, knowing that she would never do so if her children's livelihood did not depend upon that scholarship. What should this student mother do?

It may be useful to note various dimensions of the complexity that arises with asking "what are we to do?"

- What happens when one source of moral wisdom seems to say one thing and another source says something to the contrary?

- How is it possible that one kind of norm (e.g., the virtue of honesty) pushes me one direction but another kind of norm (e.g., the rule of protecting life) pushes me in another?

- What do we do when more than one norm applies and the two seem to conflict?

- What if my rational mind says one thing but my deep, gut-level response says another?

- How do big overall norms, such as "love your neighbor," play out in specific situations, especially if they could be interpreted validly as leading to opposing conclusions?

- What if every option will have some negative consequences?

- One person's experience may practically scream out that a particular path is wrong while another's experience cries out quite the opposite.

- What if the norms of my society—accepted as moral and assumed as a solid ground for moral deliberation—are, in fact, not moral if judged from outside the perceptive lens of that society? This, as we have seen in the previous chapter, is a story of human history.

- What if the consequences of doing what seems to be the right thing are actually more damaging than would be the consequences of doing nothing?

These complexities are millennia old. Unraveling them and responding to these questions have shaped the field of ethics. They are what make ethics—and the intentionality, method, sensitivity, and self-awareness entailed in ethics—so important for morality.

To sort through these conundrums and suggest a process for the normative task in moral discernment, we offer five resources:

- A set of overarching guidelines for moral deliberation

- The interplay of cognition and emotion

- Sources of moral wisdom

- The moral norm of neighbor-love

- Moral theory

The remainder of this chapter explores these five resources. In the process, we note new moves called forth by the unprecedented circumstance in which humankind now finds itself—climate crisis is threatening Earth's capacity to regenerate life.

GUIDELINES FOR MORAL DISCERNMENT BY FINITE AND FALLIBLE CREATURES (HUMAN BEINGS)

FIRST: Bear in mind that there is no singular Christian perspective on any moral issue. Inquiries into moral issues by Christians have yielded multiple and conflicting results since the earliest years of the church.

SECOND: Refrain from absolutizing moral decisions or stands. Human beings cannot know with certainty what God is doing in the world; yet, paradoxically and in the face of uncertainty, we are to act in accord with God's mission and activity based upon faithful discernment regarding it. Said differently, we disbelieve any claim to absolute knowledge of God's ways or will, as well as any claim that God's people are, therefore, excused from seeking to live in congruence with it. Allow, therefore, for moral uncertainty and ambiguity, that strange and often uncomfortable balance between moral uncertainty and the need to take a stand. Allow for provisional answers. Practice the humility that says, "I do not know the full answer, but at this time I must conclude that A is more morally viable than B. I may be wrong and I am certainly limited in my knowing."

Ambiguity streams in from varied sources. One is the reality of seeking to base life on the ways and will of a God who cannot be fully known. Joseph Sittler said it well:

> And this will of God is now confronted both as a known and as an unknown. It is known in Christ who is the incarnate concretion of God's ultimate and relentless will-to-restoration; and it remains unknown in the fact that the actual service of this will is presented to the believer not as a general program given in advance but as an ever-changing and fluctuant obligation to the neighbor in the midst of history's life.[4]

Another wellspring of moral ambiguity is the inherent fallibility and finitude of human beings. We might decide with apparent certainty that we know what God would want, or how God would have us act. However, our apparent certainty betrays the reality: we may be wrong, and if we are right, our knowledge is certainly only partial.

Yet another reason not to assume absolute certainty in moral discernment is the human tendency to correlate our desires with God's will. Sittler, noting the ease with which humans assume that our ethical crusades match God's purposes, cites Abraham Lincoln's second inaugural address. It demonstrates sharply the fallacy and danger of equating our will with God's. "Both (northerners and southerners)

---

4. Sittler, *Structure of Christian Ethics*, 73.

read the same Bible, and pray to the same God; and each invokes his aid against the other."[5]

Protestant Christianity is grounded in the conviction that all things human are finite and fallible; absolute truth does not reside in human beings or institutions, including religious authorities. Accordingly, Christians live in a perpetual paradox: On the one hand, we are called to discern to the best of our abilities what ways of life, private and public, best cohere with the love of God manifest in Scripture and in Jesus Christ. And we are to act in those ways. Yet simultaneously, we must recognize that we cannot know with certainty and fullness the ways and will of God. Said differently, we must act with conviction born of careful prayerful discernment, while recognizing that our knowledge could be mistaken and surely is incomplete.

Christian claims to know with certainty what is right and true in God's eyes are the antithesis of this conviction. Such elevation of human capacity is called idolatry. We are warned against it throughout Scripture. It defies the central Reformation insistence on human fallibility and finitude. The fundamentalist claim to absolute certainty has made its mark on mainstream denominations. Far too many Christian voices claim absolute certainty about God's will. A strong doctrine of human finitude and fallibility offers freedom from religious absolutism, and establishes boundaries on claims to religiously grounded truth. Invalid are all claims to know absolutely the will of God or God's truth, without acknowledging the possibility that one's understanding of that will or that truth may be faulty and certainly is limited.

THIRD: Stay away from universalizing. Just because something is morally good or bad in one context does not make it necessarily so in another. For example, while a particular area of biotech research might be deemed moral in a country with adequate research safety standards, that same research may not be moral where those standards are not in place.[6]

FOURTH: Maintain a critical rather than positivist perspective. By "critical," we do not mean "critical of." Rather, critical here means

5. Ibid., 14.
6. See the report of the National Bioethics Advisory Commission, "Essential Requirements for the Ethical Conduct of Clinical Trials," accessed April 18, 2017, http://tinyurl.com/y7v45gb5: "The Commission has found some evidence that disclosures relating to diagnosis and risk, research design, and possible post-trial benefits are not always clearly presented in clinical trials conducted in developing countries, even though the current U.S. regulations include such requirements."

noting and questioning any assumption that something is normal, natural, inevitable, or God's will, and therefore moral. People throughout history have used "natural," "normal," "inevitable," or "God's will" to justify human constructs that served the interests of those maintaining the constructs. (We need think no further than slavery and the subordination of women.) To note and question assumptions does not necessarily mean to conclude that they are faulty. It means to notice and test our assumptions—to render them conscious—and then, if found faulty, to revise or abandon them.

EMOTION AND COGNITION IN MORAL DISCERNMENT

Neuroscience, while a young science only on the cusp of grasping the wonder of the human brain, has arrived at a consensus that instructs us about moral discernment or decision-making. Experiments that look at neural activity in different regions of the brain reveal two processes when people are confronted with circumstances that require judgment and choice. One is fast and intuitive. It takes place by and large in areas of the brain associated with emotional processing.[7] The other process is slow, rational, and deliberate. This takes place in areas associated with cognitive processing.[8]

The two processes—emotional and cognitive—may be given different weight as we engage in moral deliberation. But both are sufficiently engaged that scientists studying moral choice refer to them as the dual system or dual process of moral decision-making.[9] While each is a distinct force, emotional processing and cognitive processing interact to effect decisions. Our immediate gut feelings and responses join our cognitive biases and reflection to arrive at decisions.

Neuroscience focused on the interaction of the two hemispheres of the brain, and not on moral decision-making only, further illumines the dual process that moral psychology describes. Iain McGilchrist's *The Master and His Emissary: The Divided Brain and the Making of the Western World* serves well as a summary.[10]

The two hemispheres are, in effect, two modes of being. The right

---

7. The medial prefrontal cortex and the amygdala.

8. The dorsolateral prefrontal cortex and the parietal lobe.

9. See the extensive review of studies and books in Tamsin Shaw, "The Psychologists Take Power," *New York Review of Books* 63, no. 3 (February 25, 2016): 38–41.

10. Iain McGilchrist, *The Master and His Emissary: The Divided Brain and the Making of the*

hemisphere registers everything immediately and at once, with no designs on anything. It registers the flood of information our environment provides and our senses take in. It cares for whatever happens in our lived world as we experience it in the moment. The left hemisphere, by way of contrast, is the organizer for what the right hemisphere registers. It gives order, purpose, and direction, which the right hemisphere does not. It divulges the meaning and appropriation of the right hemisphere's unlimited data. It does so, reports McGilchrist, in order to effect control and act with ends in view. "Being useful" is the work of the left hemisphere; simply "being," or dwelling in "being," experiencing "being," is the stance of the right hemisphere.

McGilchrist is quick to add that these two hemispheres are not two brains. They are not independent spheres. They always interact in dynamic ways, ways that are affected by the worlds of which they are part. They are responsive, interrelated, living entities, not machines.

The emotional processes register our initial moral response, even our initial moral judgment. They register the moral gravity we intuit or sense when these processes come upon something that seemingly "demands" our response. Every ounce of our being is engaged as our deepest values and strongest loyalties surface.

Consider this example: Thomas Friedman's usual column for the *New York Times* is on foreign affairs. But he felt compelled to set that aside when then-President George W. Bush proposed opening the Arctic National Wildlife Refuge to drilling for oil and gas. Friedman didn't find the president's cost-benefit argument for drilling to be the right kind of argument. Nor was the argument that drilling could take place without harming the wilderness. The right kind of argument, Friedman said, is that of Richard Fineberg, an Anchorage-based environmental consultant. For Fineberg, wilderness is "immutable."

> It is like perfection; there are no degrees to it. Oil development in a wilderness, no matter how sensitive, changes the very nature of it. It means it's no longer wilderness. If the drill worshippers prevail in the Arctic Refuge, then there will be no place on this continent where a unique environment will be safe from greed and short-term interests.[11]

Western World (New Haven: Yale University Press, 2009); this discussion draws especially from ch. 4, "The Nature of the Two Worlds," 132–75.

11. Thomas Friedman, "Foreign Affairs; Drilling in the Cathedral," *New York Times*, March 2, 2001, http://tinyurl.com/yb6k8lsh.

Friedman won't give any ground to "the drill worshippers" argument that they can extract the oil without harm to the wilderness—without, in other words, changing it. "[That's] like saying you can do online trading in church on your Palm Pilot without disturbing anyone. It violates the very ethic of the place."[12]

"The very ethic of the place" is what our moral emotions register. They are not trivial or untutored. They express what have, by way of years of moral formation, become our most basic values. They locate the initial burden of proof and form our initial judgments, if not necessarily our final ones. They may even register what we regard as sacred and uncompromising, our moral bottom lines.

Of course, Friedman's moral emotions and "very ethic of the place" are not the only ones engaged. Presumably those making the case *for* opening the Arctic Reserve to oil and gas include some for whom their initial and strongest moral emotions see in that course the way of life they cherish not just for themselves but for others as well.

Yet, first responses, while a critical part of practical moral reasoning, are not the end of moral deliberation. Friedman may be guided by his intuition about "the very ethic of the place," but he doesn't stop there. He makes an argument for it, a moral argument that depends on reason and appeals to it. He doesn't simply declare where his loyalties thump down and regard that as sufficient. He engages in reasoned deliberation with the readers of the *New York Times* in view. If they are not in his camp, he wants to convince them on grounds they respect. If they are already sympathetic to his cause, he wants to strengthen their case and their resolve. In a word, cognitive processes join emotional ones in moral discourse. They comprise a dual system for moral decision-making.

This ongoing, often unconscious dance between emotional engagement and cognition informs moral discernment. Sound ethical decision-making seeks to be conscious of both and intentional about their interaction. Both play a role as we engage the sources of moral wisdom.

Vital for us is that the Bible tutors both emotional and cognitive processes of moral decision-making as these take place within and across the brain.

---

12. Friedman, "Drilling in the Cathedral."

SOURCES OF MORAL WISDOM

Overview

We have said that Christian ethics, understood in the broadest sense, entails coming to know ever more fully and then holding in one breath two things—the realities of life on Earth and God with God's vision, or intent, for life on Earth. The descriptive task in moral discernment—described above—focuses largely on the former.

In the normative task, we turn to the latter. How do we come to know more adequately what we cannot know fully but with which we are to spend a lifetime engaging in ever-deeper relationship: God and God's intent for this world and presence in and with it? This includes coming to know more closely the faith traditions in which people have sought throughout the centuries to know God and witness to God's creative, redeeming, sustaining relationship with this good Earth.

How are we to discern what actions, lifestyles, ideas, public policies, institutional arrangements, forms of business, and more would cohere with the love of God revealed in Jesus? What would best reflect God's will, nature, and purpose? What kinds of behaviors and ways of life best enable us to be God's hands and feet on Earth? If God works through human beings, then where do we turn for knowledge of what God is seeking to do through us as individuals, as communities? The places we turn to gain such understanding—either consciously or not—are understood in Christian ethics as sources of moral guidance, authority, or wisdom. The process begs humility. We must discern to the best of our ability, knowing all along that we may be wrong and that our knowledge will be inherently limited.

Traditionally, Christian ethics draws upon four sources that are articulated and prioritized differently by different traditions within Christianity. They are Scripture, the traditions of the churches throughout the ages, other bodies of human knowledge, and experience.[13]

Two factors in recent decades reveal flaws in this configuration of sources and call for revisions.

---

13. The third of these has been understood differently in different Christian traditions. It is known in Catholic moral theology as "reason" and was articulated as such by Wesley. It also has been defined as philosophy, the sciences, or descriptive accounts of reality.

First was the rise of liberation theologies and postcolonial theologies. They made clear that while much of the Bible is written from the underside of power and privilege (Exodus slaves, prophets opposing kings, Jesus), dominant interpretations, passed on throughout the centuries, have come primarily through the lens of history's winners. Their perspectives have shaped interpretations of Scripture's moral meaning and of church teachings. Therefore, prodded by Jesus to heed perspectives from the margins, contemporary Christians situated in dominant cultural streams will seek to read our traditions and our Scripture from standpoints of people who are on the losing side of reigning power structures. We will learn from people whose understanding may challenge life as we know it and may reveal even our unintentional participation in structures of injustice.

The ecological crisis points to a second dangerous flaw in the traditional understanding of four sources. It largely ignores the Earth. Vital wisdom to be gained by listening to Earth's whole community of life is lost to human beings in our quest to live rightly. Recent decades prove the folly of this truncated and anthropocentric perspective. Called for is a modification in the centuries-old quadrilateral of moral wisdom. A fifth source of moral wisdom will join the traditional four: it is other-than-human voices of the Earth. This revision finds support in the Christian ethical call to seek out and heed moral wisdom from the underside of power and privilege. Earth's water, soil, air, fauna, foliage, and biosphere have joined that underside; the cry of the Earth has joined the cry of the poor.[14] Human creatures are invited to learn from the other-than-human parts of creation that now groan under our weight, wisdom for living in sync with Earth's well-being.

This modification is joined with another. We will seek to "read" the initial four sources (Scripture, tradition, other bodies of knowledge, and experience) through the lens of the other-than-human. The challenge, while likely to yield priceless insight, is daunting. How shall we, who may never have imagined such a move, learn even to glimpse the Bible, Christian beliefs and practices, scientific knowledge, or human experience from perspectives that are not human-centered? One foray into this challenge is the five-volume Earth Bible series that seeks to read the Bible from perspectives of the Earth.[15]

14. See Leonardo Boff, *Cry of the Earth, Cry of the Poor* (Maryknoll, NY: Orbis, 1997).
15. Five volumes of the Earth Bible were published by Sheffield between 2000 and 2002:

The Bible

The Bible is the primary—but not the only—source for Christians in their ethical engagement with the world, both in its formative and normative dimensions. Discussion of its authority may be found in chapter 3, and the use of it in ethical reflection is taken up in chapter 4. Readers may find it helpful to reference the "Practical Guidelines for Use of Bible in Moral Discernment" found at the end of chapter 4.

Tradition

In the NT, the Greek word translated as "tradition" is used first as a verb, not as a noun. It means "to pass on" as in to "pass on the Gospel."[16] However, the verb itself has dual meaning. It also means "to betray." When Judas betrayed Jesus into the hands of the Roman authorities, the Greek verb used for "betray" is the verb translated also as "to pass on" (a tradition). A warning signal flashes across two millennia.

We are forewarned. The church will both pass on the gospel and betray it. Stark evidence confirms it—the crusades, the Inquisition, the theological justification of slavery and genocide in the Americas, fascism's appeal to God, the prohibition of women's ordination, and an endless history of atrocities done in the name of God.

Therefore, as we turn to tradition to learn more deeply the ways and will of God, we do so with a due hermeneutic of suspicion and appreciation. We seek both where our forebears in faith have conveyed the gospel and where they have betrayed it. Both are invaluable instruction for the moral life. The latter alerts us to where we, too, may be claiming as God's will what in fact is quite the opposite.

Norman Habel, ed., *Readings from the Perspective of Earth*, Earth Bible 1 (Sheffield: Sheffield Academic, 2000); Norman Habel and Shirley Wurst, eds., *The Earth Story in Genesis*, Earth Bible 2 (Sheffield: Sheffield Academic, 2000); Norman Habel and Shirley Wurst, eds., *The Earth Story in Wisdom Traditions*, Earth Bible 3 (Sheffield: Sheffield Academic, 2001); Norman Habel, ed., *The Earth Story in Psalms and Prophets*, Earth Bible 4 (Sheffield: Sheffield Academic, 2001); Norman Habel and Vicky Balabanski, eds., *The Earth Story in the New Testament*, Earth Bible 5 (Sheffield: Sheffield Academic, 2002). See also the Earth Bible Commentary series, begun in 2011, published by Sheffield Phoenix.

16. See the entry on *paradidōmi* in Frederick William Danker, Walter Bauer, William F. Arndt, and F. Wilbur Gingrich, *Greek-English Lexicon of the New Testament and Other Early Christian Literature*, 3rd ed. (Chicago: University of Chicago Press, 2000).

In other words, we make the crucial distinction between reproducing moral traditions and drawing critically upon them. Reproducing moral teachings would mean simply asking: "What does the church—or a particular part of the church—say or what has it said about a given moral question," and then accepting that teaching as normative for today. Drawing critically on tradition would question more deeply, asking such things as, Does this teaching today serve the purposes that it was intended to serve when first articulated? Were those purposes or the teaching itself co-opted—even unwittingly or unintentionally—to serve the interests of some people while damaging others? How were these purposes, the teaching, and the people who formulated it and passed it on limited by the structures of privilege and power and by the culturally produced assumptions of the time that shaped people's sense of what was right or wrong, good or evil? What have been the consequences of this teaching over time? Who has benefited and who has been hurt by it? Does it seem consistent with the gospel?

Other Bodies of Knowledge

A third source of moral wisdom commonly was known as reason. "Reason" as a source of moral wisdom has been understood variously. One understanding is that God and the good are known not only through the Bible and tradition but also through other bodies of human knowledge. Some Christian traditions have understood this third source philosophically. Most prominent of these is the natural law tradition(s) of Roman Catholicism. Natural law theories vary, even within Catholicism, but in general they find that the mind of God is written into the very universe and can be known by human reason apart from Scripture and tradition. God's purposes for human life and for the world are written into the nature and order of the universe. They are evident in human nature and can be discerned by human reason.

Protestant traditions—keenly aware of human finitude and fallibility—emphasize the inability of humans to know God or the good by reason only. Only by the power of the Holy Spirit and aided by Scripture can human beings know the ways and will of God, including the purpose for human life and what constitutes morality.

Both Catholic and Protestant traditions claim, however, that God is known not only in the Bible and the traditions of the churches but also through other forms of human knowledge. In the earliest centuries, this meant philosophy. With the rise of modern science, the natural sciences joined philosophy. Theology influenced by humanism recognized the humanities and fine arts as sources of knowing God and the good. Yet more recently, the natural, social, and behavioral sciences and most fields of inquiry are seen as capable of revealing wisdom for the moral life.

Experience

Throughout history, the notion of "experience" as a source of moral wisdom has evolved in meaning. Charles and John Wesley meant by "experience" the encounter with the living God and the heartfelt experience of God. It might be understood as experience of the Holy Spirit, or as meeting Jesus, or as being overwhelmed and enveloped by the gracious, life-transforming love of God.

While experience is still used in that sense, more commonly it refers to knowledge of life grounded in the living of it. Bodily experience, emotional experience, the joys and sorrows of everyday life are experience. Feminist theology and ethics have elevated the value of experience as a source of moral wisdom. Pentecostal and evangelical streams give authoritative standing to experience.

However, more critical feminist theologies and ethics and womanist theologies and ethics unveil the vast problems caused when dominant groups unconsciously universalize their own experience. Early stages of feminism, for example, tended to universalize white educated women's experience as "women's experience," failing to recognize the chasms separating the experience of women in highly varied social locations. The practical implications for moral reasoning are immense. "Experience" no longer can refer primarily to *my* experience or the experience of people "like me." To learn from experience will mean to learn also from the experiences of people who are highly different from me and, especially, from people who may be on the underside of the systems that bring my material excess, from people who are proposing alternatives.

Liberation theologies' insistence on "epistemological privilege of the margins" deepens and expands this understanding of experience as a source of moral wisdom. A fundamental claim of liberationist perspectives is that people on the underside of power and privilege have a particular form of insight into human reality and into God. The implications are striking.

Confirming this claim, a Lutheran theology of the cross counsels that the work and ways of God are revealed most fully in Jesus Christ and—in some way beyond full human comprehension—that Jesus Christ is known most deeply in places of brokenness and suffering. Thus, we will glimpse what God is doing to the extent that we allow ourselves to be present with profound solidarity and compassion where people and creation suffer most.

Earth

This is uncharted terrain for many who have been nurtured in the strong anthropocentrism of the modern Western world. How will we learn to hear God's voice and guidance in the Earth's waters and winds? How will we learn to "read" the other four sources from perspectives of the Earth?

Much begins with retrieval. The classic stance of Christianity in its dominant forms is that God is revealed in two books, the Book of Nature and the Book of Scripture, the Bible. This was true of Roman Catholic moral theology, for which the mind of God is written into the entire cosmos and can be known by human reason, apart from Scripture and tradition. This "natural law" as known to reason is a guide to moral wisdom. The two books pointing to God's revelatory presence and power were likewise embraced by the Protestant reformers, not least Martin Luther and John Calvin, even though the Reformation itself was powered by a rereading of Scripture.

But well before medieval Catholicism and the Protestant Reformation, nature, or Earth, was the meeting place with God in the quest for wisdom. In the first centuries, a creation-rich theology and spirituality suffused the meditations of the desert fathers and mothers and the Cappadocian theologians of the Christian East. In the fourth century and following, it found lyrical expression in Celtic Christianity and the popular Celtic culture of Ireland and the British Isles. Not least, where indigenous peoples have embraced Christianity, they have, usually against the will of their colonizers, synthesized their own nature-rooted identity and wisdom with their Christianity.

The origins of the turn to nature reach into the biblical materials themselves. Scripture points to the natural world as participating in divine revelation.[17] Even Job's "frenemy," Zophar, knows that non-human creation possesses its own wisdom: "But ask the animals, and they will teach you; the birds of the air, and they will tell you; ask the plants of the earth, and they will teach you; and the fish of the sea will declare it to you. Who among all these does not know that the hand of the Lord has done this?" (Job 12:7–9). Not only does the single longest soliloquy of God in all of Scripture appear in Job 38–41, itself a stirring tour of the natural world, but much the same is found among the longest of the creation psalms, Psalm 104. Indeed, the common theme of the whole corpus of wisdom literature in the Bible, of which Job, many psalms, and Proverbs are part, is that gaining wisdom happens in part by careful, patient observation of nature and learning to craft human response and responsibility from that knowledge. This is the tack of Jesus again and again in the parables ("A sower went forth to sow . . ." Matt 13:3, Mark 4:3, Luke 8:5) and in his teachings ("Look at the birds of the air . . . ; Consider the lilies of the field . . ." Matt 6:26). What is the nature of each creature and what might we learn in its presence?[18]

Likewise, the preamble of the Gospel of John, John's "Christmas" story, assumes the Logos—the "Word" that from the beginning was with God, was God, and through whom all things were made, and took flesh—is the wonderfully intelligible ordering of creation. Cosmic creation exhibits a rational order that can instruct those who pay close attention and take heed.[19] In different words, nature is always a teacher, though it is not always a teacher of morality. That task—discerning what is the contextually good, right, and fitting response—remains the work of human judgment. Nonetheless, nature as constant teacher means that those who ignore it or flout it are, in this wisdom tradition, fools. Not to glean wisdom from Earth, even the cosmos, is the path of folly.

17. See the fine essay by Lisa Dahill, "Rewilding Christian Spirituality: Outdoor Sacraments and the Life of the World," in *Eco-Reformation: Grace and Hope for a Planet in Peril*, ed. Lisa E. Dahill and James B. Martin-Schramm (Eugene, OR: Wipf & Stock, 2016), 177–96.

18. A profound answer to this question from a botanist is Robin Wall Kimmerer's *Braiding Sweetgrass: Indigenous Wisdom, Scientific Knowledge, and the Teachings of Plants* (Minneapolis: Milkweed, 2013).

19. See the work of biblical scholar William P. Brown, *The Seven Pillars of Creation: The Bible, Science, and the Ecology of Wonder* (Oxford: Oxford University Press, 2010). For a discussion of the moral wisdom of the wisdom traditions, see William P. Brown, "Wisdom and Folly," in *Earth-Honoring Faith: Religious Ethics in a New Key*, ed. Larry L. Rasmussen (Oxford: Oxford University Press, 2013), 332–56.

A perhaps surprising finding of Gary Ferguson echoes all these sources without drawing directly from any one in particular. Ferguson participated in a project that entailed looking at a thousand nature myths from around the world. What he discovered was this: "Nearly every tale I came across pointed to at least one of three qualities that people—spanning thousands of years—considered essential for living well in the world. The first was community. The second was mystery. The third was beauty."[20] The very purpose of moral wisdom is to aid "living well in the world." "Community," "mystery," and "beauty" are key motifs of both nature and Scripture for living well.

But is retrieval enough, not only retrieval of both books (the Book of Nature and Book of Scripture) read together but retrieval of the inherited substance of each? For us, probably not. For one thing, modern science offers knowledge that was not, and could not have been, in the repertoire of previous observers, including biblical ones. That we and the planet are all late versions of stardust—literally children of the cosmos and exploded super stars, that we are threaded with DNA and kin with all life—these are stunning relationships never seen with the naked eye and unknown until recently. Moreover, and secondly, retrieval is not enough if that means learning from the settled ways of reliable nature. At a time when Earth itself may be entering upon a new geological age, and stabilities of the climate system—of seedtime and harvest and where the seas find their limit—cannot be assumed, we will need to ask anew what we learn from Earth that shapes human responsibility in the Anthropocene. Is God doing a new thing? And are we? What do we do when not only is deep-seated human power pervasive across the community of life and for generations unseen, but Earth itself responds with unleashed powers that paradoxically render human control less possible and predictable, rather than more?[21]

Yet, if retrieval means retrieval of method as well as of content, the fundamentals remain—namely, the careful, patient observation of nature, and the crafting of human responsibility in light of that. If we are, cumulatively, the single most powerful force of planetary nature itself, what is fitting as the way of life we lead? "But ask the animals . . . ask the birds of the air . . . ask the plants of the earth . . . ask the

20. Gary Ferguson, "A Deeper Boom," *Orion* 35, no. 5 (July/August and September/October 2016): 18.

21. See the discussion of Clive Hamilton, *Defiant Earth: The Fate of Humans in the Anthropocene* (Cambridge, UK: Polity, 2017).

fish of the sea, and they will teach you" (Job 12: 7–8) remains good advice.[22] Folly is the alternative.

In Conversation

How do and how ought these sources of moral guidance to work together? How are they to be prioritized, weighted, and allowed to inform each other? The interplay among these sources is a powerful factor in determining the outcome of moral deliberation and in shaping Christian traditions. Catholic tradition typically has emphasized reason and tradition. Protestantism was born in part by asserting the primacy of Scripture over all other ways of knowing God. Historical-critical biblical method brought other bodies of human knowledge—especially social sciences, history, archeology—to bear on interpretation of Scripture itself. Feminist theology elevated personal experience. Liberationist thought elevates the experience of those on the margins.

Ethics does not declare which should be primary. Ethics asserts the necessity of intentionality, self-awareness, and methodological integrity in turning to these sources. Thus, ethics warns against the tendency of the liberal Christian tradition to claim the Bible as primary source but effectively marginalize it, and the tendency of some evangelical Christians to read the texts literally for moral guidance and to claim no other complementary source. Ethics demands awareness of misuse of all five sources. In particular, it cautions against absolutizing any source or the conclusions drawn from it. All these sources have their wisdom. None should be overlooked or omitted.

THE MORAL NORM OF NEIGHBOR LOVE

Widespread agreement in Christian ethics holds that Jesus's call to love neighbor as self—or to love as God loves (John 13:34)—present in all four Gospels and grounded in the Hebrew Scriptures (Lev 19:18), is the overarching moral norm for human life. "Our responsibility as Christians," Martin Luther King Jr. declared, "is to discover the meaning of this command and seek passionately to live it out in

---

22. This is likely a speech of Zophar, one of Job's sometime friends. Even Zophar understands that wisdom is to be found in creation, even if his refusal to condone Job's claim on God's justice is ultimately not vindicated in the book as a whole.

our daily lives."[23] "The whole thrust of biblical religion is toward the recovery of the broken human capacity to love," writes Catholic moral theologian Daniel Maguire.[24] According to widespread understanding of the Christian story, this is the human vocation, our life's work—to receive and trust God's mysterious and marvelous love and then live it into the world.

That human beings are called to love is simple enough to say. But what is meant by that tiny and potent word is not. For millennia, Christians and Jews have sought to heed this calling. What love is and requires is the great moral question permeating Christian history. How that norm is interpreted—what it means—determines the shape of morality.

Space here does not allow exploring the norm of neighbor-love.[25] We simply make one point and then suggest a few features of neighbor-love as a biblical and theological norm. The point is this: Christian ethics depends upon this norm. Dedicating a year to the question of "What does God's call to love neighbor as self mean for us today?" would be—for a Christian community—a faithful, fruitful foray into the mystery and gift of life embraced by God.

A few features of neighbor-love may serve as a basis for readers' further exploration. First, neighbor-love is a steadfast commitment to serve the well-being of whomever is loved. Second, the structure of the text—"You will love your neighbor as yourself"—presupposes the normativity of self-love. That is, other love does not supersede respect and honoring of self. Uncovering this dimension of love has been a central contribution of feminist and womanist ethics.[26]

Third, where systemic injustice causes suffering,[27] seeking the well-being of those who suffer—actively loving—entails seeking to dismantle the sources of that injustice.[28] Dietrich Bonhoeffer called

---

23. Martin Luther King Jr., "Strength to Love," in *A Testament of Hope: The Essential Writings and Speeches of Martin Luther King, Jr.*, ed. James M. Washington (San Francisco: Harper & Row, 1991), 48. Here, King is speaking specifically of the commandment to love enemies.

24. Daniel Maguire, *The Moral Core of Judaism and Christianity: Reclaiming the Revolution* (Minneapolis: Fortress Press, 1993), 208.

25. For more extensive treatment, see Moe-Lobeda, *Resisting Structural Evil*, chapter 7.

26. See, for example, Emilie M. Townes, "To Be Called Beloved: Womanist Ontology in Postmodern Refraction," in *Womanist Theological Ethics: A Reader*, ed. Katie Geneva Cannon, Emilie M. Townes, and Angela D. Sims (Louisville: Westminster John Knox, 2011), 183–201.

27. As it does in multiple dimensions and contexts of social life.

28. Maguire, *Moral Core*, 220: "In the main biblical perspective, love and justice are not opposites but coordinates, manifestations of the same affect. . . . The various words for justice and love in both the Hebrew and Greek scriptures are linguistically interlocking."

this "seizing the wheel" of unjust power structures.[29] This includes (1) *seeing* systemic injustice for what it is and acknowledging it, (2) *resisting* it, and (3) forging more just alternatives.[30] This makes sense, given our discussion of structural sin in chapter Five.

If sin is both individual and structural, then so too is the force that counters sin: love. Neighbor-love is a guide not only for interpersonal relationships but also for the ways in which we structure our lives together through political, economic, and cultural systems.

A fourth feature of love as a biblical and theological norm pertains to the dangerous question, "Who is my neighbor?" "My neighbor," in the biblical sense, is anyone my life impacts. Given the current realities of climate change and globalization, my "neighbor" is a global reality and includes the world's tens of millions of climate refugees.[31]

The question "Who is my neighbor?" pushes further. The God revealed in Jesus is a living God, engaged with the creatures and elements of Earth. Divine love responds to the realities of history. God's love re-forms human love in response to where and how the world hungers for its healing and liberating hand. The escalating destruction of Earth's life systems in our day and the resulting human suffering cry out for new forms of love's expression. We are called to love—that is, serve the well-being of—the other-than-human parts of God's beloved creation, as well as the human.

This expanded scope of neighbor-love is not new with eco-theology and ecological ethics. Three decades before eco-theology emerged, H. Richard Niebuhr queried: "Who finally is my neighbor, the companion whom I have been commanded to love as myself?" "My neighbor," he responds, is "animal and inorganic being . . . all

29. Dietrich Bonhoeffer, "The Church and the Jewish Question," in *Dietrich Bonhoeffer Works*, vol. 12, *Berlin: 1932–1933*, ed. Larry L. Rasmussen (Minneapolis: Fortress Press, 2009), 365.

30. Walter Brueggemann ("Voices of the Night—Against Justice," in *To Act Justly, Love Tenderly, Walk Humbly*, by Walter Brueggemann, Sharon Parks, and Thomas H. Groome [New York: Paulist, 1986]), writes that doing justice implies "relentless critique of injustice" (7), "envisions a changed social system" (10), and works toward "nothing less than the dismantling of the presently known world for the sake of an alternative world not yet embodied" (11).

31. According to United Nations statistics, 21.5 million persons are displaced annually due to events related to climate change; see "Frequently Asked Questions on Climate Change and Disaster Displacement," United Nations High Commissioner for Refugees, November 1, 2016, http://tinyurl.com/y876208o.

that participates in being."[32] Bernard Brady expands upon the biblical notion of *hesed* (steadfast love) to show how love in the biblical understanding is not limited to people.[33]

Extending the boundaries of neighbor-love beyond the human opens radical new horizons. In what ways and to what extent does "neighbor-love" apply beyond humankind to the rest of nature? How? As object of love? As agent of love? As vessel of divine love? Biblical texts, read with ecological lenses, intimate all of these. How does love for human neighbor differ from love for the other-than-human neighbor? What differing moral obligations accompany love for different elements of God's creation? The point here is not to answer the questions but to call them to the fore of ethical deliberation.

Imagine a congregation dedicated for a year to studying, exploring, and practicing the rich and life-shaping gift of neighbor-love. They would be entering into Jesus's call to self-respecting, justice-seeking, Earth-honoring neighbor-love.

MORAL THEORY

What is the heart of moral experience? What matters most? If you, the reader, were to answer that question for yourself, what would your answer be?

Answers have varied widely. But they fall along familiar lines. So much so that students of ethics describe three ever-recurring patterns: duty ethics, virtue ethics, and consequences ethics. We discuss all three. Two of them—virtue ethics and consequences ethics—are nicely introduced with a real-life episode from World War II.

When the Japanese invaded China, they rounded up all the non-Chinese and put them in camps, one of which was the Weihsien Compound in Shandong province. Initially, about fifteen hundred people were interned in the camp, mostly from Europe and the United States, but also Eurasians, South Americans, and South Africans. Japanese soldiers were assigned to control all goods entering and leaving the camp, but most of the internal administrative tasks were assigned to the detainees. People little known to one another

32. Larry L. Rasmussen, "Green Discipleship," *Reflections Yale Divinity School*, Spring 2007, 69.

33. Bernard V. Brady, *Christian Love: How Christians Through the Ages Have Understood Love* (Washington, DC: Georgetown University Press, 2015).

were thus given the daunting task of creating a working community from scratch. As Langdon Gilkey, a detainee who narrated life in the compound, notes,[34] this was society reduced to a microcosm in which fundamental social dynamics were visible for all to see.

On a cold January day in 1945, an unexpected delivery arrived. One donkey cart after another passed through the camp gates to offload 1,500 parcels, each packed with food or clothing.

The American Red Cross was the source of this manna. Not surprisingly, then, many of the 200 Americans (of the 1,450 detainees in the camp at that time) laid claim to the parcels. With a nod to the country of origin, the Japanese commandant ruled that each US citizen would receive one-and-a-half parcels; all other prisoners, one each. The math worked almost to a tee. But a number of Americans protested vigorously. Americans, they said, should decide the distribution of American goods. The commandant temporarily retracted his ruling and postponed the distribution until the community had discussed the matter and reported back to him.

That discussion included an exchange between two of the Americans, an elderly missionary named Grant and the young schoolteacher Gilkey. Grant, according to Gilkey, wanted to argue the "moral" side of the affair: "'I always look at things, Gilkey, from the moral point of view.' 'Fascinated,' Gilkey comments, 'I heard him out.'"

> I want to make sure that there be a moral quality to the use we make of these fine American goods. Now as you are well aware, Gilkey, there is no virtue whatever in being *forced* to share. We Americans should be given the parcels, all right. Then each of us should be left to exercise his own moral judgment in deciding what to do with them. We will share, but not on order from the enemy, for then it would not be moral.[35]

Gilkey next contrasts Grant's understanding of "moral" with his own. Grant contended that actions that are not the free acts of individuals cannot be genuinely "moral." If we do not freely act from choice and do not express who we are, or who we strive to be, in our choices, then genuine morality is absent. We may well *act*, under compulsion, but the wellspring of such action is not authentic morality, even if beneficial consequences follow. The wellsprings of true morality are

---

34. Langdon Gilkey, *Shantung Compound* (New York: Harper & Row, 1966).
35. Gilkey, *Shantung Compound*, 109.

in character, free will, and free choice. Acts that mirror freely undertaken responsibility are "moral." Others are not.

Gilkey counters Grant by arguing that Grant's theory of morality ignores a basic moral fact: moral action has to do primarily with relations between persons in a community. Thus, moral actions are those in which the neighbor's needs are measured together with one's own as part of the same relational framework; immoral acts are those in which the neighbor is forgotten or ignored in deference to the self. Gilkey's conclusion is that moral action, certainly if it is to be called "Christian" (Grant is a Christian missionary), expresses "in the outward form of an act a concern for the neighbor's welfare, which concern is, if anything is, the substance of inner virtue."[36]

Gilkey's moral theory differs sharply from Grant's because for Gilkey, the heart of morality is not in character and individual free choice but in values that are realized in tangible social consequences and ends, values that are not only embodied in but tested *by* those consequences and ends. (Much to the same point, David Brooks says straightforwardly, "The heart of any moral system is the connection between action and consequences.")[37] In Gilkey's case, the roughly equal sharing of critical goods on the basis of common need is the salient value, a value rooted in an even more fundamental tenet—namely, the equality of persons in inescapable relationship to one another. Each person's welfare is placed in the same frame of moral reference, and on the same terms, as my own. The result for Gilkey is to find that "moral" action that expresses genuine care for neighbors in its consequences, whatever the source and even if compelled. Indeed, for Gilkey, genuine "inner virtue" is to cultivate this consequences orientation for all our actions. Our actions are judged by outcomes rather than by dispositions, motives, or unconstrained individual choice. To live the good life means to create and share in the general welfare by way of moral goods that are realized in society, goods such as equality and community.

If we step back from Grant and Gilkey,[38] we observe different moral theories at work: character ethics and consequence ethics. Each

36. Ibid., 110.

37. David Brooks, "The Responsibility Deficit," *New York Times*, September 24, 2010, http://tinyurl.com/35mddhl.

38. While we have drawn directly from Gilkey in *Shantung Compound*, the account here paraphrases the one Bruce Birch and Larry Rasmussen provided in Birch and Rasmussen, *BECL*, rev., 48–50. It was also paraphrased in Rasmussen, *Earth-Honoring Faith*, 130–33.

identifies genuine morality differently, just as each underscores a different dimension of moral experience (character for one, conduct for the other).

Character ethics is also known as "virtue" ethics, from the Greek *aretē*, a reference to excellence of moral character. Its answer to the question, How is the good life achieved? is this: choose the qualities that mark the good person and the good society and internalize these as the habits of heart, soul, and mind. When habitual, these qualities express who we are; they exhibit our moral identity and drive our actions. They create the good society from the inside out, as the outcome of the kind of persons we are and strive to be. The focus is on moral agents, from whom actions flow as water from a spring.

Not only individuals, but communities and societies, cultures and subcultures, bear moral traits. Some of these traits are self-consciously held while others are largely unarticulated and belong to the unwritten moral substratum of culture; they are just "who we are." Either way, groups, and not just individuals, express character traits. Empathy and compassion, a disposition to treat persons as equals, and an insistence on justice as fair play may be so widely shared that they are part of a shared collective character; so are honoring the elders, respecting those in authority, and making the welfare of future generations part of present decisions. Dignity, self-determination, and a willingness to sacrifice might be present as well. On the other hand, social character might also include tolerance for cheating on taxes or corruption in high places. Taking advantage of the power of public office might be so common as to be expected. Notions of justice might sanction honor killings and the death penalty in one society and find them abhorrent in another. Likewise, large inequalities of income and wealth might be tolerated, even defended, in some societies and deeply opposed in others. Whatever the particular constellation of virtues and vices, the morality that flows from cultivated personal and communal character is, for character ethics, morality at its most authentic. Here, authentic actions are conceived in reference to those who perform them, as matters of identity and integrity. The character of the moral subject is the center of attention and assessment.

Virtue ethics has numerous schools and exemplars. The one articulated by Grant is far from the best. There are ongoing debates in virtue ethics about which virtues have priority, who and what best embodies them, and what kind of moral formation and discernment cultivates the desired character. Albert Borgmann's *Real American Ethics*, for example, proposes that a good virtue ethic now must account for "economy and design." He thereby gives prominence to a matter that falls outside Grant's purview altogether. Why economy and design? Borgmann argues that greater attention must be given to "Churchill's principle": "We shape our buildings, and afterward our buildings shape us."[39] Just as we construct our habitat, so our habitat "constructs" us. In the modern world, the global corporate capitalist economy is so overwhelming a force that it promotes its own strong culture, one that instills and rewards certain virtues and values while discouraging or dismissing others. The economy effectively creates its own moral universe and brings about attitudinal as well as behavioral change through the consumerist habits it cultivates and rewards. It shapes desire and affects how we, as moral agents, view the world and act in it. It's the phantom moral cosmology of our era. In light of such a powerful moral presence as this, Borgmann concludes that we should self-consciously make economy and design the subject of virtue and character formation, rather than let individual and collective character be formed by external forces that are not truly external at all. For Borgmann, good virtue ethics thus includes a long, hard look at the way the economy is organized and public space is designed since daily behavior, whether consciously willed or simply assumed as the way things are, affects motives, dispositions, attitudes, intentions, desires, even perception itself.[40] We shape the habitat that shapes us. Good virtue ethics thus works for better *systemic* alternatives. Such attention to institutions and their behavior may not have occurred to Grant even though Grant and Borgmann are both exponents of virtue ethics.

Aristotle's ethics is a classic statement of virtue ethics. Like Borgmann, Aristotle is keenly aware that while character shapes decisions and actions, practices and actions mold the character that is at the heart of the moral life. In the words of the *Nicomachean Ethics*: "We become just by doing just acts, temperate by doing temperate

39. Borgmann is quoting from Winston Churchill, *Winston S. Churchill: His Complete Speeches 1897–1963*, vol. 7, *1943–1949*, ed. Robert Rhodes James (New York: Chelsea House, 1974), 68–69.

40. Albert Borgmann, *Real American Ethics: Taking Responsibility for Our Country* (Chicago: University of Chicago Press, 2006), 160–88.

acts, brave by doing brave acts."[41] So while the good life and the good society are created from the inside out, as the outcome of the kinds of persons we are, the "inside" is also created from without.

Now recall Gilkey. Gilkey's ethics are straightforward consequence ethics, also known as "teleological" ethics. *Telos* is Greek for end, goal, or purpose; teleological ethics are outcome-oriented and tested—thus, consequence ethics. Gilkey's morality is so solidly teleological that even the use of force is justified by the praiseworthy end it achieves. In this case, needy neighbors obtain needed supplies at the hands of the Japanese authorities. To his credit, Gilkey's own teleological ethic is keenly aware of human reverence and responsibility for the natural world. His *Maker of Heaven and Earth* (1959) and *Nature, Reality, and the Sacred* (1993) were significant steps toward an ecological theology.[42] In this respect, Gilkey's ethic is unlike the widespread utilitarian version of modern industrialism, where nature's value resides solely in its use for human ends. Gilkey thus illustrates that consequence ethics, too, takes varied forms with varied content. Moreover, like Borgmann and Aristotle, he is aware of the interplay of actions and character. Sharing the parcels at the hands of the enemy expresses in outward form "a concern for the neighbor's welfare, which concern is, if anything is, the substance of inner virtue."[43] Still, the decisive moral test is not with the doer ("inner virtue") but with the deed (shared parcels). Gilkey concludes his account: "In such a view all actions which help to feed the hungry neighbor are moral, even if the final instrument is an impersonal arm of government. Thus, as I argued to Grant, efforts designed to bring about a universal sharing were moral, efforts to block such a sharing, immoral."[44] So while virtue is present and important for Gilkey, even for it the test resides in the quality of actions as judged by their outcome. For Gilkey and all purveyors of consequence ethics, authentic morality is known by its fruits.

The parcel distribution had an amusing sequel. As the mountain of

41. Aristotle, *Nicomachean Ethics*, 2.1.4–5 (trans. H. Rackham, LCL 73).

42. Langdon Gilkey, *Maker of Heaven and Earth: A Study of the Christian Doctrine of Creation in the Light of Modern Knowledge* (Garden City, NY: Doubleday, 1959); Langdon Gilkey, *Nature, Reality, and the Sacred: The Nexus of Science and Religion* (Minneapolis: Augsburg Fortress, 1993). While these volumes prepare for ecological theology, Gilkey's attention is not to the ecosphere and what is happening to it. Their focus is the impact of modern science on the claims of theology and religion.

43. Gilkey, *Shantung Compound*, 110.

44. Ibid.

goods from the American Red Cross was sorted, two hundred pairs of boots sent by the South African Red Cross appeared. A grand total of two South Africans were in the camp at the time. The next day, they posted a notice: "Due to the precedent that has been set" (that is, of Americans insisting they be the ones to sort American goods), "the South African community is laying claim to all 200 pairs of the boots donated by their Red Cross. We shall wear each pair for three days to signal our right to what is our own property, and then shall be glad to lend some out when not in use to any non-South Africans who request our generous help."[45] The morality play continued!

A third moral theory, neither Grant's nor Gilkey's, centers on obligation, or duty. In philosophical ethics it is called "deontological ethics." This term stems from *deon*, Greek for "that which must be done." That is, life itself imposes requirements incumbent upon all. Living together mandates ground rules and inescapable relationships entail shared responsibilities.

But what are we duty bound to do? What moral bottom lines should frame and guide our decisions and actions? What obligations, if any, are binding in matters of faith and life?

A widely used text in biomedical ethics by Beauchamp and Childress offers a hypothetical case for obligation as an element of universal moral experience and as an answer to the question of where the heart of morality resides.[46]

Imagine you and a friend are mountain climbing. Your friend falls. When you reach him, it is obvious he is severely injured. In his dying moments, he begs you to keep a promise. You readily agree. He reveals he has a tidy sum of money, nearly a million dollars, that he acquired by dint of hard work and good investments. He tells you where the money is and asks that you deliver it to an uncle who helped him at a crucial moment in the past. Your friend dies.[47]

You know three things. You made a promise; only you know about the million dollars; and your friend's uncle, whom you know as well, is both rich and likely to squander your friend's earnings. Furthermore, you can easily identify needier causes, causes your friend has also supported. Would the money in their hands not be a more

45. Ibid., 113.

46. Tom L. Beauchamp and James F. Childress, *Principles of Biomedical Ethics* (New York: Oxford University Press, 1979).

47. Ibid., 29. As with the Shantung Compound case study, the discussion here includes some paraphrase of the discussion in Birch and Rasmussen, *BECL*, rev., 52–58.

fitting memorial to your friend? Should you not break your promise to your friend, even if sworn at his deathbed, if the outcome has better consequences? He will never know, of course. Neither will the uncle.

Promise keeping and truth telling are examples of fundamental duties. In answer to the moral question, What is the good life and how are we to live it? the chief concern here is not consequence determined or virtue determined but obligation determined. What are we obliged to do, given the investment of life itself in our hands? In this particular case, at issue is whether you should break your promise to your friend in order to use his money for worthier ends. Whatever your actual decision, the very existence of a strong sense that you should not break a solemn promise is testimony to obligation as a core reality of the moral life. (It is also testimony that the truths of duty ethics and consequence ethics might conflict, just as the truths of character ethics might conflict with those of duty and consequence ethics.)

Promise keeping and truth telling are hardly the only examples of ground rules. Extending trust is another. Life cannot be lived well, if at all, out of basic distrust or mistrust. If everyone and everything is untrustworthy all the time, nothing can be done, or even ventured, to anyone's lasting satisfaction. Elemental trust—keeping one's word, being reliable—is an indispensable norm.

Respect and love as equal regard are also necessary for the good life. How we treat one another counts for most everything. Equal regard as love and basic respect means we treat others in the manner we ourselves wish to be treated. Not by coincidence does the Golden Rule emerge in every culture and every age, not only as good advice to squabbling kids but as a moral principle applicable to all. Negatively stated, lack of basic respect issues in corrosive double standards. Some humans are regarded as less than human, or human in ways that are inferior to the ways of my tribe. "Mine" and "ours" trump "you" and "yours." "My" and "our" actions lose all sense of fair play and easily turn arbitrary, indifferent, or oppressive. Injustice, with its caustic effects for life together, follows.

Immanuel Kant was a supreme expositor of a consistent duty ethic.[48] His notion of the "categorical imperative" designates an obligation that is binding in all circumstances. His first formulation of

48. There are many editions of the work that contains the formulations of the categorical imperative discussed here. All are from Immanuel Kant's *Grundlegung zur Metaphysik der Sitten.*

the categorical imperative goes like this: "Act only according to that maxim whereby you can at the same time will that it should become a universal law." No double standards. Not one law for me and my tribe but another for you and yours. The test of genuine morality is whether you can will for others what you will for yourself. This again renders the Golden Rule a moral bottom line and guide. Promise keeping, truth telling, loving the neighbor as oneself, refraining from violence, might all be similarly basic obligations.

Kant's second formulation of the categorical imperative is, "So act in every case as to treat humanity, whether in your own person or in that of another, as an end, and never a means only." Regarding women as only a means to fulfill male desires, or any relationship without respect or according inherent value to persons as worthy in their own right—like slavery and discrimination—are "out." They don't pass the test of "ends, not means only."

Kant's third formulation works from his notion of a "kingdom of ends" for which we are the legislators. "Every human being must so act as if he were through his maxim always a legislating member in the universal kingdom of ends." If you, like Moses or Hammurabi, were the lawgiver, what laws would be binding upon all? What moral framework and substantive duties would govern your little kingdom (your family, your town, your neighborhood, your bio-region)? The stipulated guideline is to always act as though you were the giver of such laws as the laws for all.

Philosopher John Rawls has formulated this legislative function in a now classic way. It goes like this. If you were placed behind a veil of ignorance so that you could not know in advance your position or status in the future society where you will live out your days, what rules would you legislate? If you cannot know how your interests and your life will play out in the future, what terms would you create as the basic terms for everyone? What principles and practices would be binding upon all, if all are lined up at the same starting line in the same race? It is little surprise that Rawls arrives at justice as fairness.[49]

Nor is it a surprise that the rule of law, constitutions, and universal human rights all engage morality as both legislated duty and binding obligation. A constitution might need to be amended, rights may

A recent edition is Immanuel Kant, *Groundwork on the Metaphysics of Morals*, trans. and ed. Mary Gregor and Jens Timmermann (Cambridge: Cambridge University Press, 2012).

49. John Rawls, *A Theory of Justice* (Cambridge, MA: Belknap Press of Harvard University Press, 1971).

need to be extended, and new covenants may need to be drafted, but then these changes acquire the same standing and force as the previous formulations had. They are, within their domain, universally binding elements.

Kant wants morality that is not susceptible to the self-serving distortions we have identified elsewhere in our discussion. He knew that we consistently engage in ideological twists and turns meant to serve our limited interests. We construe our vices as virtues; we confirm our biases; we even believe our lies. Imperatives that are "categorical," or right for any and every person in similar circumstances (i.e., "universal"), minimize the influence of distorting interests. Kant's universalism thus yields guidelines that are independent of the interests of the people posing and deciding moral issues.

Contrasted with the other theories, this means that, for duty ethics, neither the virtue of the person nor the consequences of their actions is the decisive test of moral value; the fundamental requirements of life together and universal applicability are. Stealing, lying, breaking promises, raping, and torturing cannot be moral yardsticks. They cannot be recommended norms and behaviors. If they were universally practiced and approved, society would be impossible. Or if somehow society were remotely possible on such terms, then it would be a place we'd do everything possible to escape in favor of a habitat that valued respect and lived by fair play.

To summarize moral theory: we have identified notably different ways to underline what is most important in the moral life. They cluster around three realities continually present in human experience: the quality of human character, the goals and consequences of human action, and the rules that living together requires. Given various names, we have used the idiom of character or virtue ethics (areteological), consequence ethics (teleological), and duty ethics (deontological). However these realities are named, they cross all cultures and all recorded human time. The morality we are born to has these varied, recurring, enduring grammars.

Several notes finish the discussion.

Moral theory is the effort to reflect systematically upon the forms of human moral experience and their "logics" and "grammars." It highlights these different and sometimes conflicting logics and grammars in the moralities we live: facing the decisions we do, what do we most live by and how does it matter—character, consequences, or obligation?

Yet, lived moral experience is always richer and more dynamic than our descriptive theories. Theories, by nature, abstract from experience in ways that simplify it. They do so for the sake of an illuminating focus that lets us see what matters and what its explanatory power and guidance are. But however elegant the theories, we still feel the tug and tensions of all three moral realities—character, consequences, and duty—often without settled resolution. That should tell us that no one of these approaches itself captures the whole. No single theory, even when sound and consistent, encompasses the length, breadth, depth, and complexity of human morality, nor does any one resolve competing claims to lasting satisfaction.

The authors of *Earth Ethics*, having discussed these moral patterns, note that in most cases people exhibit "a mixed or pluralistic ethical approach," and for good reason. All three moral traditions bear essential insight and all three contribute to good ethical analysis for sound moral deliberation. The authors' example is that, on a single day, "an elected official could use a teleological approach to weigh the costs and benefits of different policy options, reject a bribe to favor one of these options out of a deontological obligation to act honestly, and later reject the advice of a campaign consultant to go negative by drawing on the areteological [virtue] resources of her moral character."[50]

The common use of mixed or pluralistic theory acknowledged, it nonetheless matters immensely what the mix is and where the weight falls. Different decisions and actions follow from different choices. Those choices are two-fold. Some are "internal" to a theory. (*Which* virtues count most in a given circumstance? *Which* consequences matter most? *Which* obligations are most basic?) Other choices are about the theory that dominates the mix. (Is Grant's stance most dominant, or Gilkey's, to remember our example? Is the dominant logic that of Aristotle's character ethics, Kant's obligation ethics, or the consequentialist's moral world?) Both domains of choice matter—choices internal to the theories and choices about the theory that most powers the decisions and actions.

The second note is that all three of these accounts of what matters

---

50. James Martin-Schramm, Daniel Spencer, and Laura Stivers, *Earth Ethics: A Case Method Approach* (Maryknoll, NY: Orbis, 2015), 69.

most for morality have been severely anthropocentric. While that has not always been so, and is not so in a few communities today (those of many indigenous peoples, for example), the dominant moralities and ways of life in the modern industrialized world—the past 250 years—have been unremittingly anthropocentric in both theory and practice. Whether focused on character, consequences, or duties, the reigning moralities have addressed human society as morally abstracted from the rest of the community of life. They have failed "to account for planetary well-being, which is the basis for all forms of life and any experience of human good."[51] They have thereby failed to understand that human well-being is always derivative of nature's well-being. In other words, modernity's dominant moral universe has not made the passage from the human ego to the planetary ecosphere as the indispensable context of the moral life. Nature lacks rights that parallel human rights. Even species extinction—uncreating, running Genesis backward—is not a crime. No one goes to court or jail for it. Evidently, it's only the unfortunate "collateral damage" of justified human development. At a time when human power affects all life, its parental elements included—earth, air, fire, water—this constricted anthropocentrism is the failure that has brought on the changes of apocalyptic proportions we noted in the introduction, changes that lead to a necessary rethinking of who we are in the great scheme of things and to the needed "new conversation" between Bible and ethics. It's also the failure that leads to the expanded moral universe we proposed elsewhere in this volume (see figures 5.1 and 5.2).

Where does that anthropocentrism leave moral theory?

Perhaps surprisingly, we do not have, and do not seek, a fourth theory, one reserved for other-than-human nature in our experience. The ethic we need is not some autonomous and segregated "environmental ethic" with fundamentally different moral categories. The ethic we need is an inclusive ethic tailored to the world we have and the changes we face at a time of vast anthropocene powers. Human character, ends, and obligation all pertain for this world of expanded human responsibility. None drop out as the moral universe moves its boundary from the ego to the ecosphere. But neither are other categories added, not even when present working moralities need to be reimagined, reframed, and rewritten. Other virtues and different character may well be necessary, as will other consequences

51. Ibid., 48.

as the outcome of different policies and habits. Likewise, a restatement of our obligations to present and future generations of both human and more-than-human life is needed. A major theme of this book is that these content changes are vital. But changes of substance expand the formal categories rather than replace them. The baselines of moral theory—character, consequence, obligation—remain. An adequate account of human responsibility incorporates them all.

The last note is about the intersection of the Bible and moral theory. Where does the Bible fall vis-à-vis character, consequence, and duty? It's safe to say that its moral contours are deeply invested in all three and that its moral worlds are frequently those of "mixed" and "pluralistic" grammars, but with different emphases at different times in different circumstances.

Take the Exodus account, for example. The Hebrews had lived far too long as the bottom tier in a great civilization run on slave labor by a priestly caste—Pharaoh's Egypt. Freedom came with the exodus into the wilderness. But now what? Shorn of their familiar habitat and livelihood in the fleshpots of Egypt, and absent its imposed order, how will the ragtag band of former slaves govern themselves for survival and a life together? They complain vehemently to Moses: "Why did you bring us out of Egypt, to kill us and our children and livestock with thirst?" (Exod 17:3b). So what will they do with their new freedom? In their own version of Shantung Compound, but without the Japanese (i.e., without the Egyptians), they need the requisites for living together. What will the rules be? What does life together as a functioning community require? The answer is the Ten Commandments and chapter after chapter of legislation (Exodus, Leviticus, Deuteronomy). The Ten Commandments and the Covenant Code are quintessential ground rules articulated as fundamental moral duties in the presence of the God who, unlike Egypt's gods, knows their suffering (Exod 20:12–16; Exodus 21–23). And Moses, though also remembered as deliverer and leader, is venerated above all as Lawgiver. In the wilderness, Israel and its leaders had discovered the forces in human experience that give rise to an ethic of basic obligations. If a people, any people, never lives easily with moral bottom lines, without them it does not live at all.

It should be added that these commandments and covenants belong to a moral order that, in Israel's experience, is authored by none other than the God of the universe, who sided with slaves

against the empire's gods. Commandments and covenants mani-
fested, in this case as in the case of many religions, an existence that is
rooted in God, the same God who flung the stars across the sky and
moved upon the primordial waters to order creation itself.

Here, then, is a formative instance of biblical ethics carrying the
weight of obligation ethics. The content changes with different circumstances and challenges. So, there are new covenants. The
covenant with Earth, the Noachian Covenant, is not the covenant
with Abraham, and the covenant with Abraham is not that
announced by Jeremiah. For Christians, the new covenant celebrated
in the passion, death, and resurrection of Jesus is not a twin of any of
the aforementioned, either. Yet all are covenants, all are fundamental
stipulations of what it means to be a people adhering to the Way of a
people of God. All entail commitments to abide by that Way.

What about character ethics? In a sense, the entire biblical corpus is
about character formation and the morality that flows from a spiritu-
ally nurtured life. An ethic of heart, mind, and soul suffuses Scripture.
Sometimes it is concentrated in certain texts and genres, however.
Think, for example, of the wisdom literature. It's all about growing people up and instructing them in ways that, internalized, make
for righteousness, justice, and peace. Or consider Jesus's Sermon on
the Mount (Matthew 5–8), as penetrating a character ethic as exists.
("But if your eye is unhealthy, you whole body will be full of darkness. If then the light in you is darkness, how great is the darkness!"
[Matt 6:23].) There is also Paul's instruction to the churches about the
virtues they are to nurture and embody. Discipleship itself is about
becoming a people of the Way through disciplines that form character and identity. In Judaism, it's *halakah* (sometimes called "the walk")
and *imitatio Dei* (relating to all things in the manner of God's character and care). In Islam, it's *shari'a* (the pathway to water) and sub-
mission in peace to Allah. In Christianity, it's the way of Jesus and
imitatio Christi. Nurturing excellence of character is a running stream
in all the Abrahamic Scriptures, even though the Way itself may be
as demanding as the Sermon on the Mount, the Torah instruction in
the wilderness, or the seven pillars of Islam.

And consequence ethics? The iniquity of parents rebound "to the
third and fourth generation" (Exod 20:5), just as keeping covenant
and honoring father and mother hold a promise that the days will "be
long in the land that the Lord your God is giving you" (Exod 20:12).

In a word, the fate of the people and their well-being, as well as their woe, is inextricably tied to their deeds. In what is as straightforward as what we heard from Gilkey and David Brooks, Jesus says, "Not everyone who says to me, 'Lord, Lord,' will enter the kingdom of heaven, but only the one who does the will of my Father in heaven" (Matt 7:21). Followers are known by their fruits, to recall the summary word of Jesus in the previous verse (Matt 7:20).

Yet these differing moral accents rarely, if ever, stand apart and alone. Biblical ethics is typically "mixed" and "pluralistic." Even the word of Jesus just cited as consequences ethics par excellence—"you will know them by their fruits"—belongs to the Sermon on the Mount and its unremitting attention to character—good trees bear good fruit (Matt 7:17). Likewise, the desirable outcome of living well and long on the land (consequences) is tied to covenantal obligations. Rare is the biblical teaching that is not a moral ecosystem interlacing character, duty, and consequences.

THE NORMATIVE TASK IN MORAL DISCERNMENT: IN SUM

In exploring the normative task, we began with complexities and conundrums inherent in it. To sort through these complexities, we offered five resources—a set of overarching guidelines for moral deliberation, the interplay of cognition and emotion, five sources of moral wisdom, the moral norm of neighbor-love, and moral theory in three forms.

THREE TASKS OF MORAL DISCERNMENT: A REVIEW

Moral discernment—otherwise known as moral decision-making, moral deliberation, or practical moral reasoning—has three tasks:

- The descriptive task: seeking to uncover what is really going on
- The constructive task: identifying various options or alternatives in response to the situation
- The normative task: deciding which option/alternative seems to be morally preferable

Each task has a related question:

- What is?
- What could be?
- What ought to be?

Moral discernment, however, is not an end in itself. It is for the purpose of moral action.

MORAL ACTION

Daily life is colored by largely unacknowledged instances of *not* doing what we have determined that we ought to do. History, too, is replete with people and groups not doing what they knew to be morally right. In discussing the gap between ethical decisions and their enactment, Joseph Sittler writes: "That men do not perform as they profess, that they do not live up to their announced belief—this is old and obvious stuff."[52]

In chapter 4, we noted that, while moral decision-making or discernment is central to ethics, if understood as the *entirety* of ethics, it is dangerously limited. Ethics must attend also to moral agency, the capacity (courage, will, motivation, material conditions, etc.) to do and be what we ought. Where moral consciousness is the awareness of the gap between what is and what ought to be, moral agency is the capacity to act to lessen that gap.

What factors enable people to act on what they determine to be right? What are the ingredients of moral agency? Wherein lies the moral-spiritual power to do and be what we determine we ought? What forces nurture that power? What forces and factors dissolve or squash it? These questions of moral agency are critical.

In any given situation, a pair of questions opens the door to deeper understanding of moral agency in that situation. Having discerned, to the best of our ability, what we ought to do in a given situation, "What forces and factors threaten to disable our moral-spiritual agency to move in that direction?" And, "What are sources of moral and spiritual power to counter the disabling forces?" The

---

52. Sittler, *Structure of Christian Ethics*, 18–19.

second may be asked differently: "How may we be empowered in our path toward living as we should?"

Responding to these questions and acting as a result may be seen as the transformative task of ethics, following the descriptive, constructive, and normative tasks.

We arrive then at the sixth and final question in the process of ethics outlined in chapter 4. It is the question of moral action: "What actions are called for?" That is, after having engaged in moral deliberation (in its descriptive, constructive, and normative dimensions), and having dared to examine forces that may enable and disable our capacity to act, what actions are we called to take?

This final question returns us to the simple table with which we began in chapter 5.

Tasks of Ethics	Accompanying Questions
Descriptive	What is?
Constructive	What could be?
Normative	What ought to be?
Formative	What morally forms and malforms us?
Transformative	What disables and enables the moral-spiritual power to do and be what we discern that we ought?
Practical	To what actions do these questions point?

MORAL DISCERNMENT AND ACTION: IN SUM

It may be useful to close by sketching in simple terms the process for moral deliberation and action unfolded in this chapter. The sketch begins with articulating the problem at hand and the various ethical issues or sub-questions that may be raised by it.

A PROCESS FOR MORAL DELIBERATION AND ACTION

1. Statement of the moral dilemma

   • This may involve a single ethical question, or it may be a more complex matter evoking several ethical questions. If the latter, then it is wise to identify all of the questions entailed and then to clarify which is being addressed in a given process of deliberation.

2. Descriptive task of ethics (descriptive analysis)

   - "Reality revealing questions" for observing the situation at hand
   - "Reality revealing questions" for broader social analysis

3. Constructive task of ethics (various alternative resolutions to the question)

4. Normative task of ethics (ethical evaluation of the alternative resolutions) informed by:

   - Guidelines for moral discernment
   - Sources of moral wisdom
   - Overarching norm of justice-seeking, Earth-honoring, self-respecting neighbor-love
   - The interplay of emotion and cognition
   - Moral theory

5. Conclusion/resolution (tentative or conclusive)

6. Testing the conclusion by identifying, arguing, and responding to the more/most viable opposing positions/arguments

7. Identifying actions to be taken

8. Identifying factors that enable and disable moral agency for those actions

People of faith are blessed with a sacred calling: to live in ways that reflect the infinite love of God and that align our lives with God's activity in the world. Heeding that calling is the aim of moral discernment and action.

Within the beauty, confusion, and wreckage of the human story on Earth, how will we discern what God is doing, through whom, where, and how? Amidst the complexity and ambiguity of life's realities—from the personal to the international—how are we to know what ways of doing and being cohere with the love of God? By what means will we test the moral assumptions of a given time and place?

What ought we—as individuals, communities, societies—do and be in any given situation? Where will we find the moral-spiritual power to do and be what we ought?

This calling and these questions give rise to moral discernment and moral action. This chapter has explored these processes.

PART III

The Bible, Ethics, and the Moral Life

8.

Witness and Practice

How does Scripture play out in the lives of persons and communities? This volume has, until now, included numerous examples that illustrate disciplined work in Christian ethics and biblical studies. Here we take a turn and go to the "real life" use of Scripture as Christians engage the compelling issues in front of them. Apart from such prime-time engagement, even good scholarly work means little. Practice—lived life—is the test that counts.

The examples in this chapter illustrate that practice. They align with what this book proposes as essential to a Bible and ethics conversation fitted to our time. So, for instance, several treatments are those of persons and communities seeking enhanced human moral responsibility in light of the deep human imprint on all of life. Consequently, these treatments illumine not only on-the-ground Bible and ethics exchange; they also show the weighty consequences that follow from shifts in ethical method and content together with ways of approaching and appropriating Scripture. Practice discloses theory.

LAUDATO SI'

Consider the June 18, 2015, papal encyclical of Pope Francis, *Laudato Si': On Care for Our Common Home*. Two years in the making, its themes signaled the priorities in place from the very moment the pope, for the first time in Roman Catholic history, took the papal name of Francis. At his election, he told six thousand journalists,

"Francis was a man of poverty, who loved and protected creation." Concern for the poor and for creation, themselves strong biblical themes, would be the central themes of his papacy. They clearly became central to the encyclical as it was prepared in dialogue with scientists, economists, diplomats, and business and labor leaders, together with members of Roman Catholic religious orders, theologians, and ethicists. It was immediately hailed as one of the most important statements of the Vatican in recent years. Not least, and unlike numerous encyclicals before it, the audience was not only the Catholic faithful; the encyclical was consciously directed to all peoples of the planet.[1]

How does *Laudato Si'* engage Bible and ethics in a new conversation? Not to be missed is that this pope is the first from the Global South. He personifies what we noted in the introduction—the shift in the center of gravity of Christianity and the ecumenical church away from the Euro-Western world. Likewise, the central themes of his papacy—the poor and the Earth—were carried to Rome from his years as "the Bishop of the Poor" or "the Bishop of the Slums" in Buenos Aires where he, then Jorge Mario Bergoglio, SJ, experienced firsthand that environmental and social deterioration were joined at the hip and affected vulnerable peoples most of all. The cry of the poor and the cry of the Earth were, and are, recurring cries of the churches of the South.

Not to be missed, either, is that this encyclical has, as one of its backstories, Latin American liberation theology. It is arguably the first liberation theology encyclical. That matters not only for its key themes but for its sources. Among them is the vital role of the Bible. For decades, many of the faithful have gathered in "base communities" in Central and South America for Bible study together in light of the most pressing issues their communities faced. Sometimes study and reflection were led by priests, sometimes by lay leaders. But always Scripture as read and interpreted together intersected lived life, above all at the points of concrete suffering and with a view to overcoming it.

The encyclical belongs to the new conversation of Bible and ethics.

That said, the encyclical does not change the overarching question for ethics. That is always and everywhere the same: how are we to

---

1. The encyclical, together with a helpful introduction and guide, is available as *On Care for Our Common Home: Laudato Si'*, ed. Sean McDonagh (Maryknoll, NY: Orbis, 2016).

live? But the question is answered differently in different traditions. The pope grounds his response in two prominent moral norms of Roman Catholic social thought: the dignity of the human person and the common good. These norms frame how Catholics attentive to their own moral tradition "do ethics."

Yet, as soon as the pope surfaces these norms, he gives them a methodological reach and expanded content they have not enjoyed in official Catholic teaching and practice. The pope is keenly aware that while he draws on prior Catholic teaching, he is taking it to a different level and, by virtue of issuing an encyclical, giving it greater authority. (An encyclical is official, authoritative church teaching.)

The pope makes these changes in the face of "the cry of the earth and the cry of the poor,"[2] knit together as planetary creation in jeopardy at human hands. Facing this dual "cry," Francis broadens the first norm, the dignity of the human person, to include the dignity of all creaturely life. In making his case for this—what ethics calls the reasoning process of "justification"—the pope cites the German bishops: where not only humans but other creatures are concerned, "we can speak of the priority of *being* over that of *being useful*."[3]

"Being useful" reflects the ethic Francis names "a distorted anthropocentrism." Here nature's value is only as a means to human ends. This is the wholly utilitarian morality of the modern industrial world. Such anthropocentrism is the bounded content assumed in the first of our two graphs of moral responsibility, the smaller circle of responsibility resting inside the larger circle of the ecosphere.[4]

The priority of "being," by contrast, accords the natural world an intrinsic or inherent value of its own, apart from its human use. "Being" finds "dignity" present throughout the ecosphere, human society included. This is our second graph, where the circle of human responsibility matches the circle of human consequences across the whole community of life.

In a way that parallels the extension of dignity, the pope's second norm, the common human good, is enhanced to include the planetary good. Care for the planet as "our common home" entails moral responsibility for the primal elements themselves—earth (soil), air, fire (energy), water. Indeed, no human good is even possible apart

2. Francis, *Laudato Si'*, para. 49.
3. Ibid., para. 69.
4. Ibid.

from the health of these planetary goods. "Being" is *necessarily prior to* "being useful." Independent of "being," "being useful" is impossible.

With these methodological extensions, the core concern of Roman Catholic social thought, namely, social justice, is itself transformed. Social justice becomes creation justice. As creation justice, the content and foci of justice shift so as to align with expanded human responsibility for the endangered planet. "Being" as planetary creation and its health has moral priority over "being useful" (to human society) as the basis of justice. "Being" as "useful" for achieving human good is vital, of course, but it is necessarily derivative of justice for the planet ("being").

Attention to the core biblical norm of "neighbor love" shows similar results. Through most of Christian history, "neighbor" is the "nigh one," the person at hand, literally "the nearby farmer." The neighbor almost invariably is a human neighbor. Yet in the Hebrew Bible, "neighbor" stretches to include not only the ancestors and those "unto the third and fourth generation" (Exod 20:5) but the land as well, since the origin, journey, and destiny of the people of God is indissolubly linked to the land and its life. When the land and its life flourishes, so do the people. When it languishes, "the gladness of the earth is banished" and "the merry-hearted sigh" (Isa 24:11, 7). When human violence issues in the shedding of blood as Cain kills Abel, *'ădāmâ* (earth, topsoil), from which *'ădām* is created, cries out (Gen 4:10). Indeed, Hebrew has no set-apart word for humans as a separate species. Nor do we have a "day" of our own in the first creation story (Gen 1:1–2:4). We are created with the rest of the mammals, all from *'ădāmâ* and all with the same breath of life. As if to underscore this, the very first of the covenants in the Hebrew Bible, one called "everlasting," is between God and "every living creature of all flesh that is on the earth" (Gen 9:16). The papal encyclical has it right: "Clearly, the Bible has no place for a tyrannical anthropocentrism unconcerned for other creatures."[5] They are neighbors who are kin.

Still, it is a further stretch when, even earlier than the German bishops, theologian H. Richard Niebuhr treats "neighbor" in the biblical and Christian tradition as "all that participates in being." The neighbor is "the near one and the far one; the one removed from me by distances in time and space, in convictions and loyalties. [The neighbor] is man and he is angel and he is animal and inorganic being, all

5. Ibid., 68.

that participates in being."[6] This is the neighbor in a million guises as the articulated form of creation across time and space, the cosmic Word incarnated as creaturely *sarx* ("flesh") (John 1:14). It is also the neighbor to whom justice is due as creation justice. Justice, in quest of the common good of the land and its peoples, and pursued in a way that respects inherent dignity, is the fullest possible flourishing of creation. Neighbor love expressed as creation justice yields the flourishing of creation.

Yet our primary topic is not neighbor love and justice. It is how the timely enhancement of specific moral norms in light of present planetary challenges—the dignity of the human person, the common good, and the meaning of neighbor and neighbor love—draws upon and affects the reading of both Christian ethics and the Bible.

Take a closer look at the dynamic. The papal encyclical, as a matter of conscious ethical method, undertakes the *descriptive* task of Christian ethics in chapter 1. That chapter, entitled "What is Happening to Our Common Home," answers the first question of ethics. Namely, "What is?" or "What is going on?" The pope writes:

> Theological and philosophical reflections on the situation of humanity and the world can sound tiresome and abstract, unless they are grounded in a fresh analysis of our present situation, which is in many ways unprecedented in the history of humanity. So, before considering how faith brings new incentives and requirements with regard to the world of which we are a part, I will briefly turn to what is happening to our common home.[7]

Then follows attention to "pollution and climate change," "the issue of water," "loss of biodiversity," "decline in the quality of human life and the breakdown of society," and "global inequality," together with "weak responses" to them and "a variety of opinions" about them. Francis's conclusion is that, whatever the responses, one thing is clear: our home is "falling into serious disrepair," "the present world system is certainly unsustainable from a number of points of view," and there are evident signs that we are reaching "a breaking point."[8]

Following the descriptive analysis, the attention shifts to constructive and normative response: What could and should be done? On

6. H. Richard Niebuhr, *The Purpose of the Church and Its Ministry: Reflections on the Aims of Theological Education* (New York: Harper, 1956), 38.

7. Francis, *Laudato Si'*, para. 17.

8. Ibid., para. 61.

what grounds, drawing on what sources and resources? Where do we turn for guidance? So chapter 2 of the encyclical is entitled "The Gospel of Creation." An initial section makes the case for "The Light Offered by Faith." It includes what every ethical method does—it draws upon sources, whether named or not. Good method identifies the sources of the individual's or the community's constructive and normative responses. "If we are truly concerned to develop an ecology capable of remedying the damage we have done," the pope writes, "no branch of the sciences and no form of wisdom can be left out, and that includes religion and the language peculiar to it."[9]

The language "peculiar to [religion]" is the next section, notably titled "The Wisdom of the Biblical Accounts." The Bible is a lead source for wisdom that underlines the nature of all creation as "very good" (Gen 1:31) and the "infinite dignity" of all human beings, conceived, as humans are, "in the heart of God." Biblical wisdom speaks as well of "the rupture of sin" to the "three fundamental and closely intertwined relationships" that ground all human life, the relationships "with God, with our neighbor, and with the earth itself."[10] Those ruptured relationships are then described, but now with a turn to what can and should be done (or should not be). The above-mentioned rejection of a "tyrannical anthropocentrism" is included, as is the German bishops' teaching that "being" has priority over "being useful." A further gleaning of wisdom is that "these ancient [biblical] stories, full of symbolism, bear witness to a conviction which we today share, that everything is interconnected, and that genuine care for our own lives and our relationships with nature is inseparable from fraternity, justice and faithfulness to others."[11] Yet another wisdom teaching is the tenet of faith that "the God who liberates and saves is the same God who created the universe, and these two divine ways of acting are intimately and inseparably connected."[12] Not least is faith's tenacious hold on hope—"All it takes is one good person to restore hope!"[13]—and on the biblical conviction that "injustice is not invincible."[14]

In short, even an abbreviated treatment of the papal encyclical demonstrates not only the presence of conscious Christian ethical

9. Ibid., para. 63.
10. Ibid., para. 66.
11. Ibid., para. 70.
12. Ibid., para. 73.
13. Ibid., para. 71.
14. Ibid., para. 74.

analysis but how changes in ethical method matter in essential ways. We are also shown that the Bible matters in essential, rather than marginal, ways.

BERRY AND MCKIBBEN

How does this play out elsewhere? Staying with those intent on an expanded moral universe as the shape of new human responsibility, we find several exemplars. For these figures, too, the Bible is a crucial source.

Wen Stephenson's *What We're Fighting for* Now *Is Each Other: Dispatches from the Front Lines of Climate Justice* is his quest for a viable spirituality and morality to face down the injustice of global warming. A chapter of his "dispatches" is entitled "Prophets."

Its epigraphs are two.

The first is from Bill McKibben's Earth Sunday sermon of April 28, 2013, at the Riverside Church, New York City.

> We're called not to charity, or maybe even to justice—the scale of the injustice is so enormous it's hard to imagine ever rectifying it. What we're called to is something even more basic: solidarity. . . . Our goal must be to make real the Gospel, with its injunction to love our neighbors. Not to drown them, not to sicken them, not to make it impossible for them to grow crops. But to love them.

The second draws from Wendell Berry's 1973 poem, "Manifesto: The Mad Farmer Liberation Front."

> Love the Lord.
> Love the world. Work for nothing.
> Take all that you have and be poor.
> Love somebody who does not deserve it.
> . . . .
> As soon as the generals and the politicos
> can predict the motions of your mind,
> lose it. Leave it as a sign
> to mark the false trail, the way
> you didn't go. Be like the fox
> who makes more tracks than necessary
> some in the wrong direction.
> Practice resurrection.

Stephenson digs into Berry's writings. While Berry is sometimes linked with the environmental movement, that is too narrow. Berry's life transcends environmentalism. It's "about community and love of neighbor, which means finding the right balance between human culture and the rest of creation."[15]

The 1979 essay "The Gift of Good Land" illustrates this. There, Berry consciously sets out to make "a Biblical argument for ecological and agricultural responsibility."[16] In doing so, he develops "a scriptural and moral connection between *land* and *community* and *justice*,"[17] exactly the nexus of responsibility in the Hebrew Bible. (It's McKibben's triad as well.)

Stephenson summarizes Berry's ethics in "Good Land." Good land is a gift, "a divine gift to a *fallen* people." It is not a reward—this people does not *deserve* the land. Nor do they truly *own* it. Theirs is not possession. It is tenancy. That tenancy, called "stewardship," brings with it three conditions. The first is that the tenants be "faithful, grateful, and humble," remembering that the land, like life itself, "is a gift." The second condition is that tenants "be neighborly. They must be just, kind to one another, generous to strangers, honest in trading, etc." Stephenson cites Berry at length here, adding his own emphasis.

> These are social virtues, but, as they invariably do, they have ecological and agricultural implications. For the land is described as an "inheritance": *the community is understood to exist not just in space, but also in time.* One lives in the neighborhood, not just of those who now live "next door," but of the dead who have bequeathed the land to the living, and of the unborn to whom the living will in turn bequeath it. But we can have no direct behavioral connection to those who are not yet alive. *The only neighborly thing we can do for them is to preserve their inheritance:* we must take care, among other things, of the land, which is never a possession, but an inheritance to the living, as it will be to the unborn.[18]

---

15. Wen Stephenson, *What We're Fighting for* Now *Is Each Other: Dispatches from the Front Lines of Climate Justice* (Boston: Beacon, 2015), 66.

16. Stephenson, 67, is here citing from Berry, "The Gift of Good Land," as published in Norman Wirzba's edited collection of Berry essays, *Art of the Commonplace* (Berkeley, CA: Counterpoint, 2002), 293–304.

17. This is Stephenson's summation, *What We're Fighting*, 67.

18. From Wendell Berry, "The Good Land," cited in Stephenson, *What We're Fighting*, 68. "The Good Land" is available in several places. The original, from 1979, is in a collection published in 1981. See Wendell Berry, *The Gift of Good Land: Further Essays Cultural and Agricul-*

The third condition continues the second, now with duties toward the land itself. "Good husbandry" is the imperative. What the land produces, stewards may rightly use, but above all "the fertility of the fields" must be preserved.[19]

In Stephenson's reading, Berry's scriptural and moral exegesis in the 1979 essay points to "nothing less than an ethical source, a deep spiritual wellspring, of *environmental* and *social* and *intergenerational justice*."[20]

This is Christian ethics in the making. The attentive reader will recognize method at work even in this brief account, with Scripture essential to it. The land is a gift and an inheritance; there are specific social virtues and practices of neighbor-love commensurate with that, as well as duties toward the land itself. Together these fund the environmental, social, and intergenerational justice of genuine community.

The essay does not end there. Berry, as "a person who takes the Gospel seriously,"[21] speaks in the manner of the prophet that McKibben says he is.

> It is possible—as our experience in *this* good land shows—to exile ourselves from Creation, and to ally ourselves with the principle of destruction. . . . If we are willing to pollute the air—to harm the elegant creature known as the atmosphere—by that token we are willing to harm all creatures that breathe, ourselves and our children among them. There is no begging off or "trading off." You cannot affirm the power plant and condemn the smokestack, or affirm the smoke and condemn the cough.[22]

Berry knows, of course, that we cannot "live harmlessly." But that hardly suffices as justification to continue a way of life rooted in "corporate industrialism"[23] that systematically breaks our covenant with creation and Creator.

Stephenson's own conclusion is that climate change requires *community* and that "there can be no true community without love of

tural (Berkeley, CA: Counterpoint, 1981). Stephenson is using the essay as published in Wirzba, *Art of the Commonplace*, 293–304.

19. Berry, "The Good Land," cited in Stephenson, *What We're Fighting*, 68.

20. Stephenson, *What We're Fighting*, 68 (italics are Stephenson's).

21. Ibid., 66.

22. Berry cited in Stephenson, *What We're Fighting*, 69.

23. This phrase is from Berry's 2012 Jefferson Lecture at the National Endowment for the Humanities, "It All Turns on Affection," here cited in Stephenson, *What We're Fighting*, 70.

neighbor—that is, with justice, social and generational, in place and in time."[24] Such is his takeaway from Berry's scripturally sourced ethic.[25]

A further example of retooled Christian ethics has already been mentioned: Bill McKibben.

McKibben may be today's best-known environmental activist (unless Pope Francis is also viewed in that way). Together with students at Middlebury College, McKibben founded 350.org, itself a leader in the international movement to curb carbon emissions and organize populist pressure on world leaders to reach global agreement. 350.org also led campaigns to shut down the Keystone XL pipeline and disinvest from fossil fuels while urging reinvestment in renewables. McKibben's July 19, 2012, article in *Rolling Stone*, "Global Warming's Terrifying New Math," showed that the fossil-fuel industry had five times more carbon in its proven reserves than scientists say dare be burned if planetary apocalypse is to be held at bay. This means that, short of numerous silver bullet technologies coming on line quickly, 80 percent of the known fossil fuels will need to be left where they are—in the ground. McKibben's "New Math" piece has been the most read of any *Rolling Stone* feature and one of the most influential articles published anywhere.

McKibben's work began decades earlier, however. While still in his twenties, he authored the first book on global warming and climate change. *The End of Nature* (1989) was more than a report on available science, however. It was "a philosophical essay" and "a piece of lay theology" (McKibben's words),[26] which argued that something of "world and worldview-altering significance" was happening,[27] namely, the end of nature as we have conceived nature and lived in relationship with it.

An idea, a relationship, can go extinct, just like an animal or a plant. The

24. Stephenson, *What We're Fighting*, 69.
25. The resonance of Berry's work with deep biblical understanding and good theology has not gone unnoticed. See his influence on the writings of Ellen Davis and Norman Wirzba, both at the Duke University Divinity School. Davis is the Amos Regan Kearns Professor of Bible and Practical Theology. The foreword to her *Scripture, Culture, and Agriculture: An Agrarian Reading of the Bible* is written by Wendell Berry. Wirzba is professor of Theology, Ecology, and Agrarian Studies. He has edited works of Berry's essays. Berry wrote the foreword to Wirzba's *Living the Sabbath: Discovering the Rhythms of Rest and Delight*.
26. As McKibben described it in his sermon, "God's Taunt," at the Riverside Church, New York, April 28, 2013.
27. Stephenson, *What We're Fighting*, 60.

idea in this case is "nature," the separate and wild province, the world apart from man to which he adapted, under whose rules he was born and died. In the past, we spoiled and polluted parts of that nature, inflicted environmental "damage." . . . We never thought that we had wrecked nature. Deep down, we never really thought we could.[28]

Nature's life apart from ours, its independence, has been its meaning. That is now gone, and humankind collectively is the single most powerful force *of* nature itself. Well before anyone ventured "the Anthropocene" to name this emerging age, McKibben argued its reality and danger. We have effected a civilization-altering relationship for which we are not prepared. The basic "think withs" of our relationship to the rest of the community of life are inadequate and at risk of becoming irrelevant. So is our conventional sense of our own responsibility.

As McKibben himself struggled for the right understanding, idea, and words to match this new reality, he composed a little work on Job. Titled *The Comforting Whirlwind*, its attention is to Job and God's single longest soliloquy in the Hebrew Bible. Job is on the receiving end of a voice out of a whirlwind or tornado that McKibben calls "God's taunt." "Where were you when I laid the foundation of the earth?" "Have you commanded the morning since your days began, and caused the dawn to know its place?" "Have you entered into the springs of the sea, or walked in the recesses of the deep?" "Who has cut a channel for the torrents of rain and a way for the thunderbolt?" "Can you bind the chains of the Pleiades?"[29] On it goes for three chapters, all of them mocking the size and pretense of the human presence in the cosmos.

Job is from the Bible's wisdom literature. And, indeed, in that corpus, humanity's stature in the universe merits little attention. While the very purpose of wisdom is for human instruction, that we might live long and well on the land, there is, as biblical scholar William Brown notes, no strong anthropic principle here. That is, the universe is not finely tuned or designed to yield hominids and the line of *Homo sapiens*. If anything, creation's principle is "sophic" (from the Greek word for wisdom, *sophia*). The cosmos is "finely and firmly constructed for Wisdom's sake, for her growth, delight, and play,

28. Bill McKibben, *The End of Nature* (New York: Random House, 1989), 41, cited in Stephenson, *What We're Fighting*, 60.
29. Questions excerpted from Job 38.

far beyond humanity's. The cosmos exists in delightful intelligibility,"[30] whether or not *Homo sapiens* is present. "Wisdom has two partners: God and creation."[31] Our kind appears within that frame, a single, lovely detail in a distant corner, a twig on a great tree, a dot among the galaxies that requires a big arrow with the words, "You are here."[32]

While *The Comforting Whirlwind: God, Job and Scale of Creation* appeared in 2005, *The End of Nature*, written sixteen years earlier, had already anticipated "God's taunt." There, McKibben writes: "God seems to be insisting that we are not the center of the universe, that he is quite happy if it rains where there are no people—that God is quite happy with the places where there are no people, a radical departure from our most ingrained notions."[33]

"God's taunt" appears again as the Earth Sunday sermon at the Riverside Church from which Stephenson's epigraph, cited above, is taken. But now McKibben's point is quite another—not our miniscule size in the far-flung universe but our huge presence on the planet. Taking the liberty of both the preacher and the biblical prophet, McKibben brings earlier texts to bear in a new way on the present moment. He begins with the familiar recollection of Job, chapter 38 and following.

[God's soliloquy] is, on the one hand, beautiful—a tour of the vast natural world, from the morning stars to the gazelle, from the edge of the ocean to the eagle's nest. But it is delivered in a sarcastic, taunting voice, as if God is annoyed at having been bothered for an explanation. If you're so smart, he tells Job, where do you keep the thunderstorms? Can you whistle up a blizzard? Do you tell the proud waves, here you shall break and no further.

And Job, of course, has to answer as all mortals. No, he says, that's your department. I can't make the weather. You are big and I am small. Can I sit down now?[34]

But then things take a turn. The sermon's next line is: "Or rather, Job

30. W. Brown, *Seven Pillars*, 169.
31. Ibid., 176.
32. This draws from Rasmussen, *Earth-Honoring Faith*, 354–56.
33. Stephenson, *What We're Fighting*, 62, citing McKibben, *End of Nature*, 76.
34. Bill McKibben, "God's Taunt," Sermon at the Riverside Church, New York City, April 28, 2013, on the texts, Job 38:1–11 and Matt 19:16–22.

has to answer as all mortals up until our time. Because all of a sudden we have gotten rather large."[35]

McKibben then revisits that "vast natural world," this time detailing the changes wrought at human hands. The "rather large" presence of modern mortals is actually huge—a huge human world on a suddenly small planet.

But Job 38:1–11 is only the first of McKibben's sermon texts. His second is the parable of the rich young ruler in Luke 18:18–30. Approaching Jesus to ask how he should live, he is told he should sell what he has, give it to the poor, and follow Jesus. This sends the rich young ruler away "sorrowful, for he had great possessions." McKibben, again in the manner of prophetic example for the present, turns the tale to further describe what is happening to Earth, this time at the hands of the fossil fuel industry. He finishes with the summary comment of Exxon's CEO, Rex Tillerson, in an interview with Charlie Rose, "My philosophy is to make money." "That's an apt summation of too much of our society," McKibben responds. Then follow the words included in Stephenson's epigraph: "But here, in this place [church], we stand in some counterpoint. Our goal must be to make real the Gospel, with its injunction to love our neighbors. Not to drown them, not to sicken them, not to make it impossible for them to grow our crops. But to love them."[36]

The final paragraphs are these.

This divestment campaign alone will not win the fight to guard creation; we will need many other fronts. Some of us will have to go back to jail; others with an engineering bent will have to build the new renewable infrastructure. We'll need to push Congress for a price on carbon—but that won't get done till we've weakened the power of the fossil fuel industry. There's work for all, though it comes with no guarantee that we will win. We have waited a long time to get started and the momentum of physics is large. Having lost the Arctic we have no room for complacency.

But we do have room for faith. The pleasure always of bringing this message to church comes from the helpful feeling one's allowed to summon, a feeling one can't rightfully raise in a science classroom or a policy think tank. Here we're allowed to believe that if we do all that we can—if we best the rich young ruler and force ourselves to think beyond our bankbooks—then God, even that grumpy and sarcastic God of Job's

35. Ibid.
36. Ibid.

whirlwind, may still be willing to meet us halfway. Let us pray that that is the case, and then let us get to work.[37]

McKibben, like Wendell Berry and the pope, has made every effort to spur an alternative to the dangerous course we are on. As he, and they, answer the basic question of ethics, How, then, are we to live? he, too, engages the fundamental questions and tasks of Christian ethics—the descriptive, constructive, and normative; what is, what could be, and what should be. And he does so in ways that display an ethical method that is biblically sourced and informed.

This brings to a close our discussion of three figures engaging Bible and ethics up close—Pope Francis, Wendell Berry, and Bill McKibben. The examples are admittedly a skewed set. All are figures making the effort to find their way to a different way of life than the one that brings climate change. And all are figures for whom Scripture matters in that cause.

The next examples pertain to other issues. The same intention holds, however—namely, to show the presence and importance of Christian ethics consciously engaged with Scripture, whatever the issue as undertaken by whomever.

THE EVANGELICAL SOUTH

Two examples follow. One is from the Bible Belt South of the United States. The second is from the Global South, in northeastern Brazil.

EXPANDED DEMOCRACY

The first example draws from a momentous chapter in US, and even world, history, remembered as the Civil Rights Movement of the 1950s and 1960s.

Yet "the Civil Rights Movement" is a misnomer. From the beginning, it was a black-led people's movement for the expansion of political, social, and economic democracy in America. Arguably its high point, the March on Washington of August 28, 1963, was not the March on Washington for Civil Rights. It was, word for word, the March on Washington for Jobs and Freedom. "Jobs and Free-

37. Ibid.

dom" includes civil rights but was, from the very outset, intentionally broader.

This is immediately evident in Martin Luther King's fabled "I Have a Dream" speech. King, noting that the huge crowd was gathered in the shadow of the Lincoln Memorial, begins with the "great beacon of hope" that was the Emancipation Proclamation of 1863. Then, without pause, he turns to describe reality a century later.

> One hundred years later, the Negro still is not free; one hundred years later, the life of the Negro is still sadly crippled by the manacles of segregation and the chains of discrimination; one hundred years later, the Negro lives on a lonely island of poverty in the midst of a vast ocean of material prosperity; one hundred years later, the Negro is still languishing in the corners of American society and finds himself in exile in his own land.[38]

Civil rights were essential, and many died for them in the course of the movement. But political, social, and economic democracy was more. To those who asked, "When will you be satisfied?" King replies

> We can never be satisfied as long as the Negro is the victim of the unspeakable horrors of police brutality. . . . We cannot be satisfied as long as the Negro's basic mobility is from a smaller ghetto to a larger one. . . . We can never be satisfied as long as our children are stripped of their selfhood and robbed of their dignity by signs stating "for whites only." We cannot be satisfied as long as a Negro in Mississippi cannot vote and a Negro in New York believes he has nothing for which to vote. No, we are not satisfied, and will not be satisfied until justice rolls down like waters and righteousness life a mighty stream.[39]

The movement to expand democracy was national and not limited to the South. But its initial battles, and many of its most decisive ones, were there. And while it evolved as broadly ecumenical and interfaith, the predominant presence of the black churches, many of them evangelical and Pentecostal, meant that it was a Bible-saturated movement from the beginning. Biblical stories and the cultural memory funded by them were sources that gave the movement its identity, energy, and direction. Not by coincidence are the volumes of the acclaimed trilogy of the movement's history

38. King, *Testament of Hope*, 217.
39. Ibid., 218–19. The last phrase is a quotation of Amos 5:24.

titled *Parting the Waters*, *Pillar of Fire*, and *At Canaan's Edge* (allusions to Exod 14:21–23; Exod 13:21–22, 14:24; and Deut 34:1–5, respectively). Nor by coincidence is *Bearing the Cross* the title of a major biography of Martin Luther King Jr.[40]

This Bible and ethics drama was hardly this preacher's doing alone, however. The black churches King and many others mobilized had for centuries drawn from Scripture, the Christian OT and the NT Gospels above all, as the most important sources for an identity and a Christianity that stood in stark contrast to the identity and Christianity of their owners and bosses.

Consider the black sacred music that initially sprang from slave utterances in the secret "hush harbors."[41] These spirituals and chants for deliverance came to number in the hundreds, and ranged from voicing the slave experience ("I've been 'buked an' I've been scorned," "Nobody knows the trouble I've seen, nobody knows but Jesus") to soulful songs of solace ("There is a balm in Gilead," "Are you burdened, worn and weary, Just tell Jesus, tell Him all," "Sweet, sweet spirit") to the underground railroad and yearning for freedom ("Hush, hush, somebody's callin' my name"; "Go down, Moses, tell ol' Pharaoh to let my people go"; "Deep river") to death and heaven ("Free at last, free at last, thank God Almighty I'm free at last," "Swing low, sweet chariot"). Some are folk songs ("Jesus in the Morning, Jesus in the noon time, Jesus when the sun goes down"), some are praise songs ("Blessed assurance"), some are pleas for holding on and holding out ("Keep me from sinking down, O Lord, O Lord, keep me from sinking down," "Precious Lord, take my hand"), some are songs of conversion ("Ah tol' Jesus it would be all right if He changed mah name") or songs of courage and resolve ("I shall not be moved, Like a tree planted by the water, I shall not be moved"). *But not a one is without biblical allusion or story*.[42] The music, piety, lore, and wis-

40. See Taylor Branch, *Parting the Waters: America in the King Years, 1954–63* (New York: Simon & Schuster, 1989); Taylor Branch, *Pillar of Fire: America in the King Years, 1963–65* (New York: Simon & Schuster, 1998); Taylor Branch, *At Canaan's Edge: America in the King Years, 1965–68* (New York: Simon & Schuster, 2006); David J. Garrow, *Bearing the Cross: Martin Luther King, Jr., and the Southern Christian Leadership Conference* (New York: William Morrow, 1986).

41. See the discussion of these as "moral haven" in chapter 9 of this volume.

42. See Howard Thurman, *Deep River and the Negro Spiritual Speaks of Life and Death* (Richmond, IN: Friends United Press, 1975); and Black Catholic Hymnal Committee, *Lead Me, Guide Me: The African American Catholic Hymnal* (Chicago: GIA Publications, 1987).

dom of millions of blacks cannot be fathomed apart from the Good Book as formative of their character, conduct, and culture.

What King and the Southern Christian Leadership Conference accomplished, together with a plethora of other predominately black organizations, was to awaken and channel the reflex morality embedded in this religious and cultural legacy into the battle for social, political, and economic equality and against segregation. As "the only consistent tradition of prophetic ministry in America,"[43] the black social gospel joined the old-time religion of the slave quarters and, with middle-class black leadership, tapped the long-nurtured ethos of the black churches to empower the struggles of the black masses.

Rarely has the prophetic-liberative tradition of the Bible, together with the story of Jesus and his passion, entered the public square with such force as it did in the Civil Rights *cum* Democracy Movement. Moral ends accomplished by moral means, as funded and framed by a biblically saturated spirituality, was its hallmark. Without this spirituality, the movement to realize democracy would likely have been stillborn, had it been conceived at all.

In September 1954, at age twenty-five, King began his pastorate at the Dexter Avenue Baptist Church in Montgomery, Alabama. His wife, Coretta (Scott), had completed her studies at the Oberlin Conservatory of Music in June, and King could meet his one remaining PhD requirement—writing his dissertation—anywhere. Little did he and Coretta, newly pregnant with their first child, know that in the next year he would be thrown into what would become a prime catalyst sparking the Civil Rights/Democracy Movement, the Montgomery Bus Boycott of 1955–56, set off when Rosa Parks refused to move to the back of the bus and was arrested for it (no black was permitted to sit parallel with a white).[44]

King's later recounting of the boycott, "An Experiment in Love," goes directly to our focus on the Bible for "witness and practice."[45]

King had already taken interest in the philosophy of nonviolent resistance, or noncooperation and passive resistance, as it was also named. But none of those phrases were heard in the first days of

---

43. See James Washington's introduction in King, *Testament of Hope*, xiv. What will certainly stand as the definitive exposition of the black social gospel has been undertaken by Gary Dorrien; the first two of three volumes are *The New Abolition: W. E. B. Du Bois and the Black Social Gospel* (New Haven: Yale University Press, 2015) and *Breaking White Supremacy: Martin Luther King Jr. and the Black Social Gospel* (New Haven: Yale University Press, 2018).

44. Garrow, *Bearing the Cross*, 11.

45. Hence the title of this chapter.

the protest and boycott. "The phrase most often heard was 'Christian love,'" he writes, and it "was the Sermon on the Mount, rather than a doctrine of passive resistance, that initially inspired the Negroes of Montgomery to dignified social action. It was Jesus of Nazareth that stirred the Negroes to protest with the creative weapon of love."[46] So while most of "the Negroes of Montgomery" "did not believe in nonviolence as a philosophy of life,"[47] they were willing to trust their leaders and try the technique of nonviolence as an expression of Christian love that might address the crisis in race relations.

In due course, Mohandas Gandhi, whom King called "the little brown saint of India,"[48] did become a household name. Yet even as nonviolent resistance developed, it was Christ who "furnished the spirit and motivation, while Gandhi furnished the method."[49] Together, Jesus and Gandhi supplied the power with which blacks walked long distances, month after month, for almost a year, before integrated bus service was negotiated.

Inspired by leaders like Benjamin Mays, King tutored himself further with Gandhi's writings and came to understand Gandhi's *satyagraha* as a profoundly significant way to embody Christian love as collective nonviolent power. (*Satya* means truth that equals love, and *graha* is force: thus, *satyagraha* is truth-force or love-force). Nonetheless, even more than his study of *satyagraha*, it was the day-by-day experience of the boycott that clarified King's thinking about the Sermon on the Mount as the practical enactment of Christian love. (Perhaps not coincidentally, the Hindu Gandhi, too, embraced the Sermon on the Mount and credited it as one of the most influential bodies of teachings for his life.)[50]

This was no sentimental love. Called *agapē* in NT Greek, this was a "neighbor-regarding concern for others" and "community-creating love." Morally, it did not distinguish between friends and enemies; rather, it placed all persons in the same moral framework and eschewed double standards.

Nor does *agapē* love "stop at the first mile, but it goes the second

46. From "An Experiment in Love," excerpted in King, *Testament of Hope*, 16. The excerpt is from King's *Stride toward Freedom: The Montgomery Story* (New York: Harper & Row, 1958).
47. King, *Testament of Hope*, 17.
48. Ibid.
49. Ibid.
50. See Jeremy Holtom, "Gandhi's Interpretation of the Sermon on the Mount," in *The Oxford Handbook of the Reception History of the Bible*, ed. Michael Lieb, Emma Mason, Jonathan Roberts, and Christopher Rowland (Oxford: Oxford University Press, 2011).

mile to restore community."[51] "The cross," King continues, "is the eternal expression of the length to which God will go in order to restore broken community. The resurrection is a symbol of God's triumph over all the forces that seek to block community. The Holy Spirit is the continuing community creating reality that moves through history."[52] *Agapē* will have its way as power for inclusive community.

Then King invokes a vocabulary and cosmology that has been latent in the campaign: "If I meet hate with hate, I become depersonalized, because *creation* is so designed that my personality can only be fulfilled in the context of community."[53] In a word, segregation and inequality *defy creation*. That is their grave error and sin. Nonviolence and *agapē* love, by contrast, "means a recognition of the fact that all life is interrelated . . . humanity is involved in a single process."[54]

The "Letter from Birmingham Jail" (1963) would put it famously: "We are caught in an inescapable network of mutuality, tied in a single garment of destiny. Whatever affects one directly affects all indirectly."[55] Such is the ecology of creation and community.

King's cosmology is even more expansive. "The universe is on the side of justice." That is the bend of its arc. "There is a creative force in this universe that works to bring the disconnected aspects of reality into a harmonious whole."[56]

This gives Christian believers and nonviolent resisters sustaining confidence. In their struggle for justice, they have "cosmic companionship."[57]

Please note: none of this is from a sermon. Nor is it from an exercise in theology and ethics. It's all from the account of a bus boycott. That's a fair measure of how broadly and deeply the Bible penetrates the witness and practice not only of King but of the movement more broadly. And if we carried the story from these beginnings in 1955 through the "Letter from Birmingham Jail" and the "I Have a Dream"

51. Matt 5:41.

52. King, *Testament of Hope*, 20.

53. Ibid. (italics ours).

54. Ibid.

55. Ibid., 290. The letter was published often but is best known as part of Martin Luther King Jr., *Why We Can't Wait* (New York: Harper & Row, 1964). "Letter from Birmingham Jail" also lists Jesus, Amos, Paul, Martin Luther, John Bunyan, Abraham Lincoln, and Thomas Jefferson as "extremists" who understood the ecology of just community and sacrificed for it.

56. Ibid., 20.

57. Ibid.

speech, and then, only two weeks after that, to the bombing of the 16th St. Baptist Church in Birmingham and the deaths of four little girls attending Sunday School, all in 1963, we would arrive at this same conclusion about the pervasive presence and power of Scripture. Just as we would if we continued to the eve of King's assassination in 1968. At the Bishop Charles Mason Temple in Memphis, Tennessee, headquarters of the largest African American Pentecostal denomination in the United States, the Church of God in Christ, King delivered his last and most apocalyptic words—"It is no longer a choice between violence and nonviolence in this world; it's nonviolence or nonexistence."[58] In that sermon, "I See the Promised Land,"[59] King invoked Moses atop Mount Nebo, peering into the promised land he would not live to see. King, after recalling his own journey, finished with these words.

> And then I got into Memphis. And some began to say the threats, or talk about the threats that were out. What would happen to me from some of our sick white brothers?
>
> Well, I don't know what will happen now. We've got some difficult days ahead. But it doesn't matter with me now. Because I've been to the mountaintop. And I don't mind. Like anybody, I would like to live a long life. Longevity has its place. But I'm not concerned about that now. I just want to do God's will. And He's allowed me to go up to the mountain. And I've looked over. And I've seen the promised land. I may not get there with you. But I want you to know tonight, that we, as a people will get to the promised land. And I'm happy, tonight. I'm not worried about anything. I'm not fearing any man. Mine eyes have seen the glory of the coming of the Lord.[60]

The next day, King was shot dead. He was in Memphis to join the garbage worker's strike ("I Am a Man" was their slogan). He, with other leaders on the Committee of 100, was also planning a second March on Washington, "The Poor People's Campaign." Announced in 1967, the focus was economic and human rights for poor Americans of diverse backgrounds. The Committee of 100 put forward an Economic Bill of Rights with five planks:

1. "A meaningful job at a living wage"

58. Ibid., 280.
59. Ibid., 279–86.
60. Ibid., 286.

2. "A secure and adequate income" for all those unable to find or do a job

3. "Access to land" for economic uses

4. "Access to capital" for poor people and minorities to promote their own businesses

5. Ability for ordinary people to "play a truly significant role" in the government

The Poor People's Campaign came to pass in May 1968, only a month after King's death, and extended into the summer. The heart of it was the three thousand person, six-week encampment on the Mall, called "Resurrection City."[61]

We should not lose the salient point. From beginning to end, from 1954 to 1968, the pattern is continuous and our conclusion the same. Namely, the black social gospel of the Exodus journey of freedom, the harsh judgment and inspiring vision of the eighth- and sixth-century BCE prophets ("Let justice roll down . . ."), and the life, death, and resurrection of Jesus Christ, together with the nonviolent practice learned from "the little brown saint of India," authorized and sustained the struggle for social, political, and economic democracy.

There were other authorities. And it's safe to say that rarely, if ever, does any successful, broad-based movement draw upon only one. For the black-led struggle, it was, beyond Scripture, the US Constitution and the Declaration of Independence. Invoked repeatedly, the point was that America had not lived up to its own values and now the promissory note had come due.

That was never proclaimed more powerfully, or anchored more appropriately, than in the "I Have a Dream" speech on the steps of the Lincoln Memorial at the March on Washington for Jobs and Freedom. One of the great feats of oratory in US history, it included a lengthy explanation for why tens of thousands had gathered.

> When the architects of our republic wrote the magnificent words of the Constitution and the Declaration of Independence, they were signing a promissory note to which every American was to fall heir. This note was the promise that all men, yes, black men as well as white men, would be

---

61. See Garrow, *Bearing the Cross*," 575–624. The work of the Committee of 100 can be found at "1968 Poor People's Campaign," Tipping Point North South, accessed April 5, 2017, http://tinyurl.com/ya6o6zon.

guaranteed the unalienable rights of life, liberty, and the pursuit of happiness.

It is obvious today that America has defaulted on this promissory note in so far as her citizens of color are concerned. Instead of honoring this sacred obligation, America has given the Negro people a bad check; a check which has come back marked "insufficient funds." We refuse to believe that there are insufficient funds in the great vaults of opportunity of this nation. And so we've come to cash this check, a check that will give us upon demand the riches of freedom and the security of justice.

We have also come to this hallowed spot to remind America of the fierce urgency of now. This is no time to engage in the luxury of cooling off or to take the tranquilizing drug of gradualism. Now is the time to make real the promises of democracy; now is the time to rise from the dark and desolate valley of segregation to the sunlit path of racial justice; now is the time to lift our nation from the quicksands of racial injustice to the solid rock of brotherhood; now is the time to make justice a reality for all God's children.[62]

"To make real the promises of democracy" and "to make justice a reality for all God's children" was the very raison d'être for the movement.

The cost was high—prison, beatings, suffering, and death, even death by assassination—and the work isn't finished. When King took the campaign north to Chicago, specifically to address economic disenfranchisement and inequality, he and the movement foundered on class in America, a barrier they did not breach. As The New Yorker put it, "King had begun to perceive that society tends to confine its indignation to injustices that can be attenuated without imperiling fundamental economic relationships."[63] So, fifty-plus years after the March on Washington for Jobs and Freedom, and the second March, the Poor People's Campaign, the work is not yet complete. Indeed, even the movement's victories enshrined in federal law (e.g., the Voting Rights Act) have been challenged anew.

All this said, there is little doubt of the power that the movement for expanded democracy and justice for all found in Scripture and in the nation's own founding documents.

62. King, Testament of Hope, 217–18.
63. Cited from Time Magazine, January 9, 2006, 51, in Rasmussen, Earth-Honoring Faith, 315.

FLOR DE MANACÁ

It's appropriate that our final example is also from the evangelical south, but this time the Global South, from northeast Brazil.

Biblical scholar Carlos Mesters started the Popular Reading of the Bible in 1970. Its interpretive method is captured by three elements: reality, Bible, community.

Women of the Pinheiro Baptist Church in the state of Alagoas formed a group to learn this method. They called themselves "Flor de Manacá" after the favorite flower of a revered matriarch in the church.

The women had a serious cause. In 2015, Alagoas was the state with the highest rate of murder of women in the northeast region.[64] But well before, and as long as people could remember, domestic violence had been endemic, though silenced.

Furthermore, 40 percent of the women in Brazil who told researchers they were victims of domestic violence belonged to the evangelical church of which Pinheiro Baptist was a part.[65] Here, the Bible had inestimable value but had been interpreted in ways that did not transgress the logic of patriarchy and its exercise of power and privilege. Gender inequality and violence against women were tacitly supported by biblical interpretation.

Flor de Manacá was determined to fight this domestic violence and chose to engage in the practice of biblical interpretation based on the reality-Bible-community triad of Carlos Mesters's Popular Reading of the Bible. Three questions led the way: What do you interpret? Why do you interpret? And how do you interpret?

The answer to the "what" question was: life. In the words of Odja Barros, the Baptist minister who followed the Popular Reading of the Bible process in the life of the Flor de Manacá, "The Bible did not enter into the lives of the women through the door of biblical authority, but through the door of personal and communal experience. The goal of reading the Bible was not to interpret the Bible, but to interpret their lives with the help of the Bible."[66] In a sense, their

---

64. Julio Jacobo Waiselfiz, "2015 | Homicídio de Mulheres no Brasil," Mapa da Violência, FLACSO Brasil, accessed March 17, 2017, http://tinyurl.com/y982gl9e.

65. Valeria Vilhena, *Uma Igreja sem Voz: Análise de gênero da violência doméstica entre mulheres evangélicas* (São Paulo: Fonte Editorial, 2011), 20.

66. All the materials in this account have been supplied by Pastor Odja Barros, who is a member of the Bible Study Center in Brazil (CEBI, Centro de Estudos Biblicos), an ecumenical

lives became the first book of the revelation of God, and the Bible facilitated the discovery of the word of God there. The effect was to remove patriarchy as the controlling logic and find, instead, the liberating presence of God in their lives and their daily struggles.

This was already to move into the second question, about why they engaged in this process of interpretation. Barros calls it "an ethics interpretation," meaning in this case that a new personal and communitarian ethic emerged among the women and men as the outcome of the transformation of their reality. Members told of their own experiences of violence and experienced solidarity with one another in the process. They in effect built a forum, a democratic public space, an *ekklēsia*, to use the early church's term, in which they discussed the impact and the import of the Scriptures for their lives.

The "how" of interpretation fit their reality. Bible study for the Flor de Manacá developed through a free sharing that included chants, prayers, celebrations, and parties. Symbolic and festive elements were an integral part of the interpretive process. As Barros explains, "the meaning of the Bible is not just an idea or message captured by objective reason; it is also a feeling, a consolation, a comfort felt with the heart, the senses, the emotions. Here the women interpret the Bible with their whole body, their thinking and their affections." Tensions and conflicts could arise, and did, but every effort was made to retain the *ekklēsia* as a safe space and a free space. "Now I see things differently" was not the uncommon result.

So what has happened in the ten years of Flor de Manacá and the Popular Reading of the Bible? Flor de Manacá has expanded beyond a Bible study group and become the Women's Ministry of the Church. The colors, symbols, and language of the group have been assimilated by others at Pinheiro Baptist Church, while the battle against the macho culture of gender inequality and violence has gone public, with recognition by the city and region. Within Pinheiro Baptist, a group adopting the methods of Flor de Manacá formed to battle racism, and an open dialogue on gay and lesbian issues has taken place, the outcome of which is that Pinheiro Baptist was the first Baptist church in Brazil to celebrate the full acceptance of LGBTQ members into its ministry. In short, what began as Bible study to help interpret women's lives in the face of widespread, even deadly,

center that focuses on equipping church communities to read the Bible from a liberation perspective. She was also a doctoral research student at Princeton Theological Seminary for 2017.

domestic violence ended up transforming not only gender relations but the way of being church in Alagoas State and Northeast Brazil. "Reality-Bible-community" describes more than Mesters's Popular Reading of the Bible.

CODA

In the two examples just discussed, strongly held views were in conflict with one another even though they were all biblically rooted and defended. Some of the conflicts were public, others were kept from view. Some were between communities—black and white, male and female—others were within.

It is hardly a surprise that conflicting views often match conflicting communities as they draw from the same sources for guidance. While we did not treat the use of Scripture by White Citizens' Councils, the Ku Klux Klan, state legislators, police, and other white opposition to the Civil Rights/Democracy Movement, it was frequently invoked. The "Letter from Birmingham Jail" was itself a response to nine Alabama clergy, all of them white, who published an open letter warning King that his nonviolent resistance would only incite further civil disturbances. They also urged that King and his allies allow the battle for integration to be settled in the courts.[67] Race divided, while both black and white citizens clutched the same Bibles.[68]

Pinheiro Baptist illustrates the conflict within a community and church. The congregation knew both patriarchal interpretation and liberative feminist interpretation, with the latter consciously set against the former.

While these battles of the Bible may seem regrettable, they are neither surprising nor uncommon. Nor should they be unexpected. It is the human condition on display, the same human condition Scripture itself displays and addresses.

Taking up Scripture for life, wherever and whenever it happens, will not escape that condition. So, if there is a conclusion to draw, it is this: it is vitally important that the reading and appropriation of

67. From the introduction by James Washington to "Letter from Birmingham Jail" in King, *Testament of Hope*, 289.

68. A massive, and perhaps definitive, account of white evangelicals in the United States is that of Frances FitzGerald, *The Evangelicals: The Struggle to Shape America* (New York: Simon & Schuster, 2017).

Scripture and of ethics, together with their conscious interplay, be critical, disciplined, self-aware, and accountable.

9.

The Church and the Moral Life

What is the place of the faith community itself in Christian ethics? What practical roles does it play, to form character and conduct? This chapter discusses five roles: the church as an agent of identity, of tradition, of discernment and deliberation, of action, and as a moral haven.

A COMMUNITY OF MORAL IDENTITY FORMATION

Morality is autobiographical but not solitary. It is, as noted earlier, ensemble work, the work of human communities.[1] Now we turn directly to the church as one of those communities and ask about its place.

There is no "app" for good moral judgment. It relies on a moral guidance system that is the long, slow work of moral identity formation. While a moral vision and common moral culture and ethos are necessary, they cannot suddenly be *willed* into existence, even when their necessity is recognized. They are social rather than genetic; they must be learned and passed along, generation after generation. A mature conscience and a moral vision to live by rely upon communities of character that have longevity. For Christians, that community is the church.

"Longevity" is not used lightly. Formed (and re-formed) moral identity takes time and a continuous effort. These are, by

1. See chapter 6, p. 112.

nature, protracted, the gift of one lifetime to the next. In a society enamored with technique and addicted to short timeframes, this intentional moral formation swims against the stream. So much of the harried, changing modern world, when faced with eco-social and moral challenges, adopts a problem/solution "fix"—usually a techno-logical, legal, economic, or martial fix. When we witness a serious case of public moral disorder—electoral campaigns that abandon truth-telling in the interests of winning at all costs, Wall Street insider trading and other cases of business collusion, violation of the public trust by office heads or their appointees, exorbitant legal and medical costs in a system of maldistributed services, inequality and the grow-ing disparity between the rich and the rest, loss of the common good in tandem with the pampering of private interests, and addiction to hedonistic consumerism—we tend to see the solution as some kind of "ethics fix." Codes of ethics are drawn up for professional groups, laws are drafted, ethics committees are appointed for public officeholders, new regulations are set for industry and the media, and rules are made for consumer and environmental protection. Or we reach for a solu-tion by assigning responsibility for moral education to certain insti-tutions—families, schools, and faith communities, for example. While all these measures are needed and serve important purposes, they are still "fixes." With the possible exception of the last named—families, schools, and faith communities—none faces the deep reality that soci-ety as a whole is responsible for its moral ethos. Moral identity forma-tion is everyone's business, can only be done over the long term, and can only be pursued effectively in a wide variety of ways. Identity formation, moral identity included, is not a fix, *it is the quiet vocation of soul craft.* And if it is not attended to across society as a day-in, day-out task, even the necessary social fixes themselves, such as good laws, will not work. Law itself, a Supreme Court Chief Justice liked to say, "floats on a sea of ethics."[2] In any case, a society is simply not viable if everything that should or should not be done needs to be spelled out and enforced in laws, rules, and regulations, with no shared commit-ments and moral culture, no reinforcing unwritten ethic. Moral for-mation must undergird and supplement laws, rules, and regulations.

---

2. The words of Chief Justice Earl Warren, as cited from Roger Lincoln Shinn, *Tangled World* (New York: Charles Scribner's Sons, 1965), 96.

TIME

The generational nature of moral soul craft should be underscored. Collective moral identity is long in the making and is necessary even for its own transformation as changed circumstances require. The shattering experience of Israel in exile is illustrative. In 587 BCE, the Babylonian army broke through the walls of Jerusalem and hauled the prominent citizens into exile, leaving the city in ruins, including the temple. But the subsequent exile was far more than a brutal relocation. It was a cultural, political, and religious catastrophe as well as an apocalypse.[3] All the sure marks of a national religious and civic identity were shattered, and the land of promise was gone. The prosperity many had come to regard as a birthright in Israel's heyday as a nation was destroyed, the Davidic kingship was toppled, and the center of the faith itself, the temple, was leveled. Israel's way of life, its leadership, and its faith, were all radically called into question.[4] The implied answer to the plaintive psalm "How shall we sing the Lord's song in a strange land?" (Ps 137:4) was that the people could not sing the Lord's song. Into this despondency the exilic prophets came with a word of judgment and of hope. It was judgment in that Israel's catastrophe was related to its own arrogance and injustice during its years of prosperity. It was hope in that God had yet another word, a word of forgiveness and a future beyond exile. But what grabs our attention in this mighty struggle of the people to come to terms with the worst crisis to befall them is the *way* in which it becomes possible for them to "sing the Lord's song" again. The prophets call up images of the people's identity, as these are rooted in their deepest memories, and then recast these images as images of hope and renewal.

> Look to the rock from which you were hewn,
> and to the quarry from which you were dug.
> Look to Abraham your father
> and to Sarah who bore you.(Isa 51:1–2)

Isaiah speaks of "a new exodus" and "a new creation," and Jeremiah and Ezekiel both speak of "new covenants of the heart." These are the long-held orienting images of Israel's own identity, and they now reestablish it as a community of faith existing in a drastically

---

3. See Birch, *What Does the Lord*, 83.
4. Ibid.

changed landscape. "A new exodus" recalls the people-creating event of liberation from Egypt, "a new creation" calls up the beginning of beginnings, and "new covenants of the heart" goes to Israel's binding relationship with God, of one with another, and with the land. Through this creative retrieval and re-forming, the people are able to combat resignation and despair, to hope, and to begin the task of new forms for their life together: for example, the birth of the synagogue happens in exile.

> Those who wait for the Lord
> shall renew their strength,
> they shall mount up with wings like eagles,
> they shall run and not be weary,
> they shall walk and not faint.
> (Isa 40:31)

The larger point is that "peoplehood" did not happen, and does not happen, solely by sharing common geography, events, or experience. A further ingredient is needed—a collective memory that augurs hope and fashions a common story from shared experience. In this case, surviving the exile was rendered possible when the newly dispossessed retold and recast stories of their own identity. Their collective sense included the memory of themselves as brickmakers and house servants, slaves who knew they were the children of Abraham, Isaac and Jacob, Sarah, Rebekah, Rachel, and Leah. In short, becoming a people was not a sudden event and never is. Neither was, nor is, surviving as a people.

But let us jump the centuries to contemporary examples. The first was mentioned in the previous chapter—enhanced democracy and the Civil Rights Movement. The songs and stories of slaves and ex-slaves made possible the vocation of Martin Luther King Jr. and thousands of others. Marching together for freedom as a people certainly did require the charisma and intelligence of a leader such as King, just as Moses was indispensable to the saga of the Hebrews. But the Civil Rights Movement also required generations of spirituals, the cultural and moral power of the black churches, and their memory of ancestors who kept the faith. It required teaching the children well and passing on the faith. It also required a certain constellation of events and consolidation of powers at a certain point in US history, a pregnant moment marked by what King called the "Zeitgeist"—the "spirit of the times"—and a *kairos*, a crisis rendered an opportunity. Yet the larger point remains: the moral formation necessary for overcoming oppression and beginning anew cannot first be willed in the moment of its need; it must be nurtured across generations.

Another example mentioned earlier surfaced after World War II in southern France. During the Nazi occupation, and in violation of the laws of the Vichy regime, the small village of Le Chambon gave refuge to hundreds of Jews and smuggled them by night across the border to Switzerland and safety. Neighboring villages did *not* risk their lives for strangers desperate to escape the trains to the labor camps or the death camps. So the question arose, Why did Le Chambon do so, especially since no Jews were native to the village itself? Le Chambon did have rather extraordinary leadership, centered in Pastor André and Magda Trocmé and their friends, and that was important. Le Chambon's distinctiveness, however, was that it was a Huguenot community with a long history of suffering as a persecuted religious minority, a history kept alive in its music and the stories and shrines of the martyrs. The villagers knew full well what such identity meant for moral action when persecuted strangers sought saving help. The Chambonnais, by religious conviction nonviolent resisters of evil, recognized in the Jews a persecuted people of God in grave need, and they responded in a way they "had to," a way they said was simply "natural," though it was not "natural" in the neighboring countryside. When, decades after the war, Philip Hallie, a student of Holocaust studies who went to Le Chambon to learn "how goodness happened" there, posed the oft-asked question to one of the surviving leaders: "But would your kind of resistance have worked in Nazi Germany itself, or in the USSR today?" the reply came back immediately, "Oh, no, no. You see, it takes generations to prepare."[5] The people of Le Chambon practiced soul craft in season and out of season, through peaceful years and dangerous ones.

As an aside, and before offering further examples, let it be noted that the moral identity contours of the Civil Rights Movement and Le Chambon were configured by Scripture. Biblical stories, metaphors, teachings, and examples shaped their sense of peoplehood and righteous conduct.

There are other poignant examples.

Early on, many Native Americans were taken as slaves in a kind

5. See Philip P. Hallie, *Lest Innocent Blood Be Shed* (New York: Harper & Row, 1979).

of reverse Middle Passage from the New World to the Old. Columbus had no fewer than one thousand "Indians" on board in his second trip to Spain, even though half did not survive the trip and were dumped at sea. Only a century later, thanks to other slavers, Seville was 7 percent black and Native American.[6] When Native peoples did survive, often as strangers parked on "reserved" land they had never known, they did so only by keeping or retrieving language, stories, ways, and ceremonies they were required to abandon under penalty of law. Still later, Native children were forcibly bussed off to boarding schools meant to drum the Indian out of them and educate them into a "true" American, Canadian, Caribbean, or South American settler identity. "Kill the Indian, save the child" was the motto and policy. Very often, this was done with the help of the colonizer's Bible in mission schools.

Not unlike Israel in exile, these First Nations had to refashion identity as a song sung in a strange land, a land they also had to somehow make their own. That they survived at all, against all odds, including pandemic disease, and did so with deep memory and even uncommon humor, is remarkable, even miraculous. Pope Francis, in *Laudato Si'*, holds up the legacy of this struggle and the wisdom of this collective identity for the planetary emergency we all face:

> It is essential to show special care for indigenous communities and their cultural traditions. They are not merely one minority among others, but should be the principal dialogue partners, especially when large projects affecting their land are proposed. For them, land is not a commodity but rather a gift from God and from their ancestors who rest there, a sacred space with which they need to interact if they are to maintain their identity and values. When they remain on their land, they themselves care for it best.[7]

The encyclical's call for dialogue is part of its own attempt to craft a moral identity that addresses the cry of the Earth and the cry of the poor together, and to do so with church participation and leadership. That leads to a final, extended example.

When Thomas Newcomen scooped coal into a new kind of engine—a practical steam engine—in 1712, and replaced the equiv-

---

6. Andrés Reséndez has distilled the scholarship of the past fifty years in *The Other Slavery: The Uncovered Story of Indian Enslavement in America* (Boston: Houghton Mifflin Harcourt, 2016).

7. Francis, *Laudato Si'*, para. 146.

alent of five hundred horses, he launched a new age, the Industrial Revolution. While in the early years of the industrial era, 94 percent of the world's energy was supplied by human labor and animals, and fossil fuels and water provided only 6 percent, by the time of the dramatic post-WWII global upswing of the 1950s, 93 percent of all energy was supplied by the dirty fuels of oil, coal, and gas and only 7 percent by the clean fuels of water, wind, and sun, together with human labor and animals. Even in 2016, when we knew we must leave dirty fuels behind, 80 percent of our energy was still supplied by fossil fuels. Wendell Berry remarks that the great obstacle to the successful transition to clean fuels is the conviction that we cannot change because we are dependent on what is wrong. But that, he goes on, "is the addict's excuse, and we know that it will not do."[8]

Three italicized sentences summarize.

(1) *Humanity is now the single most decisive force of nature itself.* Most systems of the natural world are currently embedded as part of human systems, or profoundly affected by human systems—the high atmosphere, the ocean depths, the polar regions. It never used to be this way, but it is now, not only "unto the children of the third and fourth generation" (Num 14:18), but for all foreseeable progeny. (2) *Nature has changed course.* After graphing long-term trends in twenty-four different areas, from Newcomen's engine and the onset of the Industrial Revolution (about 1750) to the year 2000, International Geosphere-Biosphere scientists concluded that "evidence from several millennia shows that the magnitude and rates of human-driven changes to the global environment are in many cases unprecedented." "There is no previous analogue for the current operation of the Earth system."[9] Industrial humanity has brought on a non-analogous moment, a unique epoch named by many the Anthropocene, the age of human domination. (3) *In contrast to the climate stability of the Holocene, the mark of the Anthropocene is climate volatility and uncertainty.* The importance of this contrast can hardly be overstated, since it was the relative climate stability of the late Holocene that made possible the rise and spread of human civilizations from the Neolithic era (ca. 10,000 BCE) to the present. What moral universe and

---

8. Wendell Berry, *What Are People For?* (Berkeley: Counterpoint, 1990), 20.

9. Will Steffen and Peter Tyson, *Global Change and the Earth System* (Berlin: Springer, 2004), v.

civilizational transitions are required if, instead of climate stability, climate volatility and uncertainty are the new normal?

Recall our two figures from chapter 5. Both have circles for moral responsibility and both relate to the whole planet, or "ecosphere" (the whole community of life together with its indispensable envelope of nonliving factors such as sunshine and atmospheric gases). In the first figure, the sphere of imagined moral responsibility is a circle smaller than the ecosphere. All the elements that belong to morality and ethics are present: virtue (i.e., the kind of person we are, our character), consequences (the outcome of our actions), and duty or obligation (our moral bottom lines and binding principles).[10] But character, consequences, and obligation in this smaller circle, within the larger one, are all human-to-human transactions only. Human society (the built environment), but not the natural world (the unbuilt environment), is the domain of moral responsibility. Indeed, this circle is the very context of what it means to be human: identity itself is defined *in* human-to-human terms, *on* human-to-human terms. Life is all about us. Humans are ends as well as means; the rest of nature is means only, for human ends only. In the second figure, by way of contrast, the circle of moral responsibility is coterminous with the ecosphere, itself now the sphere of our cumulative imprint. Our character, consequences, and basic obligations need to reflect this expanded moral universe. Virtue, consequences, and obligation all require a do-over. Without losing any of its fire, social justice must include creation justice as well, just as creation justice must include social justice.

A do-over of what matters most in the moral life as we wield anthropocene powers means re-formed moral identity, even collective human identity. To recall Roy Scranton in our introduction, "We will need a new way of thinking our collective existence. We need a new vision of who 'we' are."[11]

"Who 'we' are" in turn raises the questions we included in the introduction. What dialogue of Bible and ethics shapes the contours of moral imagination and human responsibility when no terrain goes untouched by both human goodness and human molestation? What dialogue facilitates human character and conduct when, as never before, our collective reach is "exercised cumulatively across generational time, aggregately through ecological systems, and nonin-

10. See the discussion of moral theory in chapter 7.
11. Scranton, *Learning to Die*, 19.

tentionally over evolutionary futures?"[12] What biblical and present understandings of ourselves help generate a capacity to take a stand not only for present and future generations of humankind but for the community of life as a whole?[13]

Answering questions about a different human identity, and moral re-formation as a whole, will take place in numerous ways, including some "fixes." But lasting impact will come through those communities of moral identity formation with claims on longevity. The church is one of those communities, and its Scriptures an enduring resource.

How is this moral re-formation to be carried out?

TASKS

Moral identity formation and re-formation is carried out in two quiet, steady ways. Both were necessary to the outcome of Israel's exile crisis, the Civil Rights Movement, Le Chambon as a city of refuge, and Native cultural revival and sovereignty. Both will also be necessary for the hard transition from industrial to ecological civilization.

The moral community's first task is to drink from its own wells in order to directly nurture moral capacities. These capacities take the form of individual and collective qualities of character. Sensitivity and empathy are examples, as are compassion and courage, *chutzpah* and humility. Like a disposition to wonder and stand in awe at the natural world, these qualities exercise decisive influences on our conduct *prior to* our specific choices on given issues, inclining us to respond in certain ways and not others. They exist as expressions of moral identity that we *bring to* our reflection on courses of action, *predisposing* us in one direction or another. They belong to our "think withs" as we think about our choices and action. The Chambonnais knew "intuitively" that one suffering people of God rescues another, despite the danger. In their judgment, this action "had to" be taken. But it "had to" be taken only because certain dispositions had already been formed among them as moral capacities. Every faith community can nurture moral identity and moral capacities directly and continuously with materials of its own collective story and identity.

We point to a few ways this is done. The church is a storytelling

12. Jenkins, *Future of Ethics*, 1.
13. See the introduction to this book.

community that forms moral capacities in the way our examples illustrate. The means include the educational program of the church, formal and informal, at all levels. Worship life and the liturgy is of equal importance. Even more important, the nurture in worship and in education go hand-in-hand as Christian symbols are "lived into" and their meanings explored for a way of life.

Baptism, for example, is drawn into dimensions of discipleship, some of them new or retrieved. In the present moment, that includes, in some churches, "watershed discipleship"[14] and care for all the waters of life as a baptismal vow itself.[15] In parallel fashion, the Eucharist is understood in relation to the hungers of the world and as the sign that mandates an inclusive community in the presence of God—everyone is welcome at the "welcome table."

The Bible itself is a critical and continuous resource for both worship and education. Scripture belongs at the heart of the church's task of directly nurturing moral capacities with its own resources.

Other church gatherings, beyond the set occasions of formal worship and education, are also places where moral capacities form. Very often, members' work together, making common cause around specific tasks and issues, is the unnamed laboratory of moral formation and the crafting of a shared unwritten ethic.

The community's second task is to be the integrating community, a place of moral "centering" for materials from worlds beyond church boundaries. The faith community gives perspective and place to the images, stories, pressures, and events that reign in our lives, whatever their source. This shapes moral identity by facilitating "integrity" as a moral integration at the center of our being. When the community functions as an integrating one, competing claims for allegiance and commitment interact with core faith claims.

This integrating work assumes that there are numerous sources of moral influence and wisdom. Some lie outside the faith community, some within. The issue is not the origin of sources or the diver-

14. The initiative in Ventura County, California, of the Bartimaeus Cooperative Ministries, founded and led by Ched Myers and Elaine Enns. See Ched Myers, ed., *Watershed Discipleship: Reinhabiting Bioregional Faith and Practice* (Eugene, OR: Wipf & Stock, 2016), an anthology of watershed discipleship activists across the nation.

15. This is one of the baptismal vows of the United Church of Santa Fe, New Mexico. For explorations of baptism as moral-spiritual formation for tending Earth's waters of life, see Dahill, "Rewilding Christian Spirituality," 177–96, and Benjamin M. Stewart, "The Stream, the Flood, and Spring: The Liturgical Role of Flowing Waters in Eco-Reformation," in Dahill and Martin-Schramm, *Eco-Reformation*, 160–76.

sity of content. Plural sources and diverse content formed the biblical materials themselves, and churches have always grafted influences that were non-Christian in origin onto their own traditions and made them their own. Augustine used Plotinus; Aquinas used Aristotle; many hymn writers, liturgists, preachers, and educators have used popular culture. The greatest example, however, is the Hebrew Bible itself. Not without controversy, it became Christian Scripture. So, the question for any faith community facing moral choices is not whether the moral content is in the Bible or in the church's traditions; the question is whether a center exists to which varied materials can be related, and whether criteria exist that take their measure. While we cannot discuss this question in full here, we can offer this guideline: the materials of any Christian ethic must take account of the prominent lines discerned in canonical Scripture. That is, content from whatever source must complement or elaborate, rather than violate, the message of the gospel. Determining compatibility and complementarity is, of course, an ongoing task that is never done once and for all for any living community of faith. Bonhoeffer's lifelong question is telling and timely: Who is Jesus Christ *for us today?*[16]

These two tasks together, the formation of moral identity from the church's own resources, and the integrating of materials from other quarters, comprise the first major role for the faith community. They cannot be carried out, however, apart from a second role.

THE CHURCH AS A BEARER OF TRADITION

Stories other than pure fiction are lived before they are told. They are multifaceted events before they achieve the coherence of narration. Still, the effort at coherence happens almost simultaneously with events themselves. Raw experience no sooner occurs than we give it reference, framework, and interpretation. We insist upon making sense of what, to an observer, might appear disparate and fragmented, even nonsensical. We are story-making creatures who live by the stories we tell. Narratives give form and meaning to our experience.

But we don't come to experience empty-handed. We already have a stock of stories in hand and stand amidst traditions that channel our response and interpret our experience. The important question, then,

16. This is Bonhoeffer's question from his early writings, such as *Discipleship*, to his final *Letters and Papers from Prison.*

is: "Of what stories am I a part, and of what traditions?"[17] How are they also a part of me? For I am already born with a past, situated within a social, environmental, and historical matrix that teems with carriers of myth and meaning. With the accident of birth, my parents, ancestors, and place on the planet have already been chosen, and I've been put on tracks already laid down. From my day of birth forward, my identity is being shaped by the communities and strata (race, class, gender, culture) to which I belong and which belong to me. Even if I reject my past, I invariably do so on terms supplied by it. In my quest for a different identity, I draw on familiar traditions, even if many of them are traditions I no longer choose to honor in full. My life is not fated, but it is one of influences I cannot simply shed. (Recall that *charaktēr* in Greek refers to the marks made by an engraving tool.[18])

But how do "traditions" work as living components of a community that bears moral traditions? We cite three functions: moral tradition works (1) as an aid for moral development, (2) as content for an ethic, and (3) as a framework of accountability. The church provides each of these. We take them in turn.

ROOTS

For moral development, as for personality development in general, we must be able to situate ourselves before we can go anywhere in a way that is not aimless wandering. From where do we come? To whom do we belong? Where do we wish to go from here?

Knowing who and where we are means knowing the tradition or traditions in which we live, move, and have our being. Moral growth and maturity require being part of a history and being aware of it as part of us. Lack of traditions, and lack of consciousness of them, results in moral drift and limbo, rootlessness.

But how do traditions work, and what is their authority? The question persists, and we must digress for a moment if we are to understand the dynamics of the church as an agent of moral development.

1. First we must underline the living character of moral traditions. To speak of the "authority of tradition" is badly misleading if we think of tradition as "a settled reality" for which the task is to figure

---

17. This section draws on Alasdair MacIntyre's chapter, "Virtue, Unity of Life and the Concept of a Tradition," in *After Virtue: A Study in Moral Theory* (Notre Dame: University of Notre Dame Press, 1981), 190–209. The question quoted above is from p. 201.

18. See pp. 112–15.

out how the whole complex works, as though it were a fixed unit.[19] There is a "givenness" about tradition, of course. "That which is handed on," whatever it may be, is the generic meaning of tradition. Yet, while tradition is a deposit, it is equally a dynamic, the dynamic process of handing on, of continuing sense-making and the appropriation and reappropriation of the past. This process includes sifting and assessing traditions, honoring some and repudiating others, and changing others and recognizing different meanings in them at different times. (This last-named usually happens in altered circumstances or in the face of new issues and challenges.)

Tradition as a dynamic also includes retrieving portions of the past that have been neglected or rejected by reigning myths, and gathering for present and future generations human moral experience that has been forgotten, denied, or denigrated. (Recall the call of Pope Francis to privilege the dismissed wisdom of indigenous peoples in the dialogue that now addresses a planet in peril.[20]) Paradoxically, tradition includes creating innovative practices that will shape future moral identities and give guidance for future moral action. "Traditioning" is a dynamic process, a continuous and creative reworking of the past and present. It is more verb than noun.

A single illustration must suffice—the shared heritage of Quakers and Pentecostals. The Religious Society of Friends, or Quakers, began with George Fox in mid-seventeenth-century England. "Friends" were one of the many dissenting Protestant groups rejecting the state church, the Church of England. Quakers lived by an unmediated relationship with God through direct and personal revelation that they variously described as "that of God in every person," "the inner light," "the inward light of Christ," or simply "the Holy Spirit." They reached back to "the priesthood of all believers" and "a holy nation" as inspired by 1 Peter. Like large portions of the ancient church, they also embraced a pacifism that refused to engage in war or swear oaths of fealty to the state or the empire. They opposed slavery and, in the church, rejected creeds, hierarchy, and most forms of religious symbolism, including the sacraments. All this, to the Quaker mind, was recovering and elaborating an early and strong, but later neglected, tradition—namely, the Christian life as essentially a nonviolent way of discipleship drawing continuously upon "that of

19. John Howard Yoder, *The Priestly Kingdom: Social Ethics as Gospel* (Notre Dame: University of Notre Dame Press, 1984), 77.
20. See p. 232 above.

God in everyone" as Friends actively engaged the grave issues of the day.

Quakers were called that because some "quaked." "I bade them tremble at the word of the Lord" is a declaration attributed to George Fox, a probable reference to either Isaiah 66:2 or Ezra 9:4.[21] If this quaking sounds "Pentecostal," it's because it is. Although the present Pentecostal movement came later, gathering its strength in the twentieth century, it, too, began as a renewal movement that placed special emphasis on direct personal experience of God, in this case, through a baptism of the Holy Spirit and a life of holiness. And, again like the Quakers, or, for that matter, any renewal movement, Pentecostals have weighed, sifted, and selected Christian traditions, including biblical ones, in keeping with their core spiritual experience. Their history and present practice illustrate the *living* character of religious and moral traditions.

2. If it is important to recognize the dynamics of Christian traditions, it is equally important to recognize the diversity of traditions that belong to myriad Christian communities. Coptic Christians of Egypt or Ethiopia possess very different legacies from those of Southern Baptists in the United States. While Orthodox Christians in India, Russia, and the Middle East share much between them, they are also markedly different from one another, not to say from Lutherans in Scandinavia, who in turn differ from Namibian and Tanzanian Lutherans. Mennonites of the western plains of Canada live the Christian life differently from Roman Catholics in Nicaragua or Brazil. Pentecostalism worldwide shares family resemblances together with staggering diversity. And we have not mentioned the rise of African Independent Churches, megachurches in the United States, or the house church movement in China. While all of the foregoing do share the same Bible, Scripture lives in different ways in these communities.

Or, from another perspective—historical rather than geographical—first-century Christian ethics changed markedly after Christianity's encounter with the Greco-Roman philosophical and cultural world in the second and third centuries and its establishment as the

---

21. Isa 66:2 reads: "All these things my hand has made, and so all these things are mine, says the Lord. But this is the one to whom I will look, to the humble and contrite in spirit, who trembles at my word." Ezra 9:4 reads, "Then all who trembled at the words of the God of Israel, because of the faithlessness of the returned exiles, gathered around me [Ezra] while I sat appalled until the evening sacrifice."

imperial faith after the fourth century. The Christian moral life in the West was different after the Renaissance and Reformation, and after the rise of the bourgeoisie and democratic capitalism, from what it was in the world of medieval and feudal Christendom. Presently, Christianity is undergoing a geographical re-centering from West to South and East, as well as an urban intermingling everywhere. Of special note is that previously minority and marginal Christian communities are on the ascendency. While there are resemblances throughout, and "Christian" remains a meaningful designation for widely shared elements, Scripture above all, it's the diversity of traditions that impresses most of all.

CONTENT

We are not stuck, then, with inherently static and fixed moral content. Moral traditions are not intrinsically rigid and they are not univocal. (When they have been treated as such, as they often have, they have impeded moral maturity.) Rather, diverse moral traditions supply many of the materials for fashioning an ethic by which to live and die. Diverse interpretations of Christian faith, together with their moralities, mean that wide-ranging views on a virtually endless number of moral issues are included in the tradition, as are embodiments of different lifestyles and a wealth of portraits, symbols, images, stories, rites, and rituals. The issue, then, is not whether to accept or reject "tradition" but to decide which criteria we should use to sort those traditions we should identify with and build upon, and which we should not. How do we choose among the many voices and diverse traditions of the faith community, including those traditions now in the process of creation in a changed and changing world? Much past morality is, after all, morally dubious, some even outrageous and deserving of abandonment. (We mentioned slavery and abusive treatment of women earlier; campaigns of demonizing and slaughter in the name of God can quickly be added.) The task of ethical critique of morality developed above is a continuous critique of moral traditions.[22] That said, the makings of an answer to the question of criteria begins with a cue from the church's own millennial testimony and experience: namely, to accord high place to Scripture as a common authority and, within Scripture, to give the Jesus story

22. See pp. 91–93.

and life in the Spirit a normative place as discerned in the believing community. Necessary moral discrimination then follows: what is compatible with this locus and its processes of discernment?

Yet the key point is not that we must sort diverse traditions. The point is the function of such moral traditions themselves and the role of the church. Traditions in the church help situate us, give us roots, and supply content for the ethic we live by. They are, in these ways, aids to moral development and maturity. Indeed, even when we break with certain strains of tradition, we usually take them seriously as heritage and a point of orientation, just as we usually draw *upon* the tradition for the reform *of* it. Recall our discussion of Pope Francis and *Laudato Si'* in which, situated in two hundred years of Roman Catholic social thought, he expanded standing moral norms of the dignity of the human person and the common human good so as to accord creation that same dignity and prioritize the planetary common good.

FRAMEWORK

Finally, moral traditions provide a framework of accountability. As part of a tradition and membership in a "people," we are set within a matrix of moral claims and concerns that provide a guiding influence. The faith tradition, functioning as moral tradition, mediates the claims of others upon us and we upon them. In the example just mentioned, "Catholic social teaching" is an identifiable point of reference and guidance as Roman Catholics grapple with planetary issues.

Sometimes moral traditions are less clearly defined, as a framework of accountability, than is an official body of teaching and practice. They may nonetheless be as real and effective. The Hebrew understanding of belonging provides an extended illustration. In this understanding, my life continues as part of the ongoing life of a people of God living toward a peaceable kingdom and beloved community. This sense of corporate belonging nurtures a sense of responsibility toward both ancestors and posterity. In a certain way, as among those who stand on the shoulders of those who have gone before, I am responsible to Abraham and Sarah and the saints. I belong to the story that was theirs, is mine, and will be that of those who come after me. They bequeathed a legacy and vocation, and I am responsible to them for the heritage placed in my hands. They depend upon me for their continuing presence and the life of their dream.

This notion of immortality and a goal for the world means that the past is not only not dead, it is not finished. I am part of its development.

Like its Jewish ancestors, the ancient church shared just this consciousness of an ongoing covenant. The letter to the Hebrews says as much: it calls the roll of the communion of saints and attests to their living by faith (ch. 11) for a future promised them by God, but which they could not yet see realized. The perils they knew were sometimes dreadful.

> Some had to bear being pilloried and flogged, or even chained up in prison. They were stoned, or sawn in half, or beheaded; they were homeless, and dressed in the skins of sheep and goats; they were penniless and were given nothing but ill-treatment. They were too good for the world and they went out to live in deserts and mountains and in caves and ravines. (Heb 11:37–38 JB)

Then the writer concludes: "These are all heroes of faith, but they did not receive what was promised, since God had made provision for us to have something better, and they were not to reach perfection except through us" (Heb 11:39–40 JB).

There is an emphatic accountability here. The faith community is charged to carry forward the hopes of the ancestors and the dreams of their God, and to realize those hopes and dreams as best they can. The Bible itself is a collection of letters from the ancestors as moral witness and exhortation for those who follow.

The same accountability stretches off into the future. We are responsible to coming generations. Their claims to well-being are claims upon us. The conditions that would make well-being possible for them are therefore ours to create as best we can. In an epoch of anthropocene powers, and whether we are conscious of it or not, we *are* creating the conditions within which they, together with the rest of the community of life, will live.

This does not neglect present generations. For both Jewish and Christian ethics, love of neighbor is obligatory *in the present moment* and is not vitiated by obligations to ancestors and posterity. Furthermore, as we have seen, "neighbor" is universal. All are neighbors, whether near at hand or far off, whether friend, stranger, or enemy.

The whole community of life is embraced, "all that participates in being,"[23] including other-than-human life.

The tradition itself, then, fosters moral accountability and functions as a framework for it, just as it aids moral development and contributes content.

SUMMING UP

We summarize as follows.

1. The faith community is a major source and resource for moral development. It is this as it sets members within moral traditions with which they identify.

2. The faith community is the source of rich and varied content for members' ethics. As the community embodies and passes on its own traditions, and helps locate, appropriate, and integrate sources from elsewhere, it supplies such a fund.

3. The faith community is the framework of accountability for the Christian moral life. As its moral traditions form and inform the ongoing life of its members, it functions as this framework.

These three together make up the role of the community as a bearer of moral tradition. Indeed, members of a faith community are already, by virtue of membership, grafted into a collective tradition that provides both substance for a present and future Christian ethic, and a process for appropriating it. The example of the Quakers and Pentecostals, and the example of Pope Francis and the authority of an encyclical, show two very different ways of locating moral sources, substance and process. The differences nonetheless reflect the liveliness of the tradition itself.

We can generalize. The rich diversity of faith communities across the globe enhances, rather than vitiates, what this chapter outlines as five commonly held church roles: the church as a community of moral identity formation, the church as a bearer of tradition, the church as a community of moral discernment and deliberation, the church as an agent of action, and the church as a moral haven. While they may sometimes be honored in the breach, or be more aspiration

---

23. Niebuhr, *Purpose of the Church*, 38.

than reality, all of these belong to the roles of every faith community in the Christian life.

It need only be added that tradition as a source for the Christian moral life is subject to the same multifaceted ethical critique Christian ethics brings to all sources. Tradition funds the Christian moral life; it can also betray it, and often does.[24]

THE CHURCH AS A COMMUNITY OF MORAL DISCERNMENT AND DELIBERATION

A previous chapter devoted extensive discussion to moral discernment and deliberation.[25] We need only spell out how this takes place in the church.

NEW KNOWLEDGE

The church is an arena for intentional moral education. This includes learning about issues. We have cited the encyclical *Laudato Si'* often as a salient example of "doing" Christian ethics. It surfaces again here because, for many, it led far deeper into planetary challenges and issues than they previously considered. The core idea of "integral ecology" lifted up interacting forces that numerous readers of the encyclical had previously siloed and treated as autonomous, as though economy and environment were separate sectors, or the poverty of human communities was unrelated to Earth made poor. *Laudato Si'* thus serves as an example of official church statements as a means of moral education, by offering those who study them new knowledge of issues or new perspectives on them. An earlier example (from 1986), on a great issue about which the Bible could have no inkling, was the United Methodist bishops' pastoral letter on peace, *In Defense of Creation: The Nuclear Crisis and a Just Peace.*[26] It was also an effective vehicle of learning, both in the fact-gathering and deliberative process of arriving at the moral stands themselves and as a base for ongoing study and action.

Citing church statements at the head of the list should not mislead

24. See chapter 7.
25. See chapter 7.
26. United Methodist Council of Bishops, *In Defense of Creation: The Nuclear Crisis and a Just Peace* (Nashville: Graded Press, 1986).

us. Though important examples, they are only one form of many used by the church as a community of moral learning. Moreover, most issues are not as global as these. The issues might be strictly local ones in which the congregation, rather than the denomination, is the forum of education, and the style of interchange is informal and conversational. A congregation or a coalition of neighborhood religious communities might grapple with a housing issue, an action on health care, aid for immigrants and refugees, some proposed city or state legislation. The salient matter is to expect the faith community to be an arena for learning about significant issues and their moral dimensions.

Learning about issues is clearly necessary. But it is not sufficient. If the papal encyclical or the Methodist bishops' pastoral letter were only a research document *about* their chosen subjects, they would, as *church* documents, have been very curious indeed. The churches have no essential factual data to which only faith communities, but not the wider public, is privy. Even when the church is the place where people first learn some essentials about important matters, that knowledge is still public knowledge (about hunger and fresh water scarcity, for example, or the possibilities and shortfalls of free market principles for the economy). Rather, the distinctive mark of the church's role is its formulation of a moral perspective drawn from Christian faith.

NORMATIVE PERSPECTIVE

This introduces the second component of the church's role in moral discernment and deliberation. The faith community can and should be the arena in which a moral perspective on an issue is fashioned. We need not repeat the discussion of five resources for this, only remind the reader of them: a set of overarching guidelines for moral deliberation, the interplay of cognition and emotion, sources of moral wisdom, the norm of neighbor-love, and three kinds of moral realities highlighting what most counts in the moral life (virtue, consequences, obligation).[27]

Nor do we need to repeat the guidelines for moral discernment available in that chapter.

Yet, coming to a normative moral perspective does not complete the process. A way must be found for the church to carry on public

27. For the discussion of each and all, see pp. 155–95.

moral discourse in a pluralistic society and world. The faith community must be able to make its views intelligible to parties that do not share the religious premises. A justifying reason such as "We recommend the following policies because they represent a Christian perspective" does not suffice. For a pluralistic world, "Christian" is not a compelling and sufficient reason. Moral accountability drawing on values and norms shared with others, of other than Christian faith, is needed. Universal human rights, for example, or freedom from oppression and equality of opportunity, or liberty and justice for all, or a healthy shared habitat, are examples. Common ground in pursuit of a shared good is necessary if the church's stand is to be joined by others. In summary, the faith community, as the place where a Christian moral stance is formed and the terms are found for public moral discourse, is the second component of the community's role as a community of moral discernment and deliberation.

MORAL REPRESENTATIVE

The third component of the church's role in moral deliberation is the church as a community of moral proxy. Here, strong biblical lines that we have already discussed as authoritative for the church's bearing come into play. The church is, for example, both local and global. It is not "national" by any definition of faith. The gospel knows nothing of the nation-state system, nor is a people of God determined by national boundaries. Indeed, if the ancient church is a guide, there is always serious tension between allegiance to the faith community and fealty to any and every Caesar. More to the point, and because the notion of "neighbor" is a universal one, church discussion of moral issues entails representation. Neighbor means *all*, including enemies and unborn generations, and "proxy" representation means that it is incumbent upon the faith community to amplify voices not normally heard. These are usually voices of the powerless, marginalized, underrepresented, or unrepresented (future generations of other-than-human life and the flourishing habitats they require is a voice rarely heard).

Those who need representation will often change as moral issues change. But the proxy role remains the same: to strengthen the voices of those not otherwise heard. This is a vocational consequence of Christian faith that can happen in ways large and small, and through both official and ad hoc institutional means as well as personal witness.

In 1934, Dietrich Bonhoeffer was a pastor in two German-language congregations in London. He had left his university teaching post in Berlin when the Nazi government took over the universities. He had thus left the post where would-be pastors were pursuing their theological studies. In September, he wrote his Swiss friend, Erwin Sutz:

> Now I am back again in our congregation, tormenting myself with trying to decide whether to go back to Germany as director of a preachers' seminary that is soon to be opened there,[28] stay here, or go to India.[29] I no longer believe in the university; in fact I have never believed in it—to your chagrin! The next generation of pastors, these days, ought to be trained entirely in church-monastic schools, where the pure doctrine, the Sermon on the Mount, and worship are taken seriously—which for all three of these things is simply not the case at the university and under the present circumstances is impossible. It is also time for a final break with our theologically grounded reserve about whatever is being done by the state—which really only comes down to fear. "Speak out for those who cannot speak"[30]—who in the church today still remembers that this is the very least the Bible asks of us in such times as these?[31]

"Speak out for those who cannot speak." That is the "the very least the Bible asks."

In the margin of his Bible, Bonhoeffer, now back in Germany, jotted the date of 9/11/38—November 9, 1938—next to Proverbs 31:8, the verse that reads, "Speak out for those who cannot speak." 9/11/38 was *Kristallnacht*—the Night of Broken Glass—named for the shards of broken glass of Jewish synagogues, stores, and buildings that littered the streets as the consequence of a pogrom carried out across Germany.

In sum, the church is a place to learn about issues, to formulate a Christian moral perspective and bring it to bear on the issues, and to represent the under- or unrepresented. All are dimensions of the

28. Finkenwalde, a seminary for pastors of the Confessing Church, which had broken with the state and state-funded training for clergy. Bonhoeffer did take this post.

29. To join Gandhi's ashram and learn the arts of discipleship for possible use in the Confessing Church, the dissenting Protestants who opposed the encroachment of Nazi influence in the church.

30. Prov 31:8.

31. Bonhoeffer, "Letter to Erwin Sutz, September 11, 1934," in *Dietrich Bonhoeffer Works*, 13:217.

church's function as a community of moral discernment and deliberation.

THE CHURCH AS AN AGENT OF ACTION

The formation of moral identity, utilizing moral traditions in the process, is a crucial role of the faith community, as is moral discernment, also using these traditions. Yet, conscience and character formation and deliberating issues are not ends in themselves. They exist to serve concrete action. The faith community is to be an embodiment of moral agency.

There is an important theological point here. In both Jewish and Christian traditions, faith's truth is finally a "performative" one. We *know* it when we *see* it, or experience it. It is real only when it is embodied. The test of any moral truth is in the concrete form it takes, and the difference it makes. Moral truth and a way of living go hand in hand. To remember Jesus in the Sermon on the Mount: "Not everyone who says to me, 'Lord, Lord,' will enter the kingdom of heaven, but only the one who does the will of my Father in heaven" (Matt 7:21).

This "performative" understanding of Christian faith necessarily assumes commitment to action. Literally nothing happens without it! Apart from action, moral identity and deliberation are without consequence and are rendered meaningless. Their presence and verification is visible only in their outcome.

But what does "action" refer to, precisely, in Christian ethics? Not every event is a moral action, nor every occurrence a moral act. A bird flying across the sky, a leaf falling to the ground, a sunset, or a moonrise is not a moral event, nor is the beating of a heart, the blinking of an eye, or waves lapping the shore. Moral action partakes of moral agency and thus includes a range of conscious activities we have discussed—choice, deliberation, discernment, disposition, motivation, intention, responsibility, and accountability. Moral action assumes that agents are aware of what they are doing, have some knowledge they feel is appropriate to the action, have some purpose in mind for the action, and have some possibility *of* acting (i.e., some degree of freedom and choice). When deeds have these characteristics and include aspects of what we discussed as core moral matters—virtue, consequences, obligation—they belong to moral, rather than nonmoral, action.

With this qualification in mind, what shall we say about the church as an agent of action? Deeds of faith, the "doing" of the Sermon on the Mount or "keeping" covenant, take place in two domains.

HOME TURF

The faith community itself is the first arena. It both *has* an eco-social ethic and *is* one. Its own internal arrangements reflect the morality it espouses. If, in the celebration of the Eucharist, it invites all to "the welcome table," then church practice cannot contradict this by failing to welcome all into the membership of the eucharistic community. If it pictures the world as a place where we share the same load, drink from a common cup, and belong together as members of a single family of God, then it is morally incumbent to find the means to share lives and resources for the community's own life together. Are the wages of church workers fair and just? What are the rights of employees? Since budgets are moral documents, where is the church's spending directed? What are the works of charity and the focal concerns of advocacy? How does it care for its own land and the resources it draws upon—food, water, energy, and so forth? The church has a role as moral agent on its own institutional turf.

THE WIDER PUBLIC

The second domain of moral action is the world beyond the doors of the institutional church. The actor is still the faith community, but now its attention is focused externally, to the public arena and its condition, rather than internally. The reach of the moral life here may begin internally, at home in the gathered community, but its extent is as the scattered community dispersed throughout society.

This is nicely pictured in the sanctuary of Christ Lutheran Church, San Diego, California. The stained glass that is the high wall behind the altar is the artist's rendition of Ezekiel 47, picked up in the Apocalypse of John in Revelation 22. The waters of life flow from the throne of God, with the trees of life along the banks, bearing fruit in every month and with their leaves for healing.[32] In this case, the mosaic ribbon of blue water flowing from the base of the high wall continues under the altar, then cascades down the steps into the main aisle, where the baptismal font is placed, with the waters of life flowing around it and on to the rear of the sanctuary and the front doors. But the life-giving stream does not end there. When it reaches the broad entrance (and exit), the river separates into a number of streams, delta-like, that, by implication and direction, flow into the surrounding community. The art captures well the meaning of the word "liturgy." From the Greek *leitourgia*, it means public service, the work of the people for the people. How apt that the presider sometimes ends worship with the words, "The service is ended, the ministry begins."

This presence in the public square continues as the church's action, now as the scattered community in the many sectors of civic life, including home and family. Two Catholic pastoral letters illustrate this with a focus upon what we earlier discussed as the vital work of "role morality."[33] The economics pastoral includes sections on working people and labor unions, owners and managers, and citizens and government,[34] while the peace pastoral includes educators, parents, youth, men and women in military service, men and women in defense industries, men and women of science, men and women of the media, public officials, and Catholics as citizens.[35] Here the church's presence is a dispersed one, via its membership throughout the eco-social order.

The complement of this is civic action by the church *as* a gathered community. We do not mean the attention internally, to the quality

32. See Ezek 47:6b–12 and Rev 22:1–2. It is worth noting that Ezekiel is a prophet of the exile and John lives in exile on the isle of Patmos. Both writers know the trauma of apocalyptic events happening to their people. Worthy of note is that, as Barbara Rossing writes, "apocalypses pull back a curtain so people can see the world more deeply—both the beauty of creation and also the pathologies of empire, experienced as plagues against creation." Barbara Rossing, "The World Is about to Turn: Preaching Apocalyptic Texts for a Planet in Peril," in Dahill and Martin-Schramm, *Eco-Reformation*, 141. Both the pathologies of empire and the beauty of creation are on display in the texts of Ezekiel and John, with creation renewed in God as vision and hope for the people.

33. See pp. 119–25.

34. See National Conference of Catholic Bishops, *Economic Justice for All: Pastoral Letter on Catholic Social Teaching the U.S. Economy* (Washington, DC: United States Conference of Catholic Bishops, 2009), para. 102–4, PDF, http://tinyurl.com/y86e9def.

35. See National Conference of Catholic Bishops, *The Challenge of Peace: God's Promise and Our Response* (Washington, DC: United States Conference of Catholic Bishops, 1983), para. 306–26.

of community life there; we mean the church's action as a corporate agent making corporate witness to what ought to happen in the world beyond church buildings. What stance does it take, for example, on neighborhood issues? If it has money to invest, where is it invested and to what ends? What stands do larger church forms—denominational, ecumenical, and interfaith coalitions, for example—take on public issues? In the United States, this was very much in evidence in the Civil Rights Movement and on some foreign policy issues (the Vietnam War, South African apartheid, US-sponsored wars in Central America). It was, and continues to be, in evidence in advocacy at local, state, and national levels on proposed legislation and regulations (abortion, health care, refugee resettlement, disaster response, education, pollution controls, hydraulic fracturing, and pipeline location, for example). What kind of life is reflected in the way the church is a corporate presence in the world? Corporate action supplements the action of the both the church as a witness on its own turf and the action of members as they are dispersed throughout the public arena in their work and other social roles. The way the church, at these various levels, embodies its ethic is the way the church serves as an agent of action and a moral witness.

THE CHURCH AS A MORAL HAVEN

ha-ven (hā'ven) *n.* 1. a sheltered anchorage; port; harbor. 2. any sheltered, safe place; refuge—*vt.* to provide a haven for[36]

ref-uge (ref'yōōj) *n.* < L. *refugere*, to retreat> 1. shelter or protection from danger, difficulty, etc. 2. a person or thing that gives shelter, help, or comfort. 3. a place of safety; shelter; safe retreat[37]

Whence the moral-spiritual power to be and do as we ought? Whence the courage of our convictions and the repair of frayed moral fiber? Where do we go, to what sheltered anchorage, what safe retreat, what haven, when, to remember a sonnet of Wordsworth, "The world is too much with us" and "we lay waste our powers"?[38] How do we begin anew?

36. *Webster's New World College Dictionary*, 2nd ed. (1986), s.v. "haven."
37. Ibid., s.v. "refuge."
38. Wordsworth, "The World Is Too Much with Us," as cited from Paul Brians, ed., *Reading about the World*, 2 vols., 3rd ed. (Orlando, FL: Harcourt College, 1999), 2:127.

The church comes by its role as a moral haven honestly. It's in the historical DNA, arising from the defining tension in the ancient church between "church" and "world" or between "Christ" and "culture."[39] It was constitutive of the church to confess that "Jesus is our Caesar" (as reported by the accusers in Acts 17:7) and "Jesus is Lord," both in defiance of the Roman Caesar as *dominus et deus* (Lord and God).

In short, the fundamental loyalty of ancient Christians as a "people of God," like Jews before and beside them as a "people of God," was loyalty to a *faith* community ("church") as the locus of the moral life, rather than to a *civic* community ("world").

This sometimes *created* rather than *resolved* moral issues. Obedience to Rome, demonstrated with a pinch of incense offered to Caesar as Lord, was not a religious and moral problem for most citizens of the empire. They adhered to the emperor cult without qualms. But for Christians it was. Christians could not betray their basic creed and commitment.

The same kind of moral problem arising from a chronic church/state tension surfaced in the choice of whether to fight in Caesar's armies. For most males in the Roman Empire, that was not a gut-wrenching decision. For Christians, it was. One outcome is that Christianity has always honored pacifism and advocated nonviolence, even when, under different circumstances, it found morally acceptable ways to honor exceptions as well ("just war" and "just revolution" theory, self-defense, etc.).[40]

39. The latter was laid out as an influential typology by H. Richard Niebuhr in *Christ and Culture* (New York: Harper & Row, 1951). He discerned five historical types: Christ against culture, Christ of culture, Christ above culture, Christ and culture in paradox, and Christ transforming culture. We do not address this variety above, only the continuing tension that all feel, to some degree, between church and world and the continuing role of the church as a moral haven.

40. Christian just war and just revolution theory are not about justifying war or revolution as a good. They are about preventing war and revolution or, if they are underway, conducting them morally, as a lesser evil. With formulations by Saint Augustine and Thomas Aquinas, there have been two primary matters of attention: *jus ad bellum* and *jus in bello*.

Jus ad bellum, seeking to prevent war or revolution, poses questions that serve as ethical analysis. Is the cause for war or revolution just (e.g., self-defense or overthrowing tyranny)? Is war or revolution a last resort (have all legal and nonviolent means been tried)? Is war or revolution declared by a proper authority? (This is normally the state, but if the state is tyrannical, organized resistance as the pro tempore alternative to the state might be the proper political authority.) Is there right intention (establishing or reestablishing peace and a just order rather than, for example, securing lands and colonizing peoples)? Is there reasonable chance of success? (The attention is risk assessment of the costs and consequences.) And are the ends and means proportional? (An officer's statement in the Vietnam War became famous regarding, in

Yet the larger point is that these normative stands of the church at the outset of its life were formative for what followed. Ongoing tension between civic and religious loyalties was never resolved once and for all. Choices always have to be made.

This church/world tension in turn creates the church's role as a moral haven, a safe place where Christians can be who they are as a community and can live a way of life of their own making. Here, fears and joys, "down" spirits and exultant ones, confession, grace, and forgiveness can be shared with those who know your name and have your back. Music fitted to the community's life and moods is composed, played, and sung. Visual arts and architecture in keeping with faith identity are present, as is preaching the word, celebrating the sacraments, and performing rites of passage from birth to death. For good reason, the space for this gathering is called a "sanctuary."

> sanc-tu-ar-y (sank' choo wer' ē) *n.* < L. *sanctus*, sacred> 1. a holy place . . . 2. a place of refuge or protection; asylum . . . 3. a reservation where animals or birds are sheltered for breeding purposes and may not be hunted or trapped.[41]

A holy place, a sacred space, as a place of refuge. There is something in the human spirit that compels having such a place. So when the church is not a refuge, some will steal away to create it.

---

this case, the disproportionality of ends and means: "Unfortunately we had to destroy the village to save it.")

Jus in bello, seeking to conduct war or revolution justly when they are undertaken as lesser evils, analyzes wartime behavior with the use of two principles—discrimination and proportionality. Discrimination asks who are, and who are not, legitimate targets. (Noncombatants, for example, have not been regarded as legitimate targets, nor have certain groups of people—women, children, and the elderly, hospital patients, or citizens participating in public events unrelated to the war or revolution.) Proportionality asks how much force is morally appropriate for resolving the conflict. (As with much just war/just revolution theory, this issue arises not only for military conflict but for police action as well.)

In summary, Christian just war and just revolution theory assumes that taking human life is seriously wrong, that states have a responsibility to defend their citizens, and that protecting innocent life may require a willingness sometimes to use deadly force. When threats arise, ethical analysis asks both about preventing its escalation into deadly conflict (the *jus ad bellum* criteria above) and about how such force might be used in a justifiable manner (the *jus in bello* criteria).

An introduction to just war and just revolution sources in Christian ethics begins with Augustine, *City of God* (London: Penguin, 1984) and with Thomas Aquinas, *On Politics and Ethics: A New Translation, Background, Interpretations*, ed. Paul E. Sigmund (New York: Norton, 1988). A more recent and widely used source in philosophy is Michael Walzer, *Just and Unjust Wars: A Moral Argument with Historical Illustrations* (New York: Basic, 1977).

41. *Webster's New World College Dictionary*, 2nd ed. (1986), s.v. "sanctuary."

Slaveholders made Christianity compulsory for their slaves. As slaves discovered stories in the Bible that named them precious children of God, offered them hope and promise, and found in Jesus the one who, on the cross, suffered harsh treatment they knew full well, they organized meetings they held in secret in the woods after dark. This is where African-American spirituals originated, many of them with double meanings—religious ideas coupled to freedom from slavery. African shouts, rhythms, and dance, none of which were allowed in the church of the masters, also belonged to gatherings that could last long into the night.

The place where these secret religious practices were held, and where joy and release and new-found energy suspended fear for a season, was called the "hush harbor" or "brush harbor."

har-bor (här′ ber) *n.* 1. a place of refuge, safety, etc.; retreat; shelter[42]

Haven as a harbor isn't always secret or occasioned by the need to escape fear. When times are reasonable and history is not a hammer, the church as haven is open to all, with a welcome to strangers, no questions asked. But here, too, it continues the kind of soul craft and healing that a haven makes possible. Serenity and joy reign in a setting of forgiveness, beauty, and the proclamation of good news. When "the world is too much with us" and "we waste our powers,"[43] this means moral-spiritual renewal and empowerment. Thus is it a moral haven.

The church is not the only such haven, of course. For many, family is that safe place of freedom and refreshment. Likewise, for many, the natural world is a sanctuary. Tellingly, some would even name it their "church," meaning their life-giving haven, their hush harbor. Wendell Berry gives it voice.

> When despair for the world grows in me
> and I wake in the night at the least sound
> in fear of what my life and my children's lives may be,
> I go and lie down where the wood drake
> rests in his beauty on the water, and the great heron feeds.
> I come into the peace of wild things
> who do not tax their lives with forethought
> of grief. I come into the presence of still water.

42. Ibid., s.v. "harbor."
43. From the Wordsworth sonnet cited above.

And I feel above me the day-blind stars
waiting with their light. For a time
I rest in the grace of the world, and am free.[44]

In sum, the Christian moral life involves the church in five distinct roles: as a community of moral identity formation, as a bearer of moral tradition, as a place of moral discernment and deliberation, as an agent of moral action, and as a moral haven. In a kind of ecclesial ecology, each aids the other and none can be dispensed with without stunting the Christian life. All are imperatives that follow from the substance of Christian faith itself and all pertain, whatever the wild diversity of church communities worldwide and whatever their forms of organization, from local congregations to global bodies.

44. Wendell Berry, "The Peace of Wild Things," from *The Selected Poems of Wendell Berry* (Berkeley, CA: Counterpoint, 1998).

10.

Summary and Challenge

This book began by describing the dramatically changed landscapes of our world. One is the planet itself, the other is Christianity and the church. These radically altered landscapes are the context for living the Christian life now.

Our specific subject, however, is the Bible and its role in life lived in this time and place. On that count, we argued for, and proceeded from, a twofold consensus: (1) Christian ethics is not synonymous with biblical ethics as the ethics of biblical communities, and (2) the Bible is nonetheless formative and normative for Christian ethics.

That consensus means little until it joins "a new conversation" set amid the deeply altered planetary and ecclesial landscapes. Unless we can say how Scripture "works" in the Christian moral life, it is only a relic. Like other relics, it may be treasured, on display, and ritually taken in hand now and again. But until there is a living response by people of the book, Scripture is abstract, lifeless, and impotent to do what it has often done in the past. Apart from consequences in the faith community's character and conduct, Scripture, to freely use Paul's words on love, is little more than "a noisy gong or a clanging cymbal" (1 Cor 13:1).

OLD CONVERSATIONS RENEWED

Still, in some important ways the "new conversation" we have entertained turns out to be not new at all but very old. That certainly pertains to many continuing categories and questions. The fundamental tasks and queries of all ethics remain the same. Recall the chart used earlier.

Tasks of Ethics	Accompanying Questions
Descriptive	What is?
Constructive	What could be?
Normative	What ought to be?
Formative	What morally forms and malforms us?
Transformative	What disables and enables the moral–spiritual power to do and be what we discern that we ought?
Practical	To what actions do these questions point?

No new conversation changes these as tasks and questions for the moral life and ethical analysis.

The same pertains to the church's roles. The previous chapter, for example, discusses five roles of the church in the moral life that have always been present in some manner and degree: the church as a community of moral identity formation, as a bearer of moral tradition, as a place of moral discernment and deliberation, as an agent of moral action, and as a moral haven. All of these continue, together, in the complex moral ecology of faith in our changed and changing world. All of them also engage Scripture in crafting our responsibility. But the roles remain the same as they have across millennia, even when the timely content—the right word and deed at the right time—may be old, new, or renewed.

Likewise, the categories for understanding morality display enduring patterns. We have described three. They cluster around qualities of character (virtue), the consequences of our actions, and obligation or duty (our moral bottom lines). The Bible informs and shapes each of these. Taken together, this means that no dimension of the Christian moral life is bypassed or omitted by Scripture, whether in the biblical accounts themselves or in the uses of Scripture in the post-canonical life of faith communities.

At the same time, content attuned to context may change, and should change, even while the formal patterns, tasks, basic questions, and categories do not. While qualities of character, desired consequences, and fundamental duties may well show deep continuity over time, they also are subject to faithful critique and questioning. That critique ferrets out where moral formation has been malformation and where lived values and duties may have betrayed the good that they sought to convey, the gospel. Thus, new challenges, awareness, and voices might revamp the constellation and accent of long-standing moral content. The Protestant ethic that was powerful in the rise of capitalism and the Industrial Revolution may not be viable when the whole community of life, and not simply human life, is the circle of responsibility. Virtues, consequences, and duties fitted for ecological civilization ask for an altered ethic, different from that fitted to industrial civilization. The anthropocentric relationship crafted by the extractive economy of the Industrial Revolution should give way to the relationship of Christian responsibility to the ecosphere as we outlined it in chapter 5. Likewise, ethics and moral sensibilities that have been developed hand in hand with the European and Euro-American colonial enterprise are reshaped by the voices of people who were enslaved or profoundly oppressed or exploited by that enterprise. Different or additional virtues, consequences, and duties are called forth, as are different or additional interpretations of the Bible. To be challenged are interpretations of the biblical witness that support such economic and social forces as imperil human communities and nature's life-giving and life-sustaining capacities.

The Bible, however, continues as an authoritative and formative source, even as we face issues the Bible did not know and even as we uncover biblical interpretations that served causes of death and destruction rather than life and liberation.

Much continues on biblical grounds themselves. The Bible assumes—and displays—that we are an adaptive, creative, and resilient species, if also "stiff-necked," arrogant, and disposed to evil as well as good impulses. Equally noteworthy, it is an unrelenting assumption of biblical materials that we are morally responsible for the world of which we are a part, and that this responsibility is learned in the communities to which we belong. Moreover, in the biblical world, we are "unfinished" agents in an "unfinished" world. We are co-participants with God in a dynamic history that evokes our responsibility for planetary creation itself. A certain power is invested in us for the ordering of life within our sphere of influence. In assuming this, the Bible consistently promotes moral agency as a fundamental human quality.

Simply put, to be human is to be morally responsible, with and before God. Who we are and how we conduct ourselves, our "being" and our "doing," fully belong to the life of faith itself. There is no separation of "religion" from "ethics," or worship from consequence.

What changes in the new conversation, then, is not the flourishing of all creation and all humanity. That is the drumbeat of Scripture from Genesis 1 through Revelation 22. Nor does the Bible change as a formative source of our identity and agency. What changes—or stays the same!—is that the crucial conversations of our moral responsibility engage Scripture anew, in pursuit of flourishing for all.

That engagement is multifaceted and may serve several purposes. One might be retrieval. What insights emerge now from the biblical texts: insights and wisdom, perhaps overlooked, or never seen at all, until we donned different lenses? Another purpose might be constructive response. What actions do we take, and what qualities of character do we nurture, if our anthropocene powers reach farther in space and deeper in time than human communities have ever experienced, and if those powers are endangering Earth's capacity to regenerate life itself? If we are, in fact, deciding the fate of future generations, how do we decide? By what norms and processes? The faith community's engagement with Scripture may also be for the purpose of resistance. What do we stand up against, in light of what we stand for? What do we say "no" to, on the basis of a biblically grounded "yes"? Resistance, retrieval, and construction are lasting, biblically inspired responses, even when the content of each may vary as "new occasions teach new duties."

WHICH BIBLICAL MATERIALS?

But to note lasting continuity as well as real change is not yet to answer a crucial question: *what* biblical materials mold character and conduct and engage the Christian moral life? It is not evasive to say, "all of them." Elements of the whole panorama participate—the narrative accounts; the law; the prophets and the psalms; visions and dreams; parables and teaching; letters of instruction, exhortation, and encouragement; theological ruminations; and devotional elements. There really is no major type of biblical material, including

apocalypse, that cannot play a significant role in the complex phe-
nomena we call moral development and the exercise of moral responsibility. Indeed, one of the pitfalls in the use of Scripture is "genre
reductionism." Different genres are, in effect, different "modes of
perception."[1] Genre reductionism thus crimps moral imagination
and discernment via the selection, whether deliberate or not, of only
certain kinds of biblical materials as pertinent. Thus, materials of
direct moral exhortation, such as prophetic oracles, the Ten Commandments, the Sermon on the Mount, or Paul's admonitions to
his congregations are chosen, but the historical narratives, psalms,
parables, miracle stories, and apocalyptic visions drop away. The
complex nature of character formation, decision-making, and action
argues against such selectivity and limitation. For that reason, we
have underlined the role of the canon as a framework of reference,
inclusion, correction, and control.

The canon, reaching across the centuries of Israel and the ancient
church, is necessarily pluralistic, even as it continues the God-
centeredness that shapes the life of the people of God over time.
Many of the plural materials—narratives, law codes, prophetic admonition, wisdom teaching, Gospel accounts, letters to young
churches—may share an imitation-of-God bearing in the OT (imitatio Dei) and an imitation-of-Christ bearing in the NT (imitatio
Christi). The character and living presence of God and the life, ministry, death, and resurrection of Jesus Christ are, in the Spirit, the
touchstone for the moral life. To love the world as God loves is worthy of imitation.

The canon preserves other elements vital to moral formation and
discernment. Its plural accounts approximate the complexities of the
moral life. They include, on full display, human conniving and failure
as well as dedication and resolve for walking the way of righteousness. Negative examples as well as positive ones appear in dramatic
relief. Here the materials are more mirror than imitation. We see ourselves more clearly. The canon thus serves as a record of the ups and
downs, high points and pitfalls, and successes and failures of the moral
journey as well as its destination.

Furthermore, the canon makes clear that the moral life is not
learned and lived alone but always in a community engaged with

1. See the discussion in ch. 4, citing Carol A. Newsom, *The Book of Job: A Contest of Moral
Imaginations* (New York: Oxford University Press, 2003), 13.

God as present in history and creation. This is also a community set apart. Its life does not rest in minimum moral standards but in those worthy of "a witness to the nations." The social arrangements of life together are to be in keeping with God as the God of the dispossessed and powerless, the alien and the prodigal. A critical, often counter-cultural, stand belongs to this identity. This is so prominent in Scripture that it cannot be sidelined or lost sight of. Some biblical norms are weightier than others (e.g., hospitality to the stranger and love of the enemy).

Of course, the canon's varied materials may work in quite different ways. The theological discourses of Paul or the probing questions and drama of Job, for example, might be the source of certain reasoned convictions that yield a basic orientation toward life. The apocalyptic visions might stimulate us to see the world differently. Some things come alive with meanings not discerned before those strange images turned recognizable worlds inside out and upside down. (Empires are invariably death-dealing, and redeemed creation, barely glimpsed around us, is beautiful beyond the singing of it.) The piety of the Bible's devotional materials might generate attitudes of wonder, mystery, humility, and reverence that carry over into our moral habits. The nature psalms and other wisdom passages might orient us differently to the natural world. We may experience it in awe and as kin and subject rather than only as useful object, even slave. Or, in yet a further example, the vivid contrast of the two creation stories of Genesis might engage moral imagination in the manner that happens when different cosmologies and worldviews sit side-by-side. In any event, at no point can we say on principle which biblical materials belong to the moral life and which do not. While Christian ethics must seek to decipher what effects different materials have, it must not succumb to genre reductionism and its tendency to substitute moralizing for moral maturation.

Speaking of moralizing that substitutes for maturation, it is vital to Scripture itself to set the moral life in the broader context of a multidimensional faith. We discussed this earlier with references to beauty and the relationship of aesthetics and ethics.[2] Without attention to the different dimensions, moods, and voices of faith, the moral life easily slips into moralizing and a constricted and oppressive world, with the Bible a kind of morals sheriff or czar.

2. See pp. 135–36.

SUMMARY AND CHALLENGE 263

Kristin Swenson, while eager to lay out a Christian ecological theology and ethic, recognizes the limits of always doubling down on moral responsibility as the *only* voice of faith. In quite dramatic fashion, she says:

> The God of earth must then, surely, be urging us occasionally to set aside concern and responsibility, even our responsibility for earth itself, in order to enjoy the wonder and mystery before us. Say, taking time to visit a place soon to be flooded by a dam or wild animals before their habitat is destroyed.
> There is value in adoration.[3]

"There is value in adoration" summarizes a biblical theme that belongs to the Christian moral life itself, as does the partner of adoration, praise. Paradoxically, this stepping away from single-minded, narrowed moral attention is part of mature moral responsibility itself. (Swenson's experience of the wonder and mystery before us includes anticipated loss—"taking time to visit a place soon to be flooded by a dam or wild animals before their habitat is destroyed."[4]) The moral architecture of Scripture includes this wide range of experience and feeling. How to "let go" and "let be" in the presence of the lilies of the field and the birds of the air can be as morally faithful as forever fixing everything.

Indeed, "Be still and know that I am God!" belongs not to a psalm of serenity and harmony but to the psalm of tumult that inspired Luther's Reformation and its movement song, "A Mighty Fortress is Our God."

God is our refuge and strength,
    a very present help in trouble.
Therefore we will not fear, though
    the earth should change,
though the mountains shake in the heart of the sea;
though its waters roar and foam,
    though the mountains tremble
    with its tumult. (Ps 46:1–3)

After this and much more of war, desolation, and conflict, as well as

---

3. Kristin Swenson, *God of Earth: Discovering a Radically Ecological Christianity* (Louisville: Westminster John Knox, 2016), 63.
4. Ibid.

peacemaking, comes the verse, "Be still, and know that I am God!" There is value in stepping away, stepping back, and refocusing. It is a different rhythm and ethos, one of re-centering and renewal. Ethos matters.

Consider the ethos of the Gospel of John, the source of perhaps the most memorized of all NT verses, John 3:16, "For God so loved the world . . ." "World" in Greek, and in John's Gospel, is *kosmos*, a word that connotes both "beauty" and "order." John's Gospel is a mystical gospel of deep incarnation. It breathes the universe of Hellenistic philosophy and Jewish wisdom literature. The *kosmos* of John 3:16 echoes the preamble of John's Gospel: "In the beginning was the Word, and the Word was with God, and the Word was God. He was in the beginning with God. All things came into being through him, and without him not one thing came into being" (John 1:1–3). "And the Word became flesh and lived among us, and we have seen his glory" (John 1:14). The "world," or creation, that God loves to the point of self-giving incarnation is one of cosmic "beauty" and "order." To overlook this is to shrink the meaning of "For God so loved the *kosmos* . . ." and miss the cosmic wonder that belongs to the moral life and shapes it. The influence may be indirect, as mystery and the mystical are, but it is real. Biblical materials, via their ethos, have their own effect on moral imagination and development.

The biblical panorama is moral architecture in still other ways. Biblical materials have, for example, been formative of long moral traditions that supply content and provide an orientation as we deliberate issues. Almost all the examples used in this volume are of people who have a place to stand and a canonical body of witness upon which they draw and to which they feel accountable. Whether they directly engage Scripture in the moment of decision-making or not, they likely engage moral traditions shaped by Scripture.

As we have noted throughout, those moral traditions, while they ought to shape and empower ways of living that reflect the God revealed in Jesus and the Spirit, have also betrayed that God. Of course, the biblical materials do not themselves make the decisions. Nor do the traditions. We do that, either consciously and explicitly or by default.

Here again, it is worth recalling how the Bible might work, and often has. The biblical traditions are pluralistic in content and open to change. They are sometimes drawn upon to transform moral identity itself, or to reorder the moral universe. This means a morally rich world and a creative frame of reference that offers innumerable images, analogies, and examples (including negative ones) for our own moral imagination. The same materials may supply the norms or standards by which to measure our choice. The Ten Commandments, the Sermon on the Mount, and Paul's admonitions to his congregations have often done this. Similarly, biblical materials may be the source for helping to establish the boundaries of morally permissible behavior. Not by coincidence, some version of the Ten Commandments and the Golden Rule turn up, time and again, as the framework without which society does not function fairly or well. They are the requirements for living together. Or, as noted above, some biblical themes are so strong—love of neighbor, hospitality to the stranger, going the second mile, forgiving seventy times seven—that they are moral bottom lines. To dismiss them is to empty the faith of its enacted meaning. In any case, the moral witness of biblical materials and the traditions shaped by them provide a rich and varied fund for discernment and deliberation, even if they can never supply all the crucial elements, such as the ethical analysis and empirical studies we emphasized earlier.

BIBLE AND COMMUNITY

Yet another theme threaded throughout this volume is that biblical materials locate the moral life and moral agency within the life of the faith community. The Bible is the charter resource for the Christian ethic as a *koinonia* ethic, a community-creating ethic rooted in a compelling experience of God.

Recall the chapter on the authority of Scripture. The use of Scripture in the community is to help form Christians as those who learn the story of ancient Israel and of Jesus well enough to experience the world from within those stories, and to act in keeping with that experience. The Bible aids in crafting a good and just life learned as part of the community's own ongoing life.

But this assumes the Bible is an indispensable authority in the Christian community. While there are numerous authorities in our lives (any decisive influence, however transient, is an authority), the Bible's authority lies in its function as a unique witness to the experience of the transforming presence and power of God. Biblical authority does not inhere in the text itself but in the community's recognition that Scripture is a source of empowerment for its life in the world. The authority of Scripture rests, then, in the power of Scripture to form and empower the community that experiences God through its responsive reading of that Scripture.[5]

Given the Bible as this kind of communal authority, what does this locus imply about the Christian life? It means that the gathered life of the church is as fundamentally moral in nature as the scattered, or dispersed, life of the church. The internal life of the gathered community as a "body" is where and how moral agency is developed and moral witness is made visible. Liturgy, preaching, Christian education, use and care of buildings and grounds, budgetary priorities, congregational nurture, and advocacy are not "preparation" for the moral life as it is lived elsewhere. They belong to the church as itself an embodied eco-social ethic. And Scripture, whether directly or indirectly, belongs to all these dimensions of ecclesial life.

A matching truth is this: the scattered life of the faith community is as fundamentally moral in nature as its gathered life. In many ways, the reason for gathering is to praise God and to empower the people for the lives they live when they are not directly present with one another in worship. *Leitourgia*, liturgy, is "the work of the people" for the life of the world. To be agents of justice-seeking love and messengers of hope means bearing witness as the people of God dispersed as the radiation of church in society. That, too, is the moral presence of the faith community. (Recall the church in San Diego where the waters of life flowed from the temple of God through the sanctuary and then, in multiple streams, out the doors and into the community.)

All this is only a partial summary of what we have undertaken in this book. Hopefully it suffices to draw the reader back into the details.

SPIRIT, CREATION, AND CHALLENGE

We would be remiss not to link back to the introduction and its description of a changing planet and the shift of the center of world Christianity from the Global North to the Global South, just as we would be remiss not to note that Christianity is growing. In 2010, 2.18 billion Christians comprised 32 percent of the world's

5. See ch. 4, pp. 40–41.

population. Half were Roman Catholic, with the majority in Asia, Africa, and Latin America. Most stunning, however, has been the rise of Pentecostal and Charismatic churches, together numbering 504 million Christians. Evangelicals are another 285 million. Not to be overlooked, either, is that approximately 78.5 million Bibles are distributed globally every year.[6]

All this noted, we authors have assumed a presence of the Spirit we did not anticipate or underscore at the outset. Nor did we see its full ecumenical reach across richly diverse Christian worlds. Yet, whether named or not, this volume has, sometimes consciously, sometimes unwittingly, linked creation and the Spirit throughout, in the biblical materials and beyond.

We have included only some examples. Indigenous peoples have long pictured God's Spirit permeating and animating the physical world. So, too, does Pope Francis, leader of 1.09 billion Christians. This is reflected in the very choice of his papal name and in the inspiration for his encyclical, *Laudato Si'*. For the pope, as for Saint Francis of Assisi, the whole created order manifests the Spirit. All creatures praise God and bear an intrinsic goodness, a goodness that calls for "care for our common home." This is care that rebukes injustice as inequality and planetary degradation.

Likewise, this "panentheism" (Paul's "all in God and God in all") is the provenance of Orthodox teaching from the ancient church to the present. In this tradition, the Spirit is spoken of as the all-pervading energy of God. This divine energy is cosmic. It animates all creation. With the material universe suffused by the Spirit, "nature" for the Orthodox is never a secular word to speak of a world independent of humanity and God, a meaning it has taken on in much of the modern Euro-West. There is no such word for nature in that sense in Hebrew, either. "Nature" with that meaning isn't found anywhere in the biblical accounts. Rather, creation is seamless, inclusive, ongoing, cosmic, and inspirited. Yet, the point for the Orthodox is that the creative energy of God as the Spirit is present as the life of the world for the world.[7] To recall the ninth-century plainsong and

6. "Christian Movements and Denominations," Pew Research Center, December 19, 2011, http://tinyurl.com/h3ek9pb.

7. For an Orthodox articulation of this from the desert fathers and mothers to the present, see John Chryssavgis, *Beyond the Shattered Image: Insights into an Orthodox Christian Ecological Worldview* (Minneapolis: Light and Life Publishing, 1999). Also see Wes Granberg-Michaelson, *Future Faith: Ten Ways Christianity is Changing in the 21st Century* (Minneapolis: Fortress Press, 2018).

a World Council of Churches theme, *Veni, Creator Spiritus*, "Come, Holy Spirit, Renew the Whole Creation."

All this said, the swelling world of Pentecostalism and the growth of other churches not only joins this broad consensus but insists on the Spirit's vivid presence in the inner life and in worship. The Spirit's *absence* in the inner life and in exuberant praise is another link to creation, but with negative consequences. In the pope's words: "The external deserts in the world are growing, because the internal deserts have become so vast."[8]

In any event, we finish not with a summary but with a challenge. On that, both the biblical materials and the Christian life are unequivocal. Both are about action. Nothing is so consistently underscored in Scripture, or so emphasized, as the *embodiment* of faith. Just as the meaning of the dance is in the dancing of it, the meaning of faith is in the spirited living of it.

---

8. Francis, *Laudato Si'*, para. 217. The pope is here quoting the previous pope, Benedict XVI, from *Homily for the Solemn Inauguration of the Petrine Ministry* (April 24, 2005).

Bibliography

Alexander, Michelle. *The New Jim Crow: Mass Incarceration in the Age of Colorblindness*. New York: New Press, 2012.

American Psychological Association. "Sexual Orientation, Parents, and Children." July 2004. http://tinyurl.com/y7aktk3m.

Aquinas, Thomas. *On Politics and Ethics: A New Translation, Background, Interpretations*. Edited by Paul E. Sigmund. New York: Norton, 1988.

Aristotle. *Nicomachean Ethics*. Translated by H. Rackham. Loeb Classical Library 73. Cambridge, MA: Harvard University Press, 1926.

Augustine. *City of God*. London: Penguin, 1984.

———. *On Christian Teaching*. Translated by R. P. H. Green. Oxford: Oxford University Press, 1997.

Barr, James. *The Bible in the Modern World*. New York: Harper & Row, 1973.

Barton, John. "Approaches to Ethics in the Old Testament." In *Beginning Old Testament Study*, edited in John Rogerson, 113–30. London: SPCK, 1983.

———. *Ethics and the Old Testament*. Harrisburg, PA: Trinity Press International, 1998.

———. *Ethics in Ancient Israel*. Oxford: Oxford University Press, 2014.

———. "Understanding Old Testament Ethics." *Journal for the Study of the Old Testament* 3, no. 9 (October 1978): 44–64.

———. *Understanding Old Testament Ethics: Approaches and Explorations*. Louisville: Westminster John Knox, 2003.

Bauckham, Richard. *Living with Other Creatures: Green Exegesis and Theology*. Waco, TX: Baylor University Press, 2011.

Beauchamp, Tom L., and James F. Childress. *Principles of Biomedical Ethics*. New York: Oxford University Press, 1979.

Bellah, Robert N., Richard Madsen, William M. Sullivan, Ann Swidler, and Steven M. Tipton. *Habits of the Heart: Individualism and Commitment in American Life*. Berkeley: University of California Press, 1985.

Berry, Wendell. *The Gift of Good Land: Further Essays Cultural and Agricultural*. Berkeley, CA: Counterpoint, 1981.

———. *The Selected Poems of Wendell Berry*. Berkeley, CA: Counterpoint, 1998.

———, *What Are People For?*, Berkeley, CA: Counterpoint, 1990.

Binder, David. "Waldheim Linked to Nazi Roundup." *New York Times*, February 18, 1988http://tinyurl.com/y9fqg3jn, A12.

Birch, Bruce C. "Biblical Studies: Ethics." *Oxford Online Bibliographies*. March 10, 2015. http://tinyurl.com/y9jzvyzf.

———. "Divine Character and the Formation of Moral Community in the Book of Exodus." In *The Bible in Ethics: The Second Sheffield Colloquium*, edited by John W. Rogerson, Margaret Davies, and M. Daniel Carroll R., 119–35. Sheffield: Sheffield Academic Press, 1995.

———. "Ethics in the OT." In vol. 2 of *The New Interpreter's Dictionary of the Bible*, edited by Katharine Doob Sakenfeld, 338–48. Nashville: Abingdon, 2007.

———. *Let Justice Roll Down: The Old Testament, Ethics, and Christian Life*. Louisville: Westminster John Knox, 1991.

———. "Memory in Congregational Life." In *Congregations: Their Power to Form and Transform*, edited by C. Ellis Nelson, 20–42. Atlanta: John Knox, 1988.

———. "Moral Agency, Community, and the Character of God in the Hebrew Bible." *Semeia* 66 (1994): 23–41.

———. "Old Testament Ethics." In *The Blackwell Companion to the Hebrew Bible*, edited by Leo G. Perdue, 301–2. Oxford: Blackwell, 2001.

———. "Old Testament Narrative and Moral Address." In *Canon, Theology and Old Testament Interpretation: Essays in Honor of Brevard S. Childs*, edited by Gene M. Tucker, David L. Petersen, and Robert R. Wilson, 75–92. Philadelphia: Fortress Press, 1988.

———. *What Does the Lord Require? The Old Testament Call to Social Witness*. Philadelphia: Westminster, 1985.

Birch, Bruce C., and Larry L. Rasmussen. *Bible and Ethics in the Christian Life*. Rev. and expanded ed. Minneapolis: Augsburg Fortress, 1989.

———. *The Predicament of the Prosperous*. Philadelphia: Westminster, 1978.

————. "These All Look to Thee: A Relational Theology of Nature." In *The Predicament of the Prosperous*, 118–23. Philadelphia: Westminster, 1978.

Black Catholic Hymnal Committee. *Lead Me, Guide Me: The African American Catholic Hymnal*. Chicago: GIA Publications, 1987.

Blount, Brian K., Cain Hope Felder, Clarice J. Martin, and Emerson B. Powery. Introduction to *True to Our Native Land: An African American New Testament Commentary*, edited by Brian K. Blount, Cain Hope Felder, Clarice J. Martin, and Emerson B. Powery, 1–10. Minneapolis: Fortress Press, 2007.

Boesak, Allan. "Babblers to the Rabble, Prophets to the Powerful: Mission in the Context of Empire." Keynote address, consultation sponsored by the Council for World Mission, Bangkok, May 29–June 2, 2017.

Boff, Leonardo. *Cry of the Earth, Cry of the Poor*. Maryknoll, NY: Orbis, 1997.

Bonhoeffer, Dietrich. *Dietrich Bonhoeffer Works*. 17 vols. Minneapolis: Fortress Press, 1996–2014.

————. "Ten Years After." In *Letters and Papers from Prison*, 1–20. Edited by Eberhard Bethge. Translated by Reginald Fuller. New York: Touchstone, 1997.

Borg, Marcus J. *Meeting Jesus Again for the First Time: The Historical Jesus and the Heart of Contemporary Faith*. San Francisco: HarperOne, 2015.

Borgmann, Albert. *Real American Ethics: Taking Responsibility for Our Country*. Chicago: University of Chicago Press, 2006.

Boring, M. Eugene, and Fred B. Craddock. *The People's New Testament Commentary*. Louisville: Westminster John Knox, 2009.

Brady, Bernard V. *Christian Love: How Christians Through the Ages Have Understood Love*. Washington, DC: Georgetown University Press, 2015.

Branch, Taylor. *At Canaan's Edge: America in the King Years, 1965–68*. New York: Simon & Schuster, 2006.

————. *Parting the Waters: America in the King Years, 1954–63*. New York: Simon & Schuster, 1989.

————. *Pillar of Fire: America in the King Years, 1963–65*. New York: Simon & Schuster, 1998.

Brians, Paul, ed. *Reading about the World*. 2 vols. 3rd ed. Orlando, FL: Harcourt College, 1999.

Brokering, Herbert, and Roland Bainton. *A Pilgrimage to Luther's Germany*. Minneapolis: Fortress Press, 1983.

Brookfield, Stephen. *Developing Critical Thinkers: Challenging Adults to*

Explore Alternative Ways of Thinking and Acting. San Francisco: Jossey-Bass, 1987.

Brooks, David. "The Moral Bucket List." *New York Times*, April 11, 2015http://tinyurl.com/y7von9hw, SR1.

———. "The Responsibility Deficit." *New York Times*, September 24, 2010http://tinyurl.com/35mddhl, A29.

Brown, Michael Joseph. "Hearing the Master's Voice." In *Engaging Biblical Authority: Perspectives on the Bible as Scripture*, edited by William P. Brown, 10–17. Louisville: Westminster John Knox, 2007.

Brown, William P. *A Handbook to Old Testament Exegesis*. Louisville: Westminster John Knox, 2017.

———. *The Seven Pillars of Creation: The Bible, Science, and the Ecology of Wonder*. Oxford: Oxford University Press, 2010.

———. "Wisdom and Folly." In *Earth-Honoring Faith: Religious Ethics in a New Key*, edited by Larry L. Rasmussen, 332–56. Oxford: Oxford University Press, 2013.

Brueggemann, Walter. "The Book of Exodus: Introduction, Commentary, and Reflection." In vol. 1 of *The New Interpreter's Bible*, edited by Leander Keck, 736–37. Nashville: Abingdon, 1994.

———. *The Prophetic Imagination*. Philadelphia: Fortress Press, 1978.

———. *The Prophetic Imagination*. 2nd ed. Philadelphia: Fortress Press, 2001.

———. "Voices of the Night—Against Justice." In *To Act Justly, Love Tenderly, Walk Humbly*, by Walter Brueggemann, Sharon Parks, and Thomas H. Groome, 5–28. New York: Paulist, 1986.

Buber, Martin. *Kampf um Israel*. Berlin: Schocken, 1933.

Cahill, Lisa Sowle. "The New Testament and Ethics: Communities of Social Change." *Interpretation* 44, no. 4 (1990): 383–95.

Calvin, John. *Commentary on Genesis*. Grand Rapids: Baker, 1989.

Cardoso, Nancy. "The Bible: Globalized Commodity in the New Strategies of Neocolonialism." Paper presented at consultation sponsored by the Council for World Mission, Bangkok, May 29–June 2, 2017.

Carey, George W. "James Wilson: Political Thought and the Constitutional Convention—The Imaginative Conservative." The Imaginative Conservative. February 27, 2014. http://tinyurl.com/y8wy6h78.

Childs, Brevard S. *Biblical Theology of the Old and New Testaments: Theological Reflections on the Christian Bible*. Minneapolis: Fortress Press, 1993.

Childs, Craig. *Apocalyptic Planet: Field Guide to the Future of the Earth*. New York: Vintage Books, 2013.

Chryssavgis, John. *Beyond the Shattered Image: Insights into an Orthodox Christian Ecological Worldview*. Minneapolis: Light and Life Publishing, 1999.

Churchill, Winston. *Winston S. Churchill: His Complete Speeches 1897–1963*. Vol. 7, *1943–1949*. Edited by Robert Rhodes James. New York: Chelsea House, 1974.

Clements, Ronald E. *Loving One's Neighbor: Old Testament Ethics in Context*. London: University of London Press, 1992.

Claassens, L. Juliana, and Birch, Bruce C., eds., *Restorative Readings: The Old Testament, Ethics, and Human Dignity*. Eugene, OR: Pickwick, 2015.

Crites, Stephen. "The Narrative Quality of Experience." *Journal of the American Academy of Religion* 39, no. 3 (1971): 291–311.

Croatto, J. Severino. *Exodus: A Hermeneutics of Freedom*. Translated by Salvator Attanasio. Maryknoll, NY: Orbis, 1981.

Crowder, Stephanie Buckhanon. *When Momma Speaks: The Bible and Motherhood from a Womanist Perspective*. Louisville: Westminster John Knox, 2016.

Dahill, Lisa E. "Rewilding Christian Spirituality: Outdoor Sacraments and the Life of the World." In *Eco-Reformation: Grace and Hope for a Planet in Peril*, edited by Lisa E. Dahill and James B. Martin-Schramm, 177–96. Eugene, OR: Wipf & Stock, 2016.

Dahill, Lisa E., and James B. Martin-Schramm, eds. *Eco-Reformation: Grace and Hope for a Planet in Peril*. Eugene, OR: Cascade, 2016.

Danker, Frederick William, Walter Bauer, William F. Arndt, and F. Wilbur Gingrich. *Greek-English Lexicon of the New Testament and Other Early Christian Literature*. 3rd ed. Chicago: University of Chicago Press, 2000.

Davis, Clive M., William L. Yarber, Robert Bauserman, George Schreer, and Sandra L. Davis, eds. *Handbook of Sexuality-Related Measures*. Thousand Oaks, CA: Sage, 2000.

Davis, Ellen F. *Scripture, Culture, and Agriculture: An Agrarian Reading of the Bible*. New York: Cambridge University Press, 2009.

De La Torre, Miguel A. *Doing Christian Ethics from the Margins*. Maryknoll, NY: Orbis, 2014.

DeYoung, Curtiss Paul, Wilda C. Gafney, Leticia Guardiola-Sáenz, George E. Tinker, and Frank Yamada, eds. *The People's Companion to the Bible*. Minneapolis: Fortress Press: 2010.

Dorrien, Gary. *Breaking White Supremacy: Martin Luther King Jr. and the Black Social Gospel*. New Haven: Yale University Press, 2018.

————. *The New Abolition: W. E. B. Du Bois and the Black Social Gospel*. New Haven: Yale University Press, 2015.

Douglas, Kelly Brown. *The Black Christ*. Maryknoll, NY: Orbis, 1994.

Ekblad, Bob. *Reading the Bible with the Damned*. Louisville: Westminster John Knox, 2005.

Evans, Rachel Held. *A Year of Biblical Womanhood: How a Liberated Woman Found Herself Sitting on Her Roof, Covering Her Head, and Calling Her Husband "Master."* Nashville: Thomas Nelson, 2012.

Farley, Edward, and Peter C. Hodgson. "Scripture and Tradition." In *Christian Theology: An Introduction to Its Traditions and Tasks*, edited by Peter C. Hodgson and Robert H. King, 61–87. Philadelphia: Fortress Press, 1985.

Ferguson, Gary. "A Deeper Boom." *Orion* 35, no. 5 (July/August and September/October 2016): 14–19.

Firestein, Stuart. *Ignorance: How It Drives Science*. New York: Oxford University Press, 2012.

Fishbane, Michael. *Biblical Interpretation in Ancient Israel*. Oxford: Clarendon, 1985.

FitzGerald, Frances. *The Evangelicals: The Struggle to Shape America*. New York: Simon & Schuster, 2017.

Fowl, Stephen E., and L. Gregory Jones. *Reading in Communion: Scripture and Ethics in Christian Life*. Grand Rapids: Eerdmans, 1991.

Francis. *On Care for Our Common Home: Laudato Si'*. Edited by Sean McDonagh. Maryknoll, NY: Orbis, 2016.

Frei, Hans W. *The Eclipse of Biblical Narrative: A Study in Eighteenth and Nineteenth Century Hermeneutics*. New Haven: Yale University Press, 1974.

Friedman, Thomas. "Foreign Affairs; Drilling in the Cathedral." *New York Times*, March 2, 2001, A1.

Galloway, Steven. *The Cellist of Sarajevo*. New York: Riverhead, 2008.

Gao, George. "Scientists More Worried Than Public About World's Growing Population." Pew Research Center. June 8, 2015. http://tinyurl.com/y7bdj9f5.

Garrow, David J. *Bearing the Cross: Martin Luther King, Jr., and the Southern Christian Leadership Conference*. New York: William Morrow, 1986.

Gilkey, Langdon. *Maker of Heaven and Earth: A Study of the Christian Doctrine of Creation in the Light of Modern Knowledge*. Garden City, NY: Doubleday, 1959.

———. *Nature, Reality, and the Sacred: The Nexus of Science and Religion.* Minneapolis: Augsburg Fortress, 1993.

———. *Shantung Compound.* New York: Harper & Row, 1966.

Gottlieb, Roger S. *The Oxford Handbook of Religion and Ecology.* Oxford: Oxford University Press, 2006.

Gottwald, Norman K. *The Tribes of Yahweh: A Sociology of the Religion of Liberated Israel 1250–1050 B.C.E.* Maryknoll, NY: Orbis, 1979.

Granberg-Michaelson, Wesley. *From Times Square to Timbuktu: The Post-Christian West Meets the Non-Western Church.* Grand Rapids: Eerdmans, 2013.

———. "Navigating the Changing Landscape of World Christianity." In *A Ministry of Reconciliation: Essays in Honor of Gregg Mast*, edited by Allen J. Janssen, 121–36. Grand Rapids: Eerdmans, 2017.

———. *Future Faith: Ten Ways Christianity is Changing in the 21st Century.* Minneapolis: Fortress Press, 2018.

Gutiérrez y Muhs, Gabriella, Yolanda Flores Niemann, Carmen G. González, and Angela P. Harris, eds. *Presumed Incompetent: The Intersections of Race and Class for Women in Academia.* Boulder: University Press of Colorado, 2012.

Habel, Norman, ed. *The Earth Story in Psalms and Prophets.* Earth Bible 4. Sheffield: Sheffield Academic, 2001.

———, ed. *Readings from the Perspective of Earth.* Earth Bible 1. Sheffield: Sheffield Academic, 2000.

Habel, Norman, and Vicky Balabanski, eds. *The Earth Story in the New Testament.* Earth Bible 5. Sheffield: Sheffield Academic, 2002.

Habel, Norman, and Shirley Wurst, eds. *The Earth Story in Genesis.* Earth Bible 2. Sheffield: Sheffield Academic, 2000.

———, eds. *The Earth Story in Wisdom Traditions.* Earth Bible 3. Sheffield: Sheffield Academic, 2001.

Hall, Douglas John. *Lighten Our Darkness: Toward an Indigenous Theology of the Cross.* Philadelphia: Westminster, 1976.

Hallie, Philip P. *Lest Innocent Blood Be Shed.* New York: Harper & Row, 1979.

Hanson, Paul D. *The People Called: The Growth of Community in the Bible.* San Francisco: Harper & Row, 1986.

Harris, Melanie L. *Ecowomanism: African American Women and Earth-Honoring Faiths.* Maryknoll, NY: Orbis, 2017.

Hauerwas, Stanley. *The Peaceable Kingdom: A Primer in Christian Ethics.* Notre Dame: University of Notre Dame Press, 1983.

Hays, Richard B. *The Moral Vision of the New Testament: Community, Cross, New Creation; A Contemporary Introduction to New Testament Ethics.* San Francisco: HarperSanFrancisco, 1996.

Hempel, Johannes. *Das Ethos des Alten Testament.* Berlin: Töpelmann, 1938.

———. "Ethics in the Old Testament." In vol. 2 of *The Interpreter's Dictionary of the Bible,* edited by George Arthur Buttrick, 153–61. Nashville: Abingdon, 1962.

Holtom, Jeremy. "Gandhi's Interpretation of the Sermon on the Mount." In *The Oxford Handbook of the Reception History of the Bible,* edited by Michael Lieb, Emma Mason, Jonathan Roberts, and Christopher Rowland, 542–56. Oxford: Oxford University Press, 2011.

Jacobs, A. J. *The Year of Living Biblically: One Man's Humble Quest to Follow the Bible as Literally as Possible.* New York: Simon & Schuster, 2007.

Jenkins, Willis. *The Future of Ethics: Sustainability, Social Justice, and Religious Creativity.* Washington, DC: Georgetown University Press, 2013.

Johnson, Allan G. *Privilege, Power, and Difference.* Boston: McGraw-Hill, 2006.

Johnson, Luke Timothy. "The Bible's Authority for and in the Church." In *Engaging Biblical Authority: Perspectives on the Bible as Scripture,* edited by William P. Brown, 62–72. Louisville: Westminster John Knox, 2007.

Johnson, Todd M., and Kenneth R. Ross, eds. *Atlas of Global Christianity: 1910–2010.* Edinburgh: Edinburgh University Press, 2009.

Junior, Nyasha. *An Introduction to Womanist Biblical Interpretation.* Louisville: Westminster John Knox, 2015.

Kant, Immanuel. *Groundwork of the Metaphysics of Morals.* Translated and edited by Mary Gregor and Jens Timmermann. Cambridge: Cambridge University Press, 2012.

Kennedy, William Bean. "Integrating Personal and Social Ideologies." In *Fostering Critical Reflection in Adulthood: A Guide to Transformative and Emancipatory Learning,* edited by Jack Mezirow, 99–115. San Francisco: Jossey-Bass, 1990.

King, Martin Luther, Jr. "Letter from Birmingham Jail." In *Why We Can't Wait,* 85–110. New York: Harper & Row, 1964.

———. *Stride toward Freedom: The Montgomery Story.* New York: Harper & Row, 1958.

———. *A Testament of Hope: The Essential Writings and Speeches of Martin*

Luther King, Jr., edited by James M. Washington. San Francisco: Harper & Row, 1991.

Kolbert, Elizabeth. *The Sixth Extinction: An Unnatural History.* New York: Henry Holt, 2014.

Kraybill, Donald B. *The Upside-Down Kingdom.* Scottdale, PA: Herald, 1978.

Kruger, Michael. "The Difference Between Original Autographs and Original Texts." The Gospel Coalition, May 14, 2013, http://tinyurl.com/ycgr37fv.

Kvam, Kristen E., Linda S. Schearing, and Valarie H. Ziegler, eds. *Eve and Adam: Jewish, Christian, and Muslim Readings on Genesis and Gender.* Bloomington: Indiana University Press, 2009.

Lathrop, Gordon. *Saving Images: The Presence of the Bible in in Christian Liturgy.* Minneapolis: Fortress Press, 2017.

Lee, Sandra S. K. "Christianity by Major Tradition, 1910–2010." In *Atlas of Global Christianity: 1910–2010,* edited by Todd M. Johnson and Kenneth R. Ross, 66–67. Edinburgh: Edinburgh University Press, 2009.

MacIntyre, Alasdair. *After Virtue: A Study in Moral Theory.* Notre Dame: University of Notre Dame Press, 1981.

Maguire, Daniel. *Death by Choice.* Garden City, NY: Image, 1984.

———. *The Moral Core of Judaism and Christianity: Reclaiming the Revolution.* Minneapolis: Fortress Press, 1993.

Marlow, Hilary, *Biblical Prophets and Contemporary Environmental Ethics.* Oxford: Oxford University Press, 2009

Martin-Schramm, James, Daniel Spencer, and Laura Stivers. *Earth Ethics: A Case Method Approach.* Maryknoll, NY: Orbis, 2015.

McFague, Sallie. *Models of God: Theology for an Ecological, Nuclear Age.* Philadelphia: Fortress Press, 1987.

McGilchrist, Iain. *The Master and His Emissary: The Divided Brain and the Making of the Western World.* New Haven: Yale University Press, 2009.

McKibben, Bill. *The End of Nature.* New York: Random House, 1989.

Medical University of Vienna. "Networks of the Brain Reflect the Individual Gender Identity." *Science Daily,* January 7, 2015. http://tinyurl.com/y8eykhmt.

Meeks, Wayne A. *The Moral World of the First Christians.* Philadelphia: Westminster, 1986.

Merton, Thomas. "Hagia Sophia." In *A Thomas Merton Reader,* 506–16. Edited by Thomas P. McDonnell. Garden City, NY: Image, 1974.

Milgrom, Jacob. *Leviticus 17–22: A New Translation and Commentary.* Anchor Bible 3A. New York: Doubleday, 2000.

Miller, Patrick D. *The Ten Commandments.* Interpretation. Louisville: Westminster John Knox, 2009.

Moe-Lobeda, Cynthia. *Healing a Broken World: Globalization and God.* Minneapolis: Fortress Press, 2002.

———. *Resisting Structural Evil: Love as Ecological-Economic Vocation.* Minneapolis: Fortress Press, 2013.

Murdoch, Iris. *Existentialists and Mystics: Writings on Philosophy and Literature.* New York: Penguin, 1997.

Myers, Ched, ed. *Watershed Discipleship: Reinhabiting Bioregional Faith and Practice.* Eugene, OR: Cascade, 2016.

Nairobi Daily Nation. "Austrians Divided over Waldheim's Nazi Issue." January 16, 1988.

Nasuti, Harry P. "Identity, Identification, and Imitation: The Narrative Hermeneutics of Biblical Law." *Journal of Law and Religion* 4, no. 1 (1986): 9–23.

National Bioethics Advisory Commission. "Executive Summary." *Ethical and Policy Issues in International Research: Clinical Trials in Developing Countries,* vol. 1 (2001). Bethesda, MD: NBAC, April 2001. PDF. https://tinyurl.com/y9po4uhq.

National Conference of Catholic Bishops. *The Challenge of Peace: God's Promise and Our Response.* Washington, DC: United States Conference of Catholic Bishops, 1983.

———. *Economic Justice for All: Pastoral Letter on Catholic Social Teaching the U.S. Economy.* Washington, DC: United States Conference of Catholic Bishops, 2009. PDF. http://tinyurl.com/y86e9def.

Newsom, Carol A. *The Book of Job: A Contest of Moral Imaginations.* New York: Oxford University Press, 2003.

Newsom, Carol A., Sharon Ringe, and Jacqueline Lapsley, eds. *Women's Bible Commentary.* 3rd ed. Louisville: Westminster John Knox, 2012.

Schneider, Keith, "Science Debates Using Tools to Redesign Life," *New York Times,* June 8, 1987, A1.

Niebuhr, H. Richard. *Christ and Culture.* New York: Harper & Row, 1951.

———. *The Purpose of the Church and Its Ministry: Reflection on the Aims of Theological Education.* With Daniel Day Williams and James M. Gustafson. New York: Harper, 1956.

Nissinen, Marti. "Biblical Masculinities: Musings on Theory and Agenda." In

Biblical Masculinities Foregrounded, edited by Ovidiu Creangă and Peter-Ben Smit, 271–85. Sheffield: Sheffield Phoenix, 2014.

Nussbaum, Martha C. "Justice for Women!" Review of *Justice, Gender, and the Family*, by Susan Moller Okin. *New York Review of Books* 39, no. 16 (October 8, 1992): 43–48.

Ogletree, Thomas W. *The Use of the Bible in Christian Ethics*. Philadelphia: Fortress Press, 1983.

Oliver, Mary. "The Summer Day." In *House of Light*, 60. Boston: Beacon, 1990.

Olson, Dennis. "'Oh LORD God, How Am I to Know?': The Pentateuch and Contemporary Understandings of Truth." *Princeton Seminary Bulletin* 23 (2002): 86–99.

———. "Revenge, Forgiveness, and Sibling Rivalry: A Theological Dialogue between Scripture and Science." *Ex Auditu* 28 (2012): 94–119.

Otto, Eckart. *Theologische Ethik des Alten Testaments*. Stuttgart: Kohlhammer, 1994.

Parker, David C. *Textual Scholarship and the Making of the NT*. Oxford: Oxford University Press, 2012.

Pew Research Center. "Christian Movements and Denominations." December 19, 2011. http://tinyurl.com/h3ek9pb.

———. "The Global Religious Landscape." December 18, 2012. http://tiny url.com/qg97qjy.

Rasmussen, Larry L. *Earth Community, Earth Ethics*. Maryknoll, NY: Orbis, 1998.

———. *Earth-Honoring Faith: Religious Ethics in a New Key*. Oxford: Oxford University Press, 2013.

———. "Economic Ethics." In *Dictionary of Scripture and Ethics*, edited by Joel B. Green, 263–69. Grand Rapids: Baker Academic, 2011.

———. "Green Discipleship." *Reflections Yale Divinity School*, Spring 2007, 68–72.

———. *Moral Fragments and Moral Community: A Proposal for Church in Society*. Minneapolis: Fortress Press, 1993.

———. "Shaping Communities." In *Practicing Our Faith*, edited by Dorothy C. Bass, 117–30. 2nd ed. San Francisco: Jossey-Bass, 2010.

Rawls, John. *A Theory of Justice*. Cambridge, MA: Belknap Press of Harvard University Press, 1971.

Reséndez, Andrés. *The Other Slavery: The Uncovered Story of Indian Enslavement in America*. Boston: Houghton Mifflin Harcourt, 2016.

Rossing, Barbara. "The World Is about to Turn: Preaching Apocalyptic Texts for a Planet in Peril." In *Eco-Reformation: Grace and Hope for a Planet in Peril*, edited by Lisa E. Dahill and James B. Martin-Schramm, 140–59. Eugene, OR: Cascade, 2016.

Sanders, James A. "The Bible as Canon." *The Christian Century* 98, no. 39 (December 2, 1981): 1250–55.

Schmemann, Serge. "Inquiry for Austria Declares Waldheim Knew of War Crimes." *New York Times*, February 9, 1988, A1.

———. "Waldheim Assails 'Slanders,' Vows Not to Step Down." *New York Times*, February 16, 1988, A1.

Schneider, Keith. "Farmers to Face Patent Fees to Use Gene-Altered Animals." *New York Times*, February 6, 1988, 1.

Schumacher, E. F. *Small Is Beautiful: Economics as if People Mattered*. New York: Harper Perennial, 2010.

Schüssler Fiorenza, Elisabeth. "Discipleship and Patriarchy: Early Christian Ethos and Christian Ethics in a Feminist Theological Perspective." *Annual of the Society of Christian Ethics* 2 (1982): 131–72.

Scranton, Roy. "The Anthropocene: A Man-Made World." *The Economist*, May 26, 2011.

———. *Learning to Die in the Anthropocene: Reflections on the End of a Civilization*. San Francisco: City Light Books, 2015.

Segovia, Fernando F. *Decolonizing Biblical Studies: A View from the Margins*. Maryknoll, NY: Orbis, 2000.

Segundo, Juan Luís. *Liberation of Theology*. Translated by John Drury. Maryknoll, NY: Orbis, 1976.

Seow, Choon-Leong. *Job 1–21: Interpretation and Commentary*. Illuminations. Grand Rapids: Eerdmans, 2013.

Shaw, Tamsin. "The Psychologists Take Power." *New York Review of Books* 63, no. 3 (February 25, 2016): 38–41.

Shinn, Roger Lincoln. *Tangled World*. New York: Charles Scribner's Sons, 1965.

Sittler, Joseph. *The Structure of Christian Ethics*. Louisville: Westminster John Knox, 1998.

Solzhenitsyn, Alexander. "Solzhenitsyn Explains 'Beauty Will Save the World.'" *Intercollegiate Review*, Fall 2015. Intercollegiate Studies Institute. http://tinyurl.com/yddkyehy.

Stephenson, Wen. *What We're Fighting for Now Is Each Other: Dispatches from the Front Lines of Climate Justice*. Boston: Beacon, 2015.

Stewart, Benjamin M. "The Stream, the Flood, and Spring: The Liturgical Role of Flowing Waters in Eco-Reformation." In *Eco-Reformation: Grace and Hope for a Planet in Peril*, edited by Lisa E. Dahill and James B. Martin-Schramm, 160–76. Eugene, OR: Cascade, 2016.

Strawn, Brent. *The Old Testament Is Dying: A Diagnosis and Recommended Treatment*. Grand Rapids: Baker Academic, 2017.

Sugirtharajah, R. S. *Exploring Postcolonial Biblical Criticism: History, Method, Practice*. Chichester: Wiley-Blackwell, 2012.

Swenson, Kristin. *God of Earth: Discovering a Radically Ecological Christianity*. Louisville: Westminster John Knox, 2016.

Taussig, Hal. *A New New Testament: A Bible for the Twenty-First Century Combining Traditional and Newly Discovered Texts*. Boston: Houghton Mifflin Harcourt, 2013.

Thurman, Howard. *Deep River and the Negro Spiritual Speaks of Life and Death*. Richmond, IN: Friends United Press, 1975.

Tipping Point North South. "1968 Poor People's Campaign." Accessed April 5, 2017. http://tinyurl.com/ya6o6zon.

Tov, Emmanuel. *Textual Criticism of the Hebrew Bible*. 3rd ed. Minneapolis: Fortress Press, 2011.

Townes, Emilie M. *Breaking the Fine Rain of Death: African American Health Issues and a Womanist Ethic of Care*. New York: Continuum, 1998.

———. "To Be Called Beloved: Womanist Ontology in Postmodern Refraction." In *Womanist Theological Ethics: A Reader*, edited by Katie Geneva Cannon, Emilie M. Townes, and Angela D. Sims, 183–201. Louisville: Westminster John Knox, 2011.

United Methodist Council of Bishops. *In Defense of Creation: The Nuclear Crisis and a Just Peace*. Nashville: Graded Press, 1986.

United Nations High Commissioner for Refugees. "Frequently Asked Questions on Climate Change and Disaster Displacement." November 1, 2016. http://tinyurl.com/y8762o8o.

Verhey, Allen. *Remembering Jesus: Christian Community, Scripture, and the Moral Life*. Grand Rapids: Eerdmans, 2002.

———. "Scripture and Ethics: Canon and Community." *Union Seminary Quarterly Review* 58, no. 1–2 (2004): 13–32.

Vilhena, Valaria. *Uma Igreja sem Voz: Análise de gênero da violência doméstica entre mulheres evangélicas*. São Paulo: Fonte Editorial, 2011.

Waiselfiz, Julio Jacobo. "2015 | Homicídio de Mulheres no Brasil." Mapa da Violência. FLACSO Brasil. Accessed March 17, 2017. http://tinyurl.com/y982gl9e.

Walzer, Michael. *Just and Unjust Wars: A Moral Argument with Historical Illustrations*. New York: Basic, 1977.

Westhelle, Vítor. "Freeing the Captives: Speaking the Truth." Paper delivered at Multicultural Theologians Seminar, Mystic Lake, MN, July 29–August 1, 2008.

Wilson, Brittany E. *Unmanly Men: Refigurations of Masculinity in the New Testament*. New York: Oxford University Press, 2015.

Wimbush, Vincent L., ed. *African Americans and the Bible: Sacred Texts and Social Texture*. New York: Continuum, 2003.

Woo, Courtney. "Religion Rejuvenates Environmentalism." *Miami Herald*, February 18, 2010. http://tinyurl.com/y7mqtzzn.

Yamada, Frank M. *Configurations of Rape in the Hebrew Bible: A Literary Analysis of Three Rape Narratives*. Studies in Biblical Literature 109. New York: Peter Lang, 2008.

Yoder, John Howard. *The Priestly Kingdom: Social Ethics as Gospel*. Notre Dame: University of Notre Dame Press, 1984.

Name and Subject Index

Scripture Index